~28

CASTRO AND STOCKMASTER:

A Life in Reuters

CASTRO AND STOCKMASTER:

A Life in Reuters

To Nick Moore
With best wishes
From
Michael Nelson

Michael Nelson

Matador
9 Priory Business Park
Kibworth Beauchamp
Leicester LE8 0RX, UK
Tel: (+44) 116 279 2299
Fax: (+44) 116 279 2277
Email: books@troubador.co.uk
Web: www.troubador.co.uk/matador

ISBN 978 1848767 768

British Library Cataloguing in Publication Data.
A catalogue record for this book is available from the British Library.

Typeset in 12pt Adobe Garamond Pro by Troubador Publishing Ltd, Leicester, UK
Printed and bound in the UK by TJ International Ltd, Padstow, Cornwall

Matador is an imprint of Troubador Publishing Ltd

To the family

Profits from the sales
of this book
will go to the charity
SOS Children, Pakistan

Contents

Illustrations

BLACK AND WHITE

COLOUR

CHAPTER ONE

There's a Bomb in my Bed

AN IRISH AND WELSH MIXTURE

Dr. Thomas Elliott Nelson, my grandfather, was a distinguished but unprosperous Ulster solicitor. The reason for his lack of prosperity was his politics. He was a Protestant and he believed in Home Rule for Ireland. The Catholics, who also believed in Home Rule, would give him business, but could not afford to pay him. The Protestants, most of whom opposed Home Rule, could afford to pay him, but would not give him business.

The parents of Thomas, who were farmers, were clearly not poor because he pursued university studies until he was 32 years old. The only documents I have inherited from him are his vellum degree certificates. They show he took a Bachelor's in Arts at the Queen's University in Ireland in Galway in 1880 when he was 26 and a Master's the following year. He did not take his bachelor's degree in Law until 1884 when he was 30 and he got a first at the Royal University of Ireland in Dublin. Two years later in 1886, when he was 32, the Royal University of Ireland conferred on him a degree of Doctor of Laws. We do not know why he took his first degree so late or whether or not he was in residence in Dublin.

Granddad Thomas, born in Castlederg in 1854, in 1890 married Margaret Jane, born in 1863, whose father described himself as a merchant. Family tradition, probably apocryphal, is that they were introduced by Charles Stewart Parnell, the Protestant Irish Home Rule leader. However, our grandmother used to tell us of Parnell's visits to her house in Strabane, County Tyrone. According to my uncle Jack Nelson, Parnell had high tea at the house of Jack's maternal grandfather, John Johnston. But at all events the Johnstons were clearly a prominent family and one of Margaret's cousins, Judge William John Johnston, became a judge of the Supreme Court of the

Irish Free State. His son was the playwright, Denis Johnston, who wrote *The Moon in the Yellow River*, which was performed at the Abbey Theatre in Dublin in 1931. The daughter of Denis is Jennifer, the novelist, who wrote the novel, *The Gates*, among others.

In 2005 I received an e-mail from Micheal Johnston, the son of Denis and brother of Jennifer, saying that Michael Thwaites, with whom he had been at Cambridge, and I at school, (together with his brother John) had told him our grandparents were cousins. I was able to confirm this. Over a lunch which his wife Pat kindly gave at their house in Dublin when I was visiting Ireland in 2007 we were able to fill a number of holes in our family trees.

The two families, who were Presbyterians, had probably come to Ireland from Scotland in the early seventeenth century as part of the Ulster Plantation. In 1609 the English government confiscated the lands of Ulster, which were farmed by Catholics, and resettled them with Protestants. The Protestants rented land to Catholics, which led to the two-tier society and the conflicts of today.

In Strabane the Nelsons lived in a house called "The Castle," which it was not. They left Strabane for Londonderry about 1903.

Thomas and Margaret had seven children, four boys and three girls, but could only afford to pay for the education of the eldest son, Jack, who went to Foyle College in Londonderry. The other sons left school at 14 and Thomas Alfred, my father, born in 1895, was put to an apprenticeship as a ship's joiner in the Londonderry shipyards. He was a joiner all his life and thoroughly disliked it. He always wanted to be a journalist.

My aunt Elizabeth Hughie, known as Ella, took me to visit my grandparents in Londonderry in 1935 when I was six. They lived on Strand Road next to a fire station, which for me was very exciting. My grandmother was rather put out when neighbours told her that I said my grandfather never washed. He was bed-ridden and, as I never saw him get up, I thought he never washed.

My father, known as Alfred, joined the British Army as a sapper in the Royal Engineers in 1914 and served in France until 1919 and fought in many of the great battles, including the Somme. He was mustard-gassed, but otherwise came through the war unscathed. In 1919 he settled in London. He bought his tobacco in a shop near where he lived in Shepherds Bush and married the young lady who served him, Dorothy Pretoria Bevan. She was the daughter of a Welshman, Regimental Sergeant-Major William Thomas Bevan, of the Welch Regiment, and Sarah Gertrude, née Taylor, of English stock. The father of William Thomas Bevan was William, a woodsman, who, not unexpectedly, was illiterate.

WORKING CLASSES KEEP OUT

Thomas Alfred and Dorothy had three children: Kathleen, born 1923, Denise born 1926 and Michael born 1929. I was born in Bromley, Kent, on 30 April 1929.

We lived in a small modern semi-detached house at 43 Southover, on the Downham estate, in Bromley, Kent, at one time the largest local government housing project in Europe. My parents moved there in 1926 and were among the first residents. It was one of the housing projects promised during World War I by the Prime Minister Lloyd George for the working classes when they returned from the war (e.g. my father). He said they would be "Homes for Heroes". The Downham estate was regarded as a garden city. Many of the residents had come from the slums of London. Although the houses were palatial compared with the slums, they had some strange features. I remember that water had to be heated in a copper in the scullery and then transferred for the weekly bath on Friday evenings to a tin bath in the kitchen by a small semi-rotary pump. Lighting was by gas.

The design of Burnt Ash elementary school which I attended was sufficiently revolutionary to warrant a feature in *The Times*. It reported that "practically every classroom opens on to raised terraces, so that, in suitable weather, the scholars will be almost in the open air." It concluded it was a "modern example of an elementary school artistically a delight, after the dull and sternly utilitarian London schools, erected where land has prohibitive values."

In 1926 residents of Alexandra Crescent, a private road in Bromley, built a seven foot wall, capped with broken glass, across the road about a third of a mile from our house. The purpose was to stop the working classes on their way to shop in Bromley High Street entering the streets of the middle classes. Controversy about the wall raged for nearly a quarter of a century. It was not taken down until 1950.

In 2009 an old Downham resident recalled on a local history website an experience with the Downham Wall: "My Gran was taken ill on a visit and my father had to climb the wall to get to the doctor, Dr. Bellingham, who lived in Alexandra Crescent. Needless to say, he cut his hand."

My father worked on a series of building projects and at one time, at least, his wages were £3.50 a week (£164 at current values based on the Retail Prices Index). The weekly rent of the Downham house was about £1 (£47 at current values). He was on the Army Reserve and the quarterly payment he got for that was a godsend and went on exceptional items like clothes. He did not have holidays and, as was then usual, worked a five and a half day week.

My sister Kathleen had Down's Syndrome, then commonly called Mongolism, and when I was three she went away to a boarding hospital called Earlswood, near Redhill in Surrey where she lived until she died at the suprisingly late age of 62. Most Down's Syndrome children died at about 14. Two girls, cousins of the present Queen, carrying the surname Bowes-Lyons, were also patients. We visited Kathleen once a month and she came home for a month's holiday in the summer. Doctors thought that the reason I had a bad stammer at the time was because of Kathleen, although I have never understood why.

Life on the Downham estate must have been extraordinarily relaxed because I have a clear memory of my father giving me the money to go by myself to the cinema. I could not have been more than six.

In 1935 my father took a job with the London County Council in Wandsworth, London, maintaining houses, the attraction being that it carried a pension with it. The family therefore moved to Wandsworth on 10 June, 1935 where my parents rented a sequence of cheap run-down flats. My sister and I went to the local elementary schools.

Life in Wandsworth was also very relaxed. I grew parsley in the garden and sold it outside East Putney station.

WAR

When war was declared on Sunday morning, 3 September 1939 I was singing in the choir of St. Michael's Church, Wandsworth, where I was the solo boy (Half a crown for weddings and five shillings for funerals). I was amazed when the rector interrupted the service to tell us that war had been declared and that we should all go home. Had he no faith that God would protect us in the church, I thought.

My father was called up into the Army, and after a short stay with an aunt in Taplow, Buckinghamshire, on 2 February 1940, we moved to Folkestone, Kent where my father was stationed. We were well in time for the fall of France and the threat of an invasion of Britain. Not that my father and his fellow soldiers could have done much to save Britain if the Germans had invaded. Supplies were in such short supply that they were issued with only five rounds of ammunition per man.

I remember thinking how extraordinary it was on a clear day to be able to see across the channel to France, which was occupied by Germans. Two incidents stuck in my memory. One day, as we stood on the cliffs at Folkestone watching the ships sailing up the channel, suddenly an enormous spout of water spurted up from one vessel and it immediately disappeared. I now knew the devastating power of modern weaponry. On another occasion some friends and I were playing near an army post when we spotted what we thought were parachutists descending from the sky. The soldiers had not noticed them so we ran to alert them. They called out the guards and started to load their rifles. But as the objects in the sky got bigger we realised they were puffs of smoke from anti-aircraft guns. Who looked the more foolish: we boys or the soldiers?

In July my father was posted to the army headquarters in Aldershot, Hampshire, so on 6 July we moved back to East Putney in the borough of Wandsworth, just in time to avoid the Battle of Britain over Hellfire Corner, which started on 10 July.

THE BLITZ

Five weeks after we moved to London the main London blitz started. It lasted from 13 August 1940 to 16 May 1941, and there were 71 major attacks on London.

We lived in a rented maisonette on the fourth and fifth floors of a large semi-detached Victorian house in Wandsworth called Avonmore, now a block of flats called Leyland, in Viewfield Road. The air-raid shelter was communal, dug into a public green opposite. But we did not need to use it because the kind owner of the house, Mrs Penrose, who occupied the ground floor, allowed us to sleep in her hall.

Wandsworth was badly bombed, with a number of high profile incidents within a mile of where we lived. The Castle Public House in Putney Bridge Road had been crowded when a bomb hit and 42 customers were killed and 141 injured. The most distressing incident was when our local fire station, about a third of a mile away on West Hill, was hit with an oil based high-explosive bomb on 16 November and six firemen killed. On 3 October a land-mine was dropped about a quarter of a mile away from where we lived in the back garden of 8 Portinscale Road, but fortunately the parachute caught in trees and it did not explode. We were located in the air raid warden post area C24, covering about half a dozen roads. Wandsworth Library still has the post's nightly reports, which show the range of bombs which fell in our little area: 9 September – three high explosives, three unexploded; 11 October – many incendiaries; 21 October – an incendiary oil bomb destroyed 5 West Hill Road, about 100 yards from us; 26 October – one high explosive and three unexploded.

There was a lull in the intensive bombing for nearly three years, although there were periodic incidents. One of the worst in the borough of Wandsworth was at a dance hall in Putney when 18 were killed and 210 injured.

A "Little-Blitz" started on 21 January 1944 and lasted for about three months. In the early hours of Saturday 19 February 1944 the sirens sounded. My parents came up to our rooms and asked Denise and me if we wanted to go to the air-raid shelter. Mrs Penrose had sold the house and we could no longer sleep in her hall. It was a cold night on the coldest winter for 50 years. The only heating in the flat was from a small coal-fired oven in the kitchen. My sister and I were unanimous that we preferred to stay in the relative warm under our blankets in our bedrooms on the fifth floor.

The drone of the German bombers and the British anti-aircraft fire could soon be heard. Crash! An incendiary bomb had come through the roof and was spewing out red-hot phosphorous shrapnel at the end of my bed. A bomb had landed in my sister's bedroom and another in a small storage room, but neither had exploded. We ran down the stairs to the kitchen on the fourth floor where my parents were extinguishing with a rug a bomb that had exploded there. The many fires all round the district caused a great demand for water, which meant that there was none in our taps. Much to my mother's annoyance my father used the rug they had recently bought to put out the fire. My parents sent us down to the shelter and, in the excitement, I failed to tell them that my bedroom was on fire. When they discovered it, the fire was well ablaze, but fortunately the water was now coming through the taps and they were able to put out the fire. If the other bombs had exploded they would not have been able to deal with them and the house would have been burned down. Around this time some incendiary bombs that did not explode were found to contain sand. So perhaps we owed the saving of the house to brave slave labourer saboteurs in Germany.

The owner of the house was actually annoyed that my parents had fought so hard to fight the fires. He wanted it to be burned down so that he would get government compensation, which he reckoned would have been far more than the house was worth.

Many were on the make during the war. One fellow-citizen of ours in Wandsworth was compensated 19 times in five months for being bombed out. When the authorities caught up with him in February 1941 he was sent to prison for three years.

Most houses had Anderson shelters in their gardens. They were shells of corrugated steel, buried to a depth of four feet into the ground. Morrison shelters were for indoor use and were like reinforced steel tables. We did not have either because the communal shelter, which was of similar design to the Anderson, but larger and sleeping about 30 people, was just across the road. We were not untypical in our reluctance to use the shelter: 60% of Londoners did not use them and, of course, many were killed. If the bomb aimer of our incendiaries had been a fraction of a second earlier or later in releasing the bombs, I would not be writing this recollection here now. We counted ourselves lucky that we did not have go to an underground station, as did as many as 177,000 Londoners, but we still did not like the discomfort of the communal shelter.

The air-raid alert on 19 February lasted 1-1/4 hours. Some 500 incendiaries were dropped in area C24 and six high explosives. The nearest high explosive to us destroyed 17 Viewfield Road, about 100 yards away. One high explosive and two phosphorous oil bombs did not explode. Mayfield Girls School on West Hill, a couple of hundred yards away, now Ashcroft Technology Academy, was destroyed by fire.

A total of 2,100 high explosive bombs and mines and 40,000 incendiary and oil bombs fell on Wandsworth during the war.

My parents were air raid wardens at post C24, but were fortunately not on duty on the night of our bombing. The main burden of being an air raid warden was sleep deprivation. When the sirens sounded my parents had to go, often in the rain in the middle of the night, to the air raid post a quarter of a mile away. Then they had to go to work the next day. My father's job was to repair the houses damaged in the bombings. Perhaps not surprisingly for a home-ruling Irishman, my father was sometimes defeatist and expressed the view that we were beaten and should give in. He did not make these comments in public. Our neighbours would have been unlikely to have taken into account that he had spent seven years devotedly serving in the British army in two world wars and had volunteered as an air raid warden. Not that defeatism was that uncommon. Harold Nicolson, Parliamentary Secretary to the Ministry of Information from 1940 to 1941, on 21 October 1940 recorded in his diaries the views of Kenneth Clark, who was Controller of Home Publicity in the Ministry of Information during the Blitz:

> He feels that if the Germans make a good peace offer after having bombed our cities rather more and taken Egypt we shall find that the popular Press take the offer up and that we shall be in great difficulty. I agree that the spirit of London is excellent but it would take little to swing the courage into cowardice.

After the war Clark wrote on how low morale in England was, "much lower than anyone dared to say."

More terrifying than high explosive or incendiary bombs was the V1 flying bomb, also called the doodlebug or buzz bomb, which started to attack Britain on 13 June 1944 day and night. It would drone overhead with a sound like an old motor-cycle or motor-mower, and then the engine would cut out. Those 14 seconds of silence before it exploded were the most terrifying I ever experienced in my life because I knew it was diving to the ground and that there was a chance that it was going to kill me. A week after the V1's raids started one hit the Guards' Chapel in Wellington Barracks during Sunday Service, killing 119 and seriously injuring 102. The nearest flying bomb which landed near our house fell on 26 June and destroyed a house at 2 Portinscale Road, about 200 yards away. Another fell near the fire station on 20 September. The allies' attacks on the launch sites in the aftermath of the Normandy invasion did not end the German attacks on England because some were launched from modified Heinkel He-III bombers. A total of 124 flying bombs fell on Wandsworth, the hardest hit of all London boroughs. They ceased on 29 March 1945.

The *Vergeltungswaffe-Ein* (Vengeance Weapon-1), powered by a pulse-jet mechanism using petrol and compressed air, was 25 feet 4 inches long and had a 16-foot wingspan and it flew at 360mph. It weighed 4,750 pounds and its warhead was made up of 1,874 pounds of Amatol explosive, a mixture of TNT and ammonium nitrate. The 125-foot concrete launch ramps were based in France from Watten in the north to Houppeville to the south. The reason Wandsworth was so badly hit was that the maximum range was 130 miles so south-west London was a favourite target. Moreover the bombs often fell short.

At 6.40 p.m. on Friday 8 September 1944 we heard a massive explosion. At the time we did not know what it was, although the rumour was that it was a gasworks explosion. That morning we had read in *The Times* a report of a press conference given by the foolish Duncan Sandys, Chairman of the Flying-Bomb Counter Measures Committee, with the headline "The Battle is Over." Not until 10 November did the government come clean on the new weapon when Winston Churchill made a statement in the House of Commons. He said that for the past few weeks the enemy had been using a new weapon, a long-range rocket. A number had landed at widely scattered points in the country. His statement was surprisingly inaccurate since the bombing had started two months earlier. The first, which we had heard at our flat in Wandsworth on 8 September, had landed about four miles away in Staveley Road, Chiswick, about 1-1/2 miles from my school in Hammersmith. There was great excitement in the playground on the following Monday morning: what was it that had exploded down the road? The rocket killed three people and injured six. Over the five-month campaign 1,359 rockets were fired at England, killing 2,754 people and injuring 6,523. Seven fell on Wandsworth.

In his book *The Storm of War: A New History of the Second World War* (London: Allen Lane, 2009) Andrew Roberts says that as the V2 was a supersonic ballistic missile flying faster than the speed of sound no air raid sirens could be sounded or warnings given, which added to the terror. In fact the reverse was true since you knew that when you heard the explosion the danger was past. The bomb was huge: 46 feet high, with a diameter of over five feet in the middle and 12 feet at the fins. It weighed 13 tons and flew at 3,600 mph.

A total of 1,301 persons were killed in Wandsworth through the war, 2,191 were seriously injured and 4,205 slightly. The population of the borough was 340,000 in 1939 and 251,510 in 1945. Properties damaged or destroyed totaled 72,701, or a staggering 96% of the total number of residences.

The Imperial War Museum has a diary written by Vivienne Hall, a shorthand-typist from Putney, which is of interest because she went through the war in the same part of London as we did and experienced similar bombings. She was 32 when the war started and was worried by her virginity and lack of sex-appeal. She worked for the Northern Assurance Co. in Moorgate. Her literary talents came out not only in her diary, but also in a play she wrote, but which she could not get produced.

At the outbreak of war she was living alone in a flat in Burstock Road, near the river, but in April 1940 moved into a flat with her mother at 21 Putney Hill. She frequently visited relatives on West Hill, which was just round the corner from where we lived. She was an Air-Raid Warden. The windows of her flat were blown out a few days after our incendiary bombs experience. She wrote of the area: "The damage is big and Putney looks a tired place about its quiet stately side-streets." She complained: "We don't like this resumption of bombing a bit and it seems to have caught us at the wrong time, we are war-winter-world weary."

She was having a bath on a Sunday in mid-June when a V1 landed in nearby Upper Richmond Road. "I forgot about washing my back and threw on some clothes. A most unpleasant feeling this – clothes on a wet soapy body."

In the Little Blitz she was convinced that Putney had become the Germans' most favoured target. "It seems quite a sensible thing as we are on the main Portsmouth road," she wrote.

We lack most of this fascinating diary from June 1940 to early December 1943. Her neurotic mother made her destroy it.

VIRTUOUS SCHOOLDAYS

School was spasmodic and for a spell none were open in London. I had taken my 11-Plus examination to get into a grammar school in Folkestone, but in the confusion of the war the documentation was lost, although I had probably failed anyway. For a time in early 1941 I was evacuated to families in Woking, Surrey, so that I could go to school. I was homesick and eventually cashed in some saving certificates at the local Post Office and bought a train ticket to London. The police contacted my parents, but when I finally arrived home, they never sent me back. Schools eventually started to open in London and I went to a school for commercial studies part-time.

But my parents were determined I should get a proper education at a grammar school and in 1942, when I was 13, my mother persuaded Frederick Wilkinson, the head-master of Latymer Upper School in Hammersmith, to take me, although I was at least two years behind my age group. He told me years later that he would never have taken me if it had not been for my mother's determination in the interview, which he still remembered. My mother paid the school fees by working as a clerk in the local office of the Ministry of Food, as she could not afford them from my father's army pay. He was invalided out of the army in 1943, diagnosed with "effort syndrome", whatever that means, and returned to his pre-war carpentering job, which still only paid modestly. I had largely caught up the two years by which I was behind my age group by March 1944, just before my fifteenth birthday. "A very different boy from the backward child he once was," the Headmaster commented in July 1945 when I was 16. I had to take the Higher School Certificate in one year instead of two because of my age and the likelihood of being called up for the armed forces.

Latymer Upper School was unusual in its special strength in the arts, particularly drama. It also had a number of particularly original masters. My favourite was A.D. Sopwith, the senior history master, who delighted in provoking original thought among his pupils.

Two of his favourites were:

If I had my way I would build a room with no walls and no floors so that if you leant on the wall you'd fall through and if you dropped your pencil, you'd lose it.

There should be two spellings and pronunciations for the place where there are cars. Where cars are repaired should be "garridge" and where they are lodged at home should be "garaage"

Money was always short. We could not afford a telephone, which was rather limiting socially. In the latter school years I worked on Saturday mornings as a clerk at Rayners, an estate agent in Putney, London, and in the Christmas holiday as a shop assistant in Meakers, a men's clothiers in Kingston, Surrey.

When I was 16 my mother took me to our local doctor, Dr Shaw, to talk about my stammer. He said there was no reason for me to stammer, I should buy a book of breathing exercises and do them. The whole family should identify themselves with my efforts. Within two weeks I was cured. It was a remarkable treatment and rid me of a serious affliction, which might have dogged me all my life. We still know Dr Shaw's daughter, Rona Rumney, and whenever I see her I do not fail to sing her father's praises.

In 2011 a film called *The King's Speech*, about the stammer of King George VI, was a great success. I knew the director, Tom Hooper, through his parents Richard and Meredith, but explained to them that I should not be going to see the film because it would bring back so many unhappy memories and because a stammerer always has the fear that the affliction will come back. The High Master of St. Paul's School, Martin Stephen, a former stammerer, was reported as saying:

> Only a stammerer knows what the fear is like. However much one thinks one has conquered it, the stammer sits for all one's life like a huge black crow perched on your left shoulder, head cocked to one side, reserving the right to put its vast beak through your ear and into your brain. You never defeat or remove a stammer: you just force it into a corner.

That was a bit over the top, but I knew what he meant.

TRAVEL AT LAST

In the summer of 1947, the first year after the war when foreign travel was allowed, the London County Council showed extraordinary imagination by giving 60 travelling scholarships to London schoolchildren. I was lucky enough to get one and spent two weeks in a boarding house at Milon la Chapelle near Paris and six weeks at a boarding house in Geneva. It opened my eyes to the world outside Britain and gave me a valuable foundation in French.

It came as a great shock to hear Monsieur Maheu, my host in France, complain to me that by supporting the French resistance the British had strengthened the communists, with possible dire political consequences for France.

One of the other students staying in the French boarding house was Camilla, daughter of the Swedish writer, Sigfrid Siwertz. The *Encyclopedia Britannica* said he was "one of the most facile and prolific of the early 20th century writers who consciously made use of a journalistic style and were often labelled as "social reporters." Camilla and I agreed to do an exchange, but the day she arrived in London I went into the army, so I never achieved my side of the exchange. How different my life might have been if I had.

In December 1947 I sat for a college scholarship in history at Sidney Sussex College, Cambridge. They only offered me a place. With great arrogance I decided I warranted a scholarship, so in January 1948 I tried for University College, Oxford. They offered me nothing. A couple of months later I tried Magdalen College, Oxford, who offered me a place, which I gladly accepted. It was a near squeak. I was due to be called up for the army and might never have gone to the university if Magdalen had not come to my rescue.

STAND BY YOUR BEDS

I was called up into the army on 3 June 1948 and when I had completed my three months' basic training I joined the Royal Army Educational Corps (RAEC). The reason was that my uncle Jack Nelson was an RAEC Colonel and my parents thought, wrongly, that that might do me some good. In the course of our Corps training my uncle was cited as an indication of what real soldiers we schoolteachers were. In the First World War he had deserted from the Educational Corps in 1915 to join the Irish Guards so that he could do some fighting. An officer from the Corps recognised him when he was on guard duty for the Irish Guards. He was arrested for desertion but eventually it was decided that he should not be court-martialled and that he could stay with the Irish Guards with promotion to Lance-Corporal. He was wounded at Cambrai in France in 1918.

Uncle Jack was a gregarious gentleman and when he retired to South Kensington in London he loved to stand on Sloane Square Underground Station and explain to his fellow passengers that the large pipe which traversed the platforms carried a river.

A clerk in the War Office had a sense of humour. When we were posted as sergeants at the end of training he decided that Nelson should go to Portsmouth. He would then be near the flagship "Victory" in the harbour, from which Admiral Horatio Nelson had won the battle of Trafalgar against the French in 1805. This was the best posting in the country because the

Garrison Headquarters, not surprisingly in this naval city, had a very small staff and did not run to a sergeant's mess. I therefore had to live in the YMCA, which was the height of luxury. My job was to visit the small Royal Army Service Corps boat units in Portsmouth and the Isle of Wight ("Soldiers who, like sailors, say 'Aye, Aye'") and teach them mainly citizenship. The army evidently agreed with Oliver Cromwell, who had said that men fought best when they knew what they were fighting for. I also had to give career guidance. That was not very onerous because most of the soldiers had already decided to become long-distance lorry drivers on demobilisation because of the freedom and the likelihood of picking up plenty of girls. The army only kept me for 14 months because I was going up to Oxford and I was discharged on 21 September 1949.

CHAPTER TWO

History *con amore*

MAGDALEN COLLEGE

William of Waynflete, Bishop of Winchester and Lord Chancellor of England, founded Magdalen College in 1458. It is perhaps the most beautiful college in Oxford, with much ground and even a deer park. It had an aristocratic reputation, exemplified by the attendance there of King Edward VIII when he was Prince of Wales. Another scion of a royal house was Prince Chichibu, son of the Emperor of Japan. According to legend when President Warren first met him he asked him what his name meant. "The Son of God" was the reply. "Oh well," said Warren, "you'll find we have the sons of many famous men here."

"You are nowe in an Earthly Paradise, if you have the grace to knowe it," William Trumble said to his son on sending him up in 1622. I certainly had the grace to know it.

After World War II the College became known for its socialist inclinations, which must have helped grammar school boys like me to gain entrance. It had many distinguished alumni, including Oscar Wilde. My twenty-first birthday party took place in his luxurious rooms on the Kitchen Stairs. The external walls of his rooms were still pitted with bullet holes from shots fired by undergraduates who had disapproved of his arty life-style.

Magdalen supported a boys' club in the East End of London and I once heard one of the boys who was visiting the College tell his friends that they were going to have tea in Oscar's Tea Rooms.

The President of the College when I went up in 1949 was Thomas Boase, a bachelor and art historian. The history of the College published for the 550th birthday in 2008 contained this unhappy tale:

...the Boase regime was marked by serious, if not yet critical decline. At the outset of his term, in 1948, the college was still the best endowed and richest in Oxford, but by 1968 it was close to the crisis soon to take it all but unawares – overtaken in the league table of estate wealth by at least five others, deeply in debt, lacking reserves, chronically averse to obtaining value for money in expenditure, and, despite considerable works undertaken in the 1960s, coping with a run down physical 'plant'.

Boase retired in 1968 and was succeeded by James Griffiths, a former Dean of Arts, who was not a great success. Not until an American, Keith Griffin, succeeded him in 1979 did the fortunes of the College start to turn round. The next president, who succeeded in 1987, was a surprise appointment. He was Anthony Smith, a television producer, who was a great success and was president until 2005. He became a good friend and invited me to stay with him in his lodgings.

I read Modern History and selected to study for a year the first six years of the reign of Richard II as my special subject under the great mediaevalist, K.B. McFarlane. I chose this because I had always been bad at Latin. I had never caught up the years of Latin I had missed during the war. To get into Oxford you had to have a credit in School Certificate Latin, but I only had a pass. When I was in the army I took the examination several times and failed to get the credit. Only at my last possible attempt, just before the start of my first term, did I succeed. But Latin continued to haunt me. At the end of the second term at Oxford you had to take preliminary examinations in French and Latin. I failed the Latin. I was allowed one more chance. If I failed again I would be sent down. So, little though I could afford it, I paid for lessons from an elderly retired school-teacher in Walton Street, ruining the summer term, and passed. Another undergraduate failed and was duly sent down. He got a job as a reporter on *The Daily Telegraph* and when I started work in Fleet Street I used to pass him in the street. He always looked the other way and I used to think, there but for the grace of God go I. I had thought the Latin source documents on Richard II would be a challenge. They were in dog Latin, so in fact they were not much of a challenge.

McFarlane, a bachelor, was a towering intellect, a perfectionist who, when he taught me, had never published a book because he did not feel he had sufficiently researched any subject. In my last year at Magdalen he published a slim volume on John Wycliffe (*John Wycliffe: and the beginnings of English nonconformity*, London: English Universities Press, 1952). Tutorials were graced by a beautiful Siamese cat, which sat on his lap being stroked.

My tutor for the nineteenth century was A.J.P. Taylor, who was disgusted that I had chosen the fourteenth century as my special subject and not one of his. "You might as well study land-tenure in Algeria," he told me. One of the reasons he disapproved was that K.B. McFarlane was an enemy because Taylor had blocked him from becoming President of the College. When I recounted this years later to Alan Bennett, the playwright, who had been supervised by McFarlane in research on Richard II, he replied that he thought land tenure in Algeria might have been quite interesting.

I still recall with pleasure the tutorials with Taylor. The setting was magical in the sitting room of Holywell Ford, an old water mill in the Magdalen deer park, with Taylor in a corduroy suit and bow-tie. The analysis of the essay you read him was always overwhelming, with extraordinary comparisons across the breadth of European history. I was also fortunate in sharing my tutorials with Roger Longrigg, a witty chap who went on to write successful novels on the mores of the fifties and sixties, of which the best known was *A High-pitched Buzz* (London: Faber, 1956).

Taylor's lectures, always at the ungodly hour of nine in the morning, were also extraordinary. He had no notes and finished the lectures exactly on the hour without ever having referred to his watch or a clock. Asked why he held his lectures at nine in the morning he replied: "Because if I were to start at eleven there is no hall in Oxford large enough to hold the audience." He followed his Oxford lecture style when he became the first of the dons to give talks on television. When he transferred to Fleet Street as the first and last director of the Beaverbrook Library, I invited him to come across the road from the Daily Express Building to have lunch at Reuters. "I never have lunch. It ruins the day," he told me. "But I will come to dinner if you invite me." Sadly he fell ill with Parkinson's disease before we could have the dinner.

I did not go to many lectures, agreeing with Samuel Johnson, who said, or rather, wrote: "People have now-a-days got a strange opinion that everything should be taught by lectures. Now I cannot see that lectures can do so much as reading from books from which the lectures are taken."

Another enemy of Taylor's was A.L. Rowse, a fellow of All Soul's. That enmity led later to a curious incident for me. Some time after A.L. Rowse died in 1997 the Heywood Hill bookshop in Curzon Street in London sold off his library. I managed to secure for only £25 his copy of Adam Sisman's biography of A.J.P. Taylor (*A.J.P. Taylor: a biography*, London: Sinclair-

Stevenson, 1994). It was full of pencilled imprecations, such as "liar" and "cheat" and also detailed notes, which he had clearly prepared for a review. I felt I had to give it to Adam Sisman, whom I knew, in return for another copy. Adam was delighted.

A don I knew, who later became very well known, was C.S. Lewis, who wrote the Narnia stories for children, of which the first was *The Lion, the Witch and the Wardrobe: a story for children* (London: G.Bles, 1950). He was the subject of the film *Shadowlands*. He used to give coffee after dinner on Sunday evenings for practising Christians, which I then was. My only recollection of the discussions was about mice, which his room was plagued with. He and I agreed that the best contraceptives for mice would be sealed bicycle inner tube valves.

In the college library I used to see quite a lot of Dr. C.T. Onions, the Librarian, who was also editor of the Oxford English Dictionary. On 6 February 1952 he came up to my table and told me that he had just heard on the radio that King George VI had died. "I have now lived through six reigns," he said. "Well, Sir," I replied, "I hope you don't live through another." "That's a bit double-edged, isn't it?" was his riposte. I used to go to the library directly after breakfast, taking with me my rations of sugar and butter. Food rationing did not end until 1952. I kept the sugar in a Fry's cocoa tin. One day Onions picked up the tin and read the label: "A food as well as a drink." He went down the library repeating the slogan to himself, presumably considering a new entry for the Oxford English Dictionary. He was preparing material for a supplement, including "filthy words", which had heretofore been excluded, but I never heard him use one. He was a remarkable man, who was Reader in English Philology at Oxford, although he had started his career as a primary school-teacher. He had ten children.

I had a grant from the London County Council of £341 a year, (£9000 at current values) but was always short of money. So in the vacations I did a variety of jobs and in my first year earned £115 (£3000 at current values). The most important job was as a night ward-orderly at Kingston Hospital. Since they were very short-staffed this really meant being a nurse. One night a man needed a catheter passing. The duty doctor did not want to get up to perform the deed and said that the student could do it. When I failed to pass the catheter, the nurses explained to the duty doctor that I was a student of history, not of medicine.

EUROPE WITHOUT A TENT

A highlight of Oxford was a three-week tour of Europe at the invitation of Malcolm Fraser, later to become Prime Minister of Australia. His biographer, Philip Ayres wrote (*Malcolm Fraser: A Biography,* Richmond, Victoria: William Heinemann, 1987): "Among the students Fraser admired was Michael Nelson, because Nelson was self-made – 'somebody who never went to Eton or Harrow or whatever, and he was typical of quite a large part of the intake who'd got there on their own guts and intelligence.' Students like Nelson, he felt, were probably more serious than many of the more privileged who were confident of jobs in the City."

Another member of the group was Nicolas Browne-Wilkinson, later to become Lord Browne-Wilkinson, the Senior Law Lord.

We limited ourselves to a budget of £30 each (£700 at current values)for the three weeks, which was enough for food but not for accommodation. A car was a rarity at Oxford in those days and Fraser was very attached to his, a Jowett Javelin. We suggested we fit a roofrack to the car so that we could carry a tent. Fraser exploded. He was not going to have any bloody roof-rack on his car. The fitting of a roof-rack would be certain to scratch the polished aluminium drip rails. It might also scratch the paint underneath the roof side rails. Since our suitcases would leave no room in the boot for a tent we would just have to rough it and sleep in barns or out in the open, as Fraser said he had done often enough in Australia. It was summer, after all.

We drove across to Harwich and on to the ferry for Ostend. The weather was excellent for the first few days, and some of the overnight stops, sleeping under the stars, very pleasant, though not the night in the Ruhr when we slept in a railway marshalling yard where the shunting trains ensured we had little sleep. Some nights we slept in the car.

Passing through a village in southern Germany we found ourselves in the middle of a wedding celebration and joined in. A pig is the symbol of good luck in Germany and, along with the other guests, we had to spend much of the evening carrying around a piglet. That was no easy feat, although Malcolm's experience with sheep made him the most skilled in the task.

A few days later Fraser ran out of shaving cream. In a small French town he stopped by a pharmacy to buy some more, and I went into the shop with him. Fraser had studied French at school but items like shaving cream were not part of his vocabulary and he was too proud to let me interpret. So he waved his hand about his face to indicate the act of lathering. He was sold a tube of toothpaste due to a misinterpretation of his gestures, and in spite of persuasion from his friends to the contrary he persisted in believing that it was some strange continental kind of shaving cream and continued to shave with toothpaste throughout the remainder of the trip.

In Paris we decided to sleep in the Bois de Boulogne. We had just settled down for the night under the stars when a police car screamed to a halt beside us. Sleeping in the park was not allowed, the gendarmes said. We pretended we understood no French, pointing to the 'GB' plate on the car, and the gendarmes finally gave up and drove away. Just after sunrise the next morning they returned to wake us and tell us that we should not be there when the day-shift gendarmerie came to work. They did not bring us coffee so we drove to the Tuileries where we cooked breakfast.

Another Australian who was a good friend and who went into politics was A.J. de B. Forbes. In the war he had served in the Royal Australian Artillery. A titled lady invited him and his wife Margaret to her English country seat for the weekend. He told me she had telephoned him to discuss the programme. "Do you shoot, Mr Forbes?" she asked him. "Only Japanese," he replied. He later became Minister for the Army.

LOTS OF PRIME MINISTERS

Out of the 100 or so undergraduates in my year at Magdalen, three became Commonwealth prime ministers. In addition to Malcolm Fraser was John Turner, who became Prime Minister of Canada - albeit briefly - and Tom Adams, who became Prime Minister of Barbados. Turner, whom we called "the kid", was a favourite of the gossip columnists because he knew Princess Margaret well. They pointed out, however, that there was no possibility of marriage because he was a Catholic.

Another high-profile contemporary at Magdalen was Christopher Chataway, the long-distance runner, who paced Roger Bannister when he ran the first sub-four minute mile. Our paths crossed again when he became Conservative Minister of Posts and Telecommunications in 1970.

At the other end of the political spectrum was Bill Rodgers, who was Labour Minister of Transport from 1976 to 1979, and who in 1980 was one of the gang of four, which broke away from the Labour Party to form the Social Democratic Party. I had met one of the other members of the gang, Shirley Catlin, later to become Shirley Williams, in odd circumstances when I was at school. In her autobiography she records falling on her head from a swing at the age of three. But she does not record falling down the steps of a school in Shepherds Bush when she was 13. She was attending a meeting of the Council for Education in World Citizenship, as was I. I was a boy scout and had my first-aid badge, so I rushed forward and had the privilege of binding up her cut knee. In later years I reminded her of the incident, but she seemed not to remember. The third member I met was Roy Jenkins, who kindly wrote a blurb for one of my books.

After the end of my last term I had to go back to Magdalen for my viva voce, the oral examination. I had dinner in a restaurant in the High with an old friend who was taking his viva voce in Philosophy, Politics and Economics (PPE). I knew he was troubled: his father had committed suicide. But I was shocked when he told me that he was working for MI5 and had told them that I had applied to join the Foreign Office, but that they should not hire me because I was a communist. I was not. He then said that he was going to commit suicide. When we got back to College after dinner I bade him goodnight and went to the rooms of his tutor, the distinguished philosopher and World War I hero (Military Cross (MC) and bar), Harry Weldon. He welcomed me in and gave me a large glass of sherry, as was his wont. I told him what the man planned. Weldon refused to do anything. "Ah, my boy," he said. "That is the blood sacrifice we pay for learning." I was not surprised to see that C.S. Lewis portrayed Weldon as a cynic. "Contempt is his ruling passion: courage his chief virtue," he wrote.

The man did not commit suicide, but went into a mental hospital where he underwent electric shock treatment. He came out after a few years and married one of the nurses, by whom he had two daughters. I lost touch with him but the poor fellow wrote me a letter in 1987, saying he had been in a mental home for 14 years. His wife had divorced him. Ironically, given our conversation over dinner in 1952, he said he had become a communist.

I got a Second Class Honours Degree in my finals. It was before the days of split second class degrees, but my tutor, John Stoye, wrote to me that I had got a "good second." At the end of each year the undergraduates donned their gowns and proceeded up to the high table in the dining room to have their tutors report on their performance to the college President in a ceremony called Collections. Not surprisingly, A.J.P. Taylor did not report to the President in my last term that I was a genius, but he did say that I treated history "con amore," which pleased me.

My Collections were tame in comparison with those of 1877 when the President of Magdalen, Frederick Bulley, asked Oscar Wilde's tutor, William Dennis Allen, at Wilde's Collections how he found Wilde's work. Allen replied: "Mr Wilde absents himself without apology from my lectures." Bulley asked Wilde whether this was any way to treat a gentleman. Wilde answered: "But Mr President, Mr Allen is not a gentleman." Bulley sent him out of the Hall.

CHAPTER THREE

Don't they Teach you to Type at Oxford?

A TRAINEE AT REUTERS

When I left Oxford in 1952 I was 23. I decided I wanted to travel, so I wrote to the three English-language international news agencies. Reuters did not reply. The Associated Press (AP) promptly wrote back saying that they did not take untrained journalists. British United Press (BUP), the subsidiary of United Press (UP), called me for an interview. When I went to see the Editor, Frank Fisher, he told me he had no job for me but had asked to see me because he also had been to Latymer Upper School. I could come to work on the desk for a day and if I was any good, he would try to get me a job in Reuters. At all events I should be able to say that I had once worked for UP. So I subbed copy for a day and he got me an interview with Alfred Geiringer at Reuters. He did not pay me for the day.

Alfred Geiringer was Manager of Comtelburo, also known as Comtel-Reuter, Reuters Commercial Services and Reuters Economic Services. He interviewed me and hired me as a trainee, described in my letter of appointment from the Secretary of Reuters, H.B. Carter, as a "junior". I started on 6 October 1952 in the newsroom on the second floor of 85 Fleet Street at a salary of £338 a year (£7240 at current values). In 2011 the average salary of a graduate trainee in Britain for the first year was £25,000 a year. I could not have existed on what Reuters paid me in 1952 if I had not been living with my parents.

The British Press progressively bought the shares of Reuters during the second quarter of the twentieth century. After World War II the competition was primarily the Associated Press (AP), a cooperative of United States newspapers, United Press (UP), owned by the Scripps-Howard US newspaper chain and Agence France-Presse (AFP), the French news agency established by the French government, which subsidised it. Although clearly a member of the big four international news agencies, Reuters found it a problem to compete against the other three and was usually in financial difficulties. The newspaper owners kept at a low level what they paid for the Reuter news service. The consequence was that the staff were badly paid and the office and living conditions around the world often appalling. Walton A. Cole, the Editor when I joined, once said to me: "This is not Shell, you know, old boy." I knew that already.

When I joined the chief executive was Sir Christopher Chancellor, who carried the title of General Manager. He had effectively succeeded Sir Roderick Jones in 1941 when Jones had been forced to resign for keeping from the Board his true relationship with the British government. Chancellor was patrician, educated at Eton and Trinity College, Cambridge, where he took a first in history. He joined Reuters in 1930 and the following year was appointed General Manager and Chief Correspondent in the Far East, with headquarters in Shanghai, at the age of 27.

Chancellor had to deal with the poverty of the organisation. He brought the Australian Associated Press and the New Zealand Press Association into ownership, which helped a little. He thought of bringing the South African and Dutch newspapers into ownership, but nothing came of it. His only acquisition was Comtelburo, a financial news agency specialising in Latin America, which had an office in New York, which Reuters bought in 1944. But he was British Empire and Europe centred and did not see that the future of Reuters had also to lie in the United States. The first trained specialist in the financial information business to be sent abroad, Derek Prag, went to Spain, but should have been sent to the United States. The second, which was myself, went to the Far East instead of to the United States. Policy was to give rights in the services to national news agencies in order to keep down overheads. Those agencies were uncommercial cooperatives in most cases and showed little interest in selling Reuter services. Reuters also lacked sales staff in the countries where it operated itself.

The meanness of the owners meant that salaries were extraordinarily low. I once complained to Lord Drogheda, Chairman of the *Financial Times*, that he was always enticing away our journalists by higher salaries. "Well, you should pay them more," he said. That was pretty rich in that he was a director of Reuters and his newspaper paid a reduced subscription for the Reuter service because it argued that it did not use as much news as the other national dailies. When I was eventually posted abroad I was put into accommodation which was worse than I had had in the British Army.

In 1992, after I had retired, I was attending the International Press Institute (IPI) Annual Conference in Budapest. I went to a café to have a coffee with Peter Preston, the sagacious Editor of the *Guardian*. "I'll pay for the coffee," Peter volunteered. "The *Guardian* owes a lot to Reuters." It did indeed. In 1984 the *UK Press Gazette* calculated that the newspaper owners had already received £152 million after tax (£364 million at current values) from sales of Reuter shares following the flotation. The share of the Guardian group was £5.1 million (£12.2 million at current values). It was ironical that the poor relation of the poor relation should have bailed out the British Press and enabled them to move to the luxuries of Docklands and other like sites.

For my first six months in London I decoded stock and commodity prices so I was truly involved in the roots of the Company. My typing was not very good. "What do they teach you at Oxford, if they don't teach you to type?" Albert Murray, the cockney head of the desk asked me. So I taught myself to touch-type. Another conversation went like this:

"What did you study at the University?"

"History."

"Well, when you consider how long it takes to transmit a news story from this place, you need a degree in history."

For the next eighteen months I sub-edited financial news and wrote stock market reports.

Comtel, as it was usually known, was the underdog to the glamorous general news service. The general news journalists looked down on their colleagues who wrote news on finance and commodities. When I tried to join the National Union of Journalists Sidney Weiland, the chairman of the Reuters section (whose title was Father of the Chapel), checked with the Fleet Street branch. He came back with a negative because they said that people who wrote financial news were not real journalists. At least I saved my union subscription.

TANGIER

On Sunday 1 August 1954 I was sent to Tangier, the British, French, Spanish tripartite zone of Morocco, to start the first lap of three months overseas training, which was planned to include Madrid and Paris. The Sunday was significant. I was advised never again to arrive anywhere on a Sunday and ruin the weekend of the Reuter representative. The office sold Paris gold prices to gold dealers and smugglers. It closed at two o'clock in the afternoon and I spent the rest of the day on the beach. Brian Marsh, the manager, who had earlier failed in a project to start dog-racing in Italy, was a friend of the American novelist, Paul Bowles, who lived in Tangier and I counted myself privileged to meet this distinguished author and his wife Jane.

But the sybaritic life was not to last and after two weeks I was summoned back to London. The manager in Bangkok, an Indian called Menon, had resigned to become manager of the Royal Bangkok Sports Club and I was to replace him. I spent a month in Singapore where, under Warren White, the correspondent of Australian Associated Press-Reuters, I learnt more about writing a news story than I had learned in two years in London.

BANGKOK

Bill O'Neill, the Reuter Manager for South-East Asia, an Irishman, was a splendid boss. He was famous for the circumstances of his internment by the Japanese in the war. When the Japanese invaded Hong Kong they interned the British, but not the Irish, who were neutral. Bill O'Neill became lonely and asked the Japanese to intern him with his British friends. They complied.

The office in Bangkok, which I took over on 2 October 1954, was in an old ramshackle wooden house in a compound on West Lane, off Silom, in the centre of town. The office was on the ground floor and the Manager's flat on the first floor. The house had not been painted for years. It had few fans and the unreliability of the electricity supply meant they often did not work. There was no mosquito netting or glass in the windows. There was little furniture and the fridge often cooked the contents instead of cooling them. There was no running water and my servant had to bring buckets up to the bathroom to fill a Shanghai jar, one of the large ceramic jars used throughout Asia to store water, just like the jars where Ali Baba found the forty thieves. I had to scoop cold water from it in lieu of a shower. With great daring I asked my bosses in London to be allowed to spend £50 on a new fridge and some more easy chairs.

The staff of about a dozen clerks, messengers and the radio operator, and their families, mostly lived in huts in the compound. George, the radio operator, was an Anglo-Thai and he and his younger brothers lived and worked in the compound. George had a beautiful daughter of 14, who later became a famous announcer on Thai TV. The atmosphere was very Somerset Maugham with me as the all-powerful *tuan*, or boss – in Thai *nai*. I once had to assert my authority on an important domestic matter. There was a large mango tree in the garden and I watched the fruit ripening with eager anticipation. One day I returned from a day out in Bangkok and to my horror all the mangoes had gone. George had picked them for himself. He told me that had always been the custom. I instructed him to bring them all to the office, where I divided them equally among all the members of the staff. Shortly after I had played Solomon the six-year old son of George came to me in tears bearing his pet monkey. George had told him he had to give it to me as a present to make up for the mango affair. Naturally, I refused and the little boy tripped away rejoicing.

George listened to the radio at night to receive transmissions from London or Singapore on a tape printer called a hellschreiber. There was much radio interference and we often received only part of the transmissions. This was also sometimes because George had gone to sleep, as I found whenever I got up in the middle of the night to check up on him. The reason he often fell asleep was that his day job was at the receiving station of the Post and Telecommunications Authority who received the Reuter general news service, which they sold to the Press and radio. We distributed the commercial news to banks and brokers by duplicated sheets, which were delivered by the messengers, and by telephone.

The hellschreiber was an extraordinary communications device invented in the late twenties by Dr. Rudolf Hell, a German. The signal was a matrix of seven by seven dots, which made up the characters, which were printed on narrow tape. Its superiority over morse, which was the other main system of communication, was that even if atmospheric interference blotted out some of the dots, the 49-dot character was still often readable. Morse had only six elements. The hellschreiber was the precursor of the fax machine. In the sixties I went to Kiel to meet the remarkable Dr. Hell and wrote about my fascinating visit in *The Times* when he died in 2002 at the age of 100.

In addition to editing the service and selling it I was also the correspondent. For reporting I was responsible to the Australian Associated Press (AAP) in Melbourne. As part of the deal under which AAP became shareholders in Reuters in 1947 they acquired rights to supervise reporting East of Burma. The correspondents were a mixture Britons, Australians and New Zealanders. The division of responsibility between Melbourne and London led to endless bickering until the arrangement ended in 1965.

There was generally not much spot news in Thailand of interest to the outside world, but it was the feature story capital of the world and I wrote at least one feature, called a situationer in Reuters, each week. These were the sort of subjects I covered:

> Priesthood: As the first of the heavy rains start young Thais don saffron robes and enter the priesthood. Few parents would approve of their daughters marrying a young man who had not been a priest.
>
> Kites: Male and female kites battle in the wind above the pagodas of Bangkok. The female kite flies staid and upright in her half of the battle-field and the male goes after her. The kite which captures the other and brings it down into its own half of the field is the winner.
>
> Cinema: Western films are dubbed live in Thai cinemas. A man and a woman, called versionists, play all the parts, showing great skill in varying the voices for each character. The advantage of this system is that the versionist can introduce local colour. So, for example, if a girl of doubtful virtue appears on the screen they can give her the name of one of the local prostitutes. The audience love it.

For me the most moving story I covered was of a visit to the cemeteries of the Railway of Death at Kanchanburi and Chungkai, north of Bangkok, which the BBC had asked for, commemorating the end of the war with Japan. The cemeteries were still unfinished. The film *Bridge Over the River Kwai* was yet to be made and little had been written about the infamous railway. Parts of it were still in use for tourists and trolley-cars took laughing holiday-makers over crazy bridges to visit waterfalls. I interviewed a Buddhist priest who as a boy had sold bananas, papayas and mangoes to the prisoners. "They were thin like skeletons," he said, "and we sold them the food very cheap."

The Thai Press varied in quality. One of the favourite stories was the dog giving birth to a baby. This was always accompanied by a photograph of a dog nuzzling up to a baby.

The biggest story in Bangkok while I was there was a conference of the South-East Asia Treaty Organisation (SEATO), attended by Anthony Eden, the British Foreign Secretary, and John Foster Dulles, the American Secretary of State. The big Reuter guns came in to cover it: Graham Jenkins, the Manager for South-East Asia, Warren White, correspondent in Singapore, both Australians, Garth Roydhouse, Parliamentary correspondent of the New Zealand Press Association, a New Zealander, Denys Corley Smith, correspondent in Saigon, and David Chipp, correspondent in Rangoon, both British. David Chipp later became the first Western correspondent in Beijing, editor of Reuters and Editor-in-Chief of the Press Association, the British domestic news agency. He remained a life-long friend.

Speaking at David Chipp's eightieth birthday party in 2007, I recalled his visit to Bangkok 52 years before. There were only four European hotels in Bangkok at that time – other hotels all doubled up as brothels – and David stayed at the Trocadero Hotel because the run-down Reuter house was unsuitable for a visitor. However, he came to lunch each day. After the first week my cook, a young Thai lady on whom her previous American employers had bestowed the name "Chief", told me: "Master Chipp bad man." I expressed some surprise and asked her why. "He come here every day for lunch but never gives me money for food." I did not comment, nor did I mention it to David, but I thought to myself that, given the large sum I gave her to feed me, she could have fed half a dozen Reuter correspondents and not been out of pocket. The next week we were covering the conference and he did not come to lunch. On the Friday I took him out to the airport for his trip back to Rangoon. When I came back to the house Chief was wreathed in smiles. "Master Chipp give me lots of money," she said. "Master Chipp very good man."

David died in 2008. The Daily Telegraph Group, the Press Association and Thomson Reuters agreed to a proposal of his Cambridge College, King's, to finance the cost of designing and printing a collection of his writings and related material. It was called *Mao's Toe: Memoirs of the Life of David Chipp, A serious Correspondent*. It was edited by a friend of David's, Damien Freeman, who was a Cambridge researcher. The reason for the title was that David had trodden on Mao Tse Tung's toe at a reception in Beijing. Chou en Lai had described him as a serious correspondent. David was gay, but had never come out. His friends were staggered to find the memoirs contained an admission that when he was in Rangoon he had fathered a son by a Burmese girl, who was part British. The cynics among his friends said it was not true and was merely a device to divert attention from his homosexuality. His family said it was not true and it was a well-known trick of Asian girls to get money from foreigners by pretending to be pregnant. But when I questioned Damien Freeman about it he insisted he had seen documentary proof among David's papers that he had paid £500 (£10,000 at current values)to the Roman Catholic orphanage where he had arranged for the child to be placed. David never saw the mother or the child again.

The annual Oxford and Cambridge dinners were important social events in Asia for those who qualified. The first I went to was in Bangkok on 14 December 1954. The British Ambassador, Sir Berkeley Gage (Trinity, Cambridge, 1925) proposed the toast of Oxford and Mom Rajawongse (Princess) Pimsai Amoranandh (Lady Margaret Hall, Oxford, 1938) proposed the toast of Cambridge. The most memorable Oxford and Cambridge dinner for me was in the E&O Hotel in Penang in 1957 when the Chinese chairman invited us after the dinner to what he described as his youth club – the City Lights dance-hall. There beside each place was a bottle of whisky and a pretty girl.

Jenkins was very tough, but established an unusually close relationship with some of the powers-that-be in Asia. "Bung" Sukarno, first President of Indonesia, held him in great respect. In his book *Memories of Times Past* Louis Heren recounted that when he was the correspondent of *The Times* in South-East Asia, General Jean de Lattre de Tassigny, commander-in-chief of the French forces in Indo-China, invited him to accompany him on a tour of Vietnam, Laos and Cambodia. De Lattre told him that he had already invited Graham Jenkins. "I have invited you because you are *The Times*. I have invited Graham because I love him," he said.

In 1949 Jenkins had been arrested by the Nationalist Chinese and sentenced to death because they did not like one of the stories he had filed. He told me that the day before he was due to be shot he was taken out of the death cell to talk on the telephone to Monty Parrott, another Reuter correspondent in China. "Hey Graham," he said. "You'd better get out of there. Reuters will stop your pay, you know." In fact the sentence was not carried out and he was beaten up and deported to Hong Kong.

I was allowed to play a minor role in the SEATO conference. I got a lot of pleasure out of besting the competition over my organisation of the communications. At that time news was sent from Bangkok by toll cable.

You went to the Post Office, queued at the counter and handed in the piece of paper on which your story was written. It could take hours to reach its destination, which was usually the Reuter office in Singapore. So some weeks before the conference I went to see the head of the Post and Telecommunications department and asked him to lease Reuters a full-time dedicated morse circuit from Bangkok to Singapore. The Thais had never leased a circuit before, but not only did he lease us one circuit, but two, in case the first frequency encountered atmospheric interference. When the other international agencies later asked for circuits there were none: they had been leased to Reuters. Our competitors had to queue up in the Post Office, while Reuters stories instantaneously winged their way to Singapore, sweeping the board.

The head of the UPI team, who was their boss for Asia, attacked the head of the Post and Telecommunications department in the *Bangkok Post* for incompetence and said Bangkok was clearly unsuitable to be the site of the headquarters of SEATO, which the Thai government were desperately bidding for. The civil servant telephoned me almost in tears, terrified that he would be arrested. So Graham Jenkins gave an interview to the newspaper praising the Thai government for its efficiency and pointing out that experienced news agencies knew that communications for such conferences had to be planned well ahead. The Post and Telecommunications chief was delighted.

The competition thought we had over-staffed the conference, which was true. The reason was that Cole was shortly to do a tour of Asia. He planned to ask the principal newspaper clients for more money and wanted to show how well we had done on the big story. This was a common trick of news agency executives, but the newspaper owners countered it with their own trick, which was to instruct their editors not to use much of the agency's news just before the arrival of the visitor.

Soon after the Bangkok SEATO Conference, in April 1955, the Bandung Conference of non-aligned countries took place in Indonesia. I interviewed at Bangkok airport Norodom Sihanouk, who was on his way to the conference. He had just abdicated as king of Cambodia in favour of his father. His reply to most of my questions was "Je ne sais pas, Monsieur." I always said he was the only king who ever called me sir.

The story the Thai government least liked covered was corruption. The head of the army, Field Marshal Sarit Thanarat, later Prime-Minister, once took me aside at a party to ask me not to write corruption stories. "Don't worry," he said. "We'll get Burma into SEATO." It was a curious quid pro quo and of course Burma never did join SEATO.

A bizarre story on which I reported was the execution on 17 February 1955 of three men for the murder of the previous king, Ananda Mahidol. He died in mysterious circumstances in 1946 and was succeeded by his brother. The men who had been convicted of the assassination were shot. They were Nai Chit, the senior royal page, Butr Paramasrin, a page of the royal bed-chamber and Chaleo Paroomros, a Senator and King Ananda's personal private secretary. Thais, as Buddhists, do not believe in killing, so the men had painted targets draped over their chests. The executioners fired at the targets, not the men.

Another out of the ordinary royal story was the birth on 2 April 1955 of Princess Sirindhorn, the second daughter of the king and queen. The palace had its own radio station and on the day the birth was expected played a stack of records, which included *Onward Christian Soldiers*. Suddenly the music was interrupted for the squalling of a baby. The microphone had been taken into the Queen's bedchamber.

Thailand was an ancient monarchy, but in 1932 the army staged a coup and General Pibul Songgram became prime minister. He held that position when I was in Bangkok. The other two strong-men were Phao Sriyanon, head of the para-military police and Sarit Thanarat, head of the army, and they were great rivals. On one occasion the police seized a consignment of opium which belonged to the army. The army sent a tank to the police station where it was being held and the police quickly returned it.

My main mission in Bangkok was to increase revenues, which I did. I sold mainly rubber prices by cold-calling on the traders in the old Chinese quarter of Bangkok. I doubled the profit overnight, not in Bangkok, but in Haadyai in the rubber producing area in the south. The telephone service was so bad that the traders there often could not get the Singapore, London and New York rubber prices on which they made their living. So I hit on the idea of installing a hellschreiber radio receiver in the office of the Danish company East Asiatic, charging them an appropriately large sum for exclusivity.

Since London decided the financial future of the Thai office was now established I was instructed to find a local replacement for me. I was fortunate to find Maitri Sirochiratana, a splendid Cambodian, and he took over on 26 July 1955 when, after a short trip to Phnom Penh in Cambodia, where I established an agency for Reuters, I was posted to Colombo, Ceylon.

COLOMBO

My time in Thailand had been a revelation to me. I had a degree in history from Oxford but knew nothing of Asian history, except where the British were involved. I knew nothing of Buddhism. I had been amazed to find that the attitude of respectable Thai girls to Europeans was one of indifference, believing that we had had bad luck not to have been born Thai.

The Reuter representative in Ceylon was Eddie Wijeyesinghe, a Sinhalese, who combined the jobs of Reuter correspondent, Manager of Reuters Economic Services and Manager of the Press Trust of Ceylon, which was a newspaper cooperative that distributed the Reuter news service to the media. My task again was to improve the services and raise revenues. I lived in the main hotel.

Eddie Wijeyesinghe was a well-known amateur actor. He was appearing in a play called *Fifty-Fifty*, which was a precursor of the appalling war which was to break out between the government dominated by the majority Sinhalese and the minority Tamils. The Tamils were calling for 50-50 representation.

One incident taught me about one of the wicked customs of some places in the Third World. Revenue had improved and I got the approval of my bosses in London to give some modest increases in the exiguous salaries. I learned that one of the clerks was not too overjoyed by his increase because he had to give half to the Chief Clerk. The Chief Clerk had hired him and the condition of the clerk's employment was that he gave half his salary and any increases to his boss. I told the Chief Clerk that if the practice did not stop, he would be fired. He was not very pleased.

The Chairman of the Press Trust of Ceylon was Esmond Wickremasinghe, Chairman of the Lake House group, the largest newspaper conglomeration on the island. He had married the daughter of the owner. He was also secretary of the ruling United National Party. To its amazement it lost the 1956 election, having been in power since independence. Wickremasinghe told me that if they had had any idea that they risked losing the election, they would have rigged the results. The shock of the results showed him the importance of polling and he introduced me to a budding pollster, also called Nelson, whom he had hired, later to become one of the biggest market research organisations in the world as Taylor Nelson Sofres.

Wickremasinghe frequently came to London and became Chairman of the International Press Institute. I saw a lot of him in the sixties and seventies and he introduced me to Sir John Kotelawala, the defeated Prime Minister, who bought a block of flats in Belgrave Square and a farm in Kent, where he kept elephants. He was very pro-British and took a very anti-Chinese line at the Bandung Conference in 1955. He told me that he had taken aside Jawaharlal Pandit Nehru, Prime Minister of India, and Mohammad Ali, Prime Minister of Pakistan, and gave them a dressing down for their anti-colonial speeches. "'Listen you buggers,' I said. 'Remember you are Commonwealth prime ministers.'" Sir John invited me to come to stay at his farm. "My wife and I would like that very much," I said. "Don't bring your wife, you silly bugger. I have other things in mind for your entertainment," he replied. I did not go to his farm.

Kotelawala had been succeeded as Prime Minister by Solomon W.R.D. Bandaranaike. He was assassinated in September 1959 and succeeded by his wife Sirimavo Bandaranaike, the first woman prime minister in the world. She eased out from office the Governor-General, Sir Oliver Goonetilleke, who came to England, where Wickremasinghe introduced us at the large block of flats Goonetilleke owned in Victoria. Kotelawala and Goonetilleke had not met since the latter's arrival in the UK as there seemed to have been some falling out. Wickremasinghe got me to organise a Reuter dinner for them at the Savoy Hotel. I was not a little surprised when the former Prime Minister greeted the former Governor-General with: "Why did you not sleep with her, you silly bugger? Then she would not have kicked you out." "Bugger" was a favourite term of affection of Kotelawala.

Wickremasinghe's teenage son Ranil was following a course at a technical college in London and my wife Helga and I had to take him around the museums at the weekends. He became Prime Minister of Sri Lanka in 1993.

A visitor I entertained in Colombo was Roy Thomson, a Canadian newspaper publisher, who had bought *The Scotsman* in 1953. He had just been in Bangkok. He told me that he had declined Maitri's offer of a girl. "Too old, eh?" said Maitri, which greatly amused Thomson. Little did I know that not only would Thomson in 1959 buy *The Sunday Times*, in 1960 become a director of Reuters and in 1965 buy *The Times*, but that one day his company would buy Reuters.

I always treasured the story of his first meeting with Cecil King, Chairman of the Mirror Group. "Got anything for sale," asked the short and dumpy Thomson. "I certainly have nothing for sale," replied the tall patrician King. "Don't be like that," said Thomson. "It's like my friend in Timmins says: 'Everything I've got is for sale, except my wife.'" "But I am not one little bit like your friend in Timmins," replied King.

I went back to Singapore on 2 February 1956 and travelled around South-East Asia advising on how revenues could be improved, and visited Bangkok, Phnom Penh, Saigon, Hong Kong and Manila.

KARACHI

On 1 July 1956 I was seconded for six months to the Associated Press of Pakistan, the local news agency, in Karachi to advise them on improving their revenues from economic services. The Reuter correspondent was Ross Birtwistle, with whom I shared a flat in a new housing development on the road to the airport. I had to share a bedroom with him. Although the office driver's name was Allah, he was a Christian. The flat was on the first floor of the building and reached by an outside staircase, which housed a cupboard. Allah got Birtwistle's permission to live in the cupboard. Birtwistle went on a prolonged visit to Iran and I went to East Pakistan. I came back early from my trip and surprised Allah's domestic arrangements. He had sublet part of the cupboard to a lodger.

Conditions in Karachi, still recovering from the aftermath of independence and the division of the sub-continent, were grim. Outside the apartment refugees lived in makeshift tents and the stench was appalling. The refugees did our laundry. It was demanding work because our white cotton drill trousers had to be washed once or twice a day to remove the betel juice which was the result of poor aim by the staff in the office as they spat the juice into the waste paper baskets. It was a country of contrasts. Travelling by train to Lahore I shared a compartment with a captain in the army. He was reading a biography of the mid-nineteenth century British prime-minister Melbourne.

On Saturday morning, 3 November 1956, Ross telephoned me at home to tell me that there was rioting outside the British High Commission in the centre of Karachi. The mob were protesting at the British invasion of Egypt following the nationalisation of the Suez Canal by their fellow Muslims there. He could not get to the High Commission because the mob was too dense between the office where he was and the scene of the riots. Could I try to get there from my side of Karachi and see what was happening?

I hired a taxi, but by the time I was near the High Commission it was unapproachable because of the crowds. When I arrived at the *maidan*, a vast open space where there were fewer people, I got out of the cab. I was greeted by a hail of stones. To my relief the taxi driver, whose cab was badly damaged, did not drive off without me and leave me to be killed, but got me back in the vehicle and by a circuitous route, delivered me to the office. Ross Birtwistle was glad to see me – a German had just been killed outside the British High Commission.

The Times reported:

> A procession of about 10,000 students yesterday demonstrated at various places in Karachi and shouted slogans condemning the Anglo-French action in Egypt. Outside the British High Commission headquarters the students clashed with the police. The police first made a lathi charge on the crowd, then used tear gas.
>
> About a dozen students were hurt and six constables were injured by stone-throwing. According to unconfirmed reports some Englishmen were manhandled by the crowds on the roads.

There was no mention of the dead German.

On the fiftieth anniversary of the incident in which I narrowly escaped death I gave a sum of money to the Pakistani children's charity, *SOS Children*, as thanks to that unknown taxi driver who saved my life.

It was not my job in Karachi to write stories, but I could not resist filing one to London. The Americans had supplied grain to Baluchistan to relieve a famine. The leaders of the state asked the government if they could meet this Amir Khan to thank him.

The most bizarre source of income for the Associated Press of Pakistan was reporting the price of New York cotton. Across the Indian sub-continent gamblers bet on the last three digits of the closing price. It was a pure numbers game, but the bookies needed to have access to fluctuating prices throughout the trading session to set the odds. Reuters transmitted the prices by radio printer and in Karachi three groups competed to deliver the prices to the bookies first. One group was the messengers employed by the agency, the second was the radio operators at the receiving station and the third other members of the staff, headed by the chief messenger. When I caught the chief messenger stealing the prices I reported him to Malik Tajuddin, the head of the agency, and told him the chief messenger should be fired. "Ah, no," he said. "He has a wife and six children. I will punish him by sending him as manager to our office in Hyderabad." There he was able to steal the prices with even greater impunity.

The Times of India had a curious experience with the cotton prices. It published the *Li'l Abner* cartoon, which it bought from Capp Enterprises of the United States. It dropped it when Capp Enterprises increased the subscription. The newspaper was inundated by complaints from all over India. The Editor investigated and found that gamblers were running systems based on the date on which the cartoon had originally been published in the United States, which was published at the bottom of the cartoon. The gamblers were convinced there was a relationship between the publication date of the *Li'l Abner* cartoon and the New York cotton price.

MALAYA

By the end of December 1956 I was back in Singapore and spent the next four months working on the economic services in Penang and Kuala Lumpur in Malaya.

I went back to Bangkok briefly on a strange assignment. A young inexperienced Australian journalist of AAP had visited Bangkok and written a grossly unbalanced story critical of the Thai government's treatment of the Muslims in the south of Thailand. The Thai government delivered a strong protest to Reuters. In such circumstances Reuters would always have issued a corrective story. But this was even more important because the Thai government paid Reuters £1800 a year (£33,500 at current values) for exclusive rights to the general news service. The thought of losing that princely sum caused London to instruct me to get on a plane to Bangkok and write a balancing story, which I was happy to do.

In 2008 a curious flashback of my time in Malaya occurred. The President of Magdalen, David Clary, invited Helga and me to a dinner in college which he was giving for Malcolm Fraser and his wife Tamie. I was seated next to the second Viscount Slim who had known Fraser in Australia. "I have not seen you since the engagement story in Kuala Lumpur in 1957," I said. He seemed embarrassed and looked across the table to see if his wife had heard. It seemed she had not.

Fred Coleman, an Australian, was the AAP-Reuter correspondent in Kuala Lumpur in 1957 and one Sunday he and I went to the beach with two Malay girls, Che Ah and her sister Che Salmah. Che Ah was the secretary at the Australian High Commission. We were due to be back in Kuala Lumpur by two o'clock. The reason was that the radio-teletype transmission to Melbourne closed at four o'clock and Coleman had to check the early proofs of *The Malay Mail* to decide what he should file before the deadline. But we dallied too long over lunch and did not get back till after three o'clock. The lead story was a winner for Australia: Major Slim, who was stationed in Kuala Lumpur and was the son of the Australian Governor-General, had become engaged to an American girl. Coleman rushed to check the story, but could not get hold of Slim. The minutes to deadline were ticking away. The English reporter who had got the story swore that Major Slim had telephoned him with the news at lunchtime. He knew him well and knew his voice. "Shall I file, or not file," Coleman asked me. "You are the correspondent, you have to decide," I told him. He filed just before the deadline.

The Australian newspapers sought the Governor-General's reaction. "I am very surprised," he said. "I have never heard of the girl, or any engagement." The engagement was the splash lead in all the Australian newspapers. The next comment was the denial by Major Slim. "I am not engaged and I never telephoned *The Malay Mail*," he said.

My Australian colleagues told me the story was clearly a *furphy*. They explained what that was to the ignorant pom: a *furphy* is a water cart made by J.Furphy & Sons of Shepparton, Victoria. Given the frequent droughts in Australia there is often nothing in it. So in Australian journalist parlance a story with nothing in it is a *furphy*.

In normal circumstances, Coleman would have been fired. But a dispute was going on at that time between AAP and Reuters and Reuters decided it would be politic not to insist on the firing.

Fifty-one years later I said to Viscount Slim: "The journalists in Kuala Lumpur decided that you had got drunk in the mess at lunchtime, you had decided to have some fun with the Press and made the telephone call." He did not comment.

This bizarre story brought to mind another strange incident in Malaya. On New Year's Eve 1956 I was not celebrating, I was standing in Reuters new office in Penang with Graham Jenkins waiting for a new teleprinter line from Singapore to start working. At the stroke of midnight the machine stuttered into life. But the news was garbage. Jenkins barked at me: "Get Lawrenson on the phone." John Lawrenson was the English trainee in Singapore. Lawrenson dragged from a New Year's Eve party in Singapore Geoffrey Thompson, the head of the telecommunications authority, to deal with the problem. Lawrenson called back. "It is due to icing on the aerials!." Jenkins roared: "Does he realise he is 50 miles from the equator?"

But Thompson was correct. The microwave circuit from Singapore to Penang went though the Cameron Highlands, which were more than 1200 metres high. Heaters were fixed to the antennae next day and the news came through loud and clear.

CHAPTER FOUR

Lessons in the Power of Positive Thinking

GEIRINGER

Home leave came in April 1957 and, after a few weeks holiday in France and Spain, I was back in 85 Fleet Street as Personal Assistant to the Assistant Manager of Comtelburo, George Cromarty Bloom, who was Geiringer's deputy.

I learned much from Alfred Geiringer when I worked under him in London after my return from Asia. The power of positive thinking dominated his life. The best example was in the late fifties when Reuters wrongly reported the British Petroleum dividend. The three London evening newspapers had banner headlines reporting Reuters error and the chaos which ensued on the stock market with millions of pounds lost and gained. The next morning Geiringer summoned his senior executives to a meeting. All awaited the rolling of heads of those responsible for the terrible error. But Geiringer conducted no inquest. All he said was: "If the financial community depends so much on Reuters service that it can gain and lose millions on the strength of one Reuters error, we are clearly not charging enough. Subscriptions to the London financial teleprinter service will be increased by a third forthwith." They were increased, no subscribers cancelled and the added revenue went straight through to Reuters bottom line.

When I told the story to Rupert Murdoch, Chairman of News Corporation, years later, he said: "That's an amazing story. I'd like to hire that guy." "But you can't do that, Rupert," I replied. "He's over 80."

Alfred Geiringer was born in Vienna on 9 May 1911. His father kept the art deco Café Geiringer in the 20th *Bezirk* of Vienna. He was a distant cousin of the composer, Gustav Mahler. In 1933 Geiringer first dipped his fingers in printer's ink by working as a stringer for a number of British and American newspapers, including the *News Chronicle* and the *New York Times*. The young journalist joined Reuters as assistant to the Chief Correspondent in Vienna in 1937.

Reuters Vienna office had incurred the wrath of Hitler and when the Germans invaded, the young man faced certain imprisonment because he was Jewish and because of his views. He escaped to London in March 1938, exiting Austria in the boot of the car of Reuters Chief Correspondent, Christopher Holme.

Lord Layton, Chairman of the *News Chronicle* and a director of Reuters, and his wife sponsored the young Austrian to the British government so that he could stay in Britain. He married their daughter, Margaret. He had a brief spell with Reuters in London in 1939/1940 and then again in 1942. In 1945 he became European Editor and then Assistant European Manager. He played a leading role in the re-establishment of Reuters in Europe after the Second World War and in the restructuring of national news agencies. Before the war many news agencies, which Reuters used as their agents, were government-controlled or subsidised.

Reuters and the world of information would be different places today if Alfred Geiringer had not worked in Reuters. Until the Second World War Reuters base was the British Empire. With the dissolution of that Empire, Reuters might well have disappeared in the face of American competition. The American competitors had a home base in the United States of 1700 daily newspapers to underwrite their costs. Reuters home base in the UK was a mere 58 newspapers.

Geiringer knew that if Reuters were to survive it had to find new sources of revenue. He believed passionately that supplying news to business could be that source of revenue and ensure the survival of the organisation he so loved. When in 1952 he was made head of Reuters Commercial Services it was the poor relation of the organisation.

I saw how twisted the priorities were when I was in Singapore. We were forbidden to start a teleprinter service for banks and brokers in Singapore because the Straits Times group objected that it would damage the circulation of its newspapers.

Derek Jameson, then a duty editor in the privileged general news services, and later to become Editor of the London *Daily Express*, described in his autobiography, *Touched by Angels* (London: Ebury Press, 1988) what happened when Geiringer's staff tried to get use of the newswires. Jameson says he would tell them, for example, that the Italians had just formed their 29th postwar government. There was no room for all that stock market rubbish. Soon the new head of Reuters Commercial Services had earned enough money from the post-war opening up of markets to be able to establish revolutionary long-wave radio communications in Europe and stock market prices were no longer delayed by the vagaries of the world of politics.

AG, as he was always known, fought for his staff and services up and down the floors of the headquarters of 85 Fleet Street. His voice could be heard booming as soon as a passenger got out of the lift. And he engendered an enthusiasm and excitement which made his staff proud to work with him. By the time he left in 1958 they were holding their heads high. Geiringer's greatest contribution to Reuters was in recruiting staff. He knew that if Reuters was to survive he had to recruit and train a new generation of young men and women graduates as specialist journalists and managers. Reuters had started recruiting graduates as trainee foreign correspondents for their general news services in 1947 through the Cambridge University Appointments Board. But none of these men were assigned to the commercial services. University Appointment Boards were not for the unorthodox Austrian. He recruited from any source that might produce talent. A young man, fresh out from Australia, called Glen Renfrew, dropped into Reuters London headquarters at 85 Fleet Street one day in 1952 and asked the front hall porter if there were any jobs going. The porter said there was a man called Geiringer who seemed to be interviewing a lot of people. He rang his secretary, she consulted her boss, who said he would see the young Australian. Renfrew explained his qualifications, which included good languages. "What do you most want to do in your life" he was asked. "Sail alone across the Atlantic," he replied. "You're hired," said Geiringer. Three decades later Renfrew was appointed chief executive of Reuters.

Alfred Geiringer put the recruits to work on the business news desks in London for a couple of years, at first as clerks tabulating market quotations and then as subeditors. In most cases he then sent them abroad to run small offices, where they combined all the jobs of journalism, selling and managing. When financial and commodity markets opened up in the sixties and computers started to appear in financial institutions, Reuters alone of the international news agencies had staff who could see the opportunities and who had the know-how to go ahead and exploit them. And the staff had, with great foresight, been recruited and trained by Geiringer a decade earlier. When he took charge of Reuters Commercial Services in 1952 Reuters had revenues of £1.4 million (£300 million at current values), which were tiny compared with competitors. In 2007 Reuters revenues were £2.6 billion.

Curiously enough Geiringer was wrong about the direction the company should take. Since the days of Paul Julius Reuter and his carrier pigeons, the company's wealth had been based primarily on selling time-critical prices and news about commodities, money and shares. Markets in Europe were controlled during and after World War II. "Voters are never again going to let speculators control the destiny of the world's economy," he argued. "Markets will never regain their importance. The future of economic news will be in industrial intelligence." He launched a mailed newsletter called *International Business Facts* and told his bosses it would get 10,000 subscribers. It got 16. He launched a global market-research operation, which gained only a handful of clients.

Alfred Geiringer left Reuters on 30 April 1958 after falling out with Cole. He was much missed for his enthusiasm, but it was time he went. Bloom, who before the war had sold market prices in Shanghai and never believed Geiringer's industry-orientated theories, succeeded him.

Resilience was Geiringer's greatest characteristic. When he left Reuters and, with great courage, founded Universal News Services, a public relations newswire, and went into other business ventures, time and again he bounced back from adversity. He offered me the job of Managing Director of one of the enterprises he had invested in, LBC News Radio, but I turned it down.

In Reuters I worked increasingly with Nigel Judah, the Deputy Chief Accountant, who became my best friend in Reuters. He attended our wedding, I was best man when he married Phoebe and became godfather to his daughter, Hettie.

Before I had gone abroad I could not afford my own accommodation and lived with my parents in their maisonette in Wandsworth. I stayed with them again on my return, but in 1958 I moved into a flat in Marsham Square, Chelsea, with two former Magdalen friends, Christopher Lush and Alec Morrison, and John Awdry, who later asked me to be godfather to the son of Juliet and himself, Simon. But the communal nature of the flat did not appeal to me and I rented a couple of rooms with shared bathroom in a grim house at 140 Holland Road, Shepherds Bush. Then Michael Goldman, a Wadham College, Oxford man, whom I had met through Oxford friends, and I decided to share accommodation and we found a very civilised flat at 35 Netherhall Gardens, Hampstead.

COLE

Chancellor left Reuters on 1 July 1959 and was succeeded as General Manager and chief executive by Cole.

The Board also appointed a permanent non-executive Chairman, departing from the practice of a rotating chairmanship. He was John Burgess, Chairman of Cumbrian Newspapers, a jolly decent gentleman, whom Garrett Drogheda described in his memoirs as "a courteous man without great cutting edge."

Cole was a Scot who had left school at 15 and gone straight into newspaper journalism. In all ways he was very large. He was very conscious of his lack of education and of his working-class background. Chancellor mocked him when one day he unwittingly wore an Old Etonian tie. On one occasion he could not get the head of the Greek news agency to understand him. "You tell him, Gerry," he told Gerald Long, Chief Correspondent in Germany. "These Latins find it difficult to understand us Scots." "I'm just talking out loud," he would say. "So my new office is like a seedy Manchester boarding house, is it, Mike," he charged me soon after he had become General Manager. I then knew who my friends were. Donald Ferguson, his personal assistant, had relayed my comment about his office to him. But he did not seem to hold it against me and sent his two daughters to represent him at my wedding.

Cole was an extraordinarily hard worker, an inspired newsman and a great salesman. Never-the-less clients often described him as "phoney Tony." He could not, or would not, see that the future of Reuters lay in the economic services, about which he knew nothing.

He was totally uncreative. In the 3 1/2 years that he was chief executive the company did not take one product initiative. Chancellor had his doubts about him. I once heard him apologising to a director at an annual lunch: "I had to make him general manager," he said. A particularly neglected area was economic services in the United States. Reuters had a base there with Comtelburo. The management was wise not to compete with Dow Jones at that time, but they could have started commodity news wires, where there was little competition.

An excellent choice as chief executive of Reuters instead of Cole would have been Ian Fraser. He had been Chief Correspondent in Germany, had left Reuters to join the merchant bank Warburgs, and eventually became chairman of the merchant bank Lazards.

I was Cole's personal assistant for a short period when the incumbent was in hospital. The work was mainly drafting letters, of which there were many, largely because he insisted in sending letters of thanks for thank-you letters. I had to have the Sunday newspapers delivered to my house by a special Reuter messenger at the crack of dawn because he always wanted to telephone me at eight o'clock to discuss them. His secretary, Maggie Alliston, explained to me that there had to be a rehearsal for the arrival of important visitors and she had to play the part of the visitor being shown into Cole's office: "My dear Ambassador. Welcome to Reuters, your Excellency."

On 19 October 1962 Reuters unveiled a plaque on the tavern in Aachen in Germany where Paul Julius Reuter had started the news agency in 1850 using carrier pigeons. Sales of the news service had been good and Cole wanted to spend the extra money he had in the kitty by taking the Board abroad and celebrating. Unfortunately what should have been a joyous occasion turned into a farce. The day before the Board was due to leave by plane fog descended over London and all planes were grounded. Cole summoned me to his office almost in tears. "I should never have given the organisation of the trip to a Canadian (Ferguson). He does not understand English weather," he said. "You'll have to take it all over." So I booked cabins on the Dover-Ostend ferry. The Continental guests were waiting in Aachen for the tardy Reuter board. Some newspapers could not resist making fun of the British the next day. One Spanish newspaper expressed surprise that Reuters was not familiar with English weather and did not know that fog often descended in the autumn.

Then to crown it all, when a lorry-load of pigeons was released to fly to Brussels they bombed the guests. The British Ambassador put up his umbrella.

The star of the group was Roy Thomson. Although he had left the Board and become a trustee, in 1967 he also came on the Board visit to Holland where the directors were guests of the Dutch news agency, ANP. By then he was Lord Thomson. When we visited a leading newspaper he did not seem much interested in the plant, but surprised everybody by asking to see the balance sheet. I did my best to translate it from the Dutch for him. He did not buy the newspaper.

MARRIAGE

In June 1959 Eise Cancrinus, my opposite number in ANP, introduced me to Helga den Ouden. We married in Holland on 26 March 1960.

Helga was born in Bucharest, Romania, on 9 May 1938, the daughter of Pieter den Ouden, who was Dutch, and Erna den Ouden Hermann, who was Romanian. Her father was an accountant with Shell and he had met her mother when he was posted to Bucharest. In 1939 her parents, older brother, Peter, and Helga moved to Indonesia. When the Japanese invaded in 1941 her father was put into a prison camp on the island of Flores in which he died. Extraordinarily, he was both born and died in a prison camp. He was born in a British prison camp in South Africa in the Anglo-Boer War. His wife, son and daughter were put in a succession of other camps in Indonesia. After the war Helga's mother wisely decided not to go back to Romania, but to settle near her late husband's family in Oegstgeest, Holland.

The forebears of Helga's Romanian family had come from Saxony to settle in Transylvania, then part of Hungary, in the Middle Ages. They spoke German and her birth certificate is in German. Her Romanian grandfather owned a number of restaurants and had a large house in Bucharest and a country place in Predeal, near Brazov.

Helga's grandfather, Reginus Anthonie den Ouden, was born in Gouda in Holland in 1868 and married Anna Josina Wilhelmina du Chatenier. She was of Huguenot stock and her family probably came to Holland from France in 1685 after the Revocation of the Edict of Nantes, which ended the right of the Protestants to worship. Reginus Anthonie was a school teacher and in April 1899 sailed, via London, for South Africa. He became headmaster of a school in Buffelsvlei, but he had to close it in May 1900 because of the Anglo-Boer War, which had broken out in the previous October between the British and the Boers, who were largely of Dutch origin. He joined the Boer government, led by Paul Kruger, as secretary of the War Commission. It was based in Machadodorp on the railway line near the Mozambique border, to where the government had withdrawn after the fall of Pretoria (The patriotic parents of my mother, on the other side in the war, named her Pretoria because she was born on 5 June 1900, the day Pretoria fell to the British). Reginus had to write reports on the War and some of them are included in his collected letters, edited by Helga's cousin, Professor drs. Freek van Veen. One letter is an appeal, which was successful, to the British general, Kitchener, to release his family from a prison camp where Helga's father had been born.

The war ended in May 1902 but, more than a year before, Reginus went to Lourenço Marques in Mozambique to board a Portuguese ship, the *Zaire*, en route to Portugal with 350 Boer refugees. They arrived on 28 March 1901 and he became the headmaster of a school for the children of the refugees in Caldas da Rainha. The story is recounted in a Portuguese book by O.J.O Ferreira *Viva os Boers*.

Reginus returned to Holland in 1902 and became headmaster of a school in Leimuiden near Schiphol. He later went into politics and became parliamentary editor of the *Standaard* newspaper.

When Helga and I became engaged Cole gave a dinner for her with the senior staff of Reuters and their wives in a private room at the Savoy Hotel in London. The custom at such dinners was for each guest to make a short speech. They were usually sycophantic and referred to the family spirit of Reuters. Helga was the last to speak and continued the family theme. "It is a great pleasure for me to be here tonight in the family way," she said. She brought the house down.

Helga and I married in her village, Oegstgeest. The ceremony took place in the town hall and the town clerk conducted the whole procedure in English. I was a little put out when, in accordance with Dutch law, he asked my parents if they gave permission for the marriage. The best man was Bob Mauthner, an old Oxford friend, who was able to make a speech both in Dutch and English. The reception was a lunch at the Beukenhof restaurant in Oegstgeest. Fifty years later we celebrated our diamond wedding anniversary with the family in the same restaurant.

Nigel Judah chartered a plane for the wedding guests from Southend in Essex to Amsterdam at a cost of £3 per person. At that price it was not the latest word in aircraft. On the way out a tyre burst on take-off and on the return flight the door between the cockpit and the cabin fell off. Fortunately one of the guests was very tall and was able to stretch out and keep it in position with his foot.

We had our honeymoon in the Pensione Paradiso in Taormina, Sicily, and in Rome. Soon after we arrived at the pension in Rome Helga received an enormous bunch of flowers from Walton Cole, who was passing through Rome. "There's something ulterior behind that bouquet," I warned my bride. A few minutes later a messenger appeared with a note. "Would I mind dropping by the office?" I spent the rest of the honeymoon there dealing with a contractual problem with an important client.

We moved into a small basement flat in Belsize Lane, Swiss Cottage, London and, after six months, bought a small modern house in The Hall, Foxes Dale, Blackheath, London.

In later years we moved to houses in Foxgrove Road, Beckenham, Kent, where we met other young people at the beginning of their careers, who remained life-long friends. The included Frank Kennedy, later to become British Consul-General in New York and a knight, and his wife Anne and Dr. Michael Butler, Reader in Virology at the University of Surrey and his wife Hazel.

CHAPTER FIVE

Computer Revolution

MANAGER OF COMTELBURO

When Bloom left Reuters to become General Manager of the Press Association on 10 October 1960, Alan Hammond, an old China hand, and I became Joint Managers of Comtelburo. The duopoly ended on 12 December 1962 when I became sole Manager of Comtelburo. I was 33.

One of the greatest problems I faced was the quality of staff. The majority of the staff had joined from secondary school at the age of 14 or 15 as messenger boys, although a number were of excellent quality despite their education being cut short. Outstanding were John Daniel, Daniel Fogel, Desmond Maberley, Cyril Smith, Peter Wade and Reg Watts. Most of the graduates Geiringer had hired had left because of the poor salaries. We therefore started a formal graduate entry scheme. Notable recruits were Nicholas Bray, Ian Capps, Gordon Hanson, Denis Lyons, Allan Maitland, Alex McCallum, John Makinson, David Marsh, Peter Montagnon, John Ransom, Tony Robinson, Martin Taylor, David Ure, André Villeneuve, Phil Wardle and David Wright.

Some moved on to careers outside Reuters. The most distinguished were Martin Taylor, chief executive of Barclays plc, and John Makinson, chairman and chief executive of the Penguin Group.

Amazingly, the Company had only one full-time salesman in the whole world. He was Joe Daffin, a former teleprinter operator in London.

I decided that central to the success of the economic services had to be that we should only exploit products where the key role was the time factor. I also believed that no successful company did specials – commissions for individual clients. Profitability should come from developing revenue rather than cutting costs. Anyone who developed a product had to sell it. We should avoid most business schools because the case-history approach looked to the past, not the future.

Helga contributed much to my work in Reuters. She managed on an exiguous housekeeping allowance and never raised objections to my frequent absences abroad. In 1963 I spent the month of August at the boarding house of Frau Doktor Riese in Heidelberg, improving my German. Helga did not complain. She went to Holland to stay with her mother.

Only as the children grew up was she able to devote the time she wished to her hobbies: pottery, batik, silk painting, water colour.

The role of wives in Reuters was brought home to me when I ran into the PR of a company in Los Angeles soon after we started to compete with Dow Jones. "You've got a funny set-up here," he said. "I rang your office to give my company's results. A woman with a foreign accent answered the phone. 'Hang on a second,' she said. 'I just have to see to the baby.'" We could only afford a one-man bureau. When the splendid correspondent, Bruce Russell, was out of the office, which doubled up with his family flat, his loyal French wife, Marie-Louise, held the fort.

A recurrent complaint in *Parting Shots* by Matthew Parris and Andrew Bryson (London: Viking, 2010), a selection of valedictory despatches by British ambassadors, is that wives were not paid for all the work they did for the Foreign Office. This was particularly the case in entertaining. I never heard that complaint in Reuters. Bob Elphick told me that when he was the BBC TV correspondent in Bonn in the mid-seventies Derrick Amoore, the Editor of BBC TV News, arranged for Bob's talented wife, Eve, to be paid when she kept the office going when he was away. But when the accountants heard about it they stopped it because they were terrified the practice would spread through the whole Corporation.

IBERIA

Soon after he became General Manager Cole appointed Gerald Long as Assistant General Manager in charge of Europe. Long and I went to Sweden and Finland to negotiate new contracts for the general news and economic services with the national news agencies. Long had a need to dominate and continually tried to put me down before the heads of the agencies. When I came back to London I told my boss, Stuart Underhill, an Assistant General Manager, that I would never again go on a trip with Long. Cole acted like the Spanish Pope Alexander VI dividing South America between Spain and Portugal. He lopped off the east and west extremities of Long's empire and gave to me responsibility for relations with Spain and Portugal and Eastern Europe and the Soviet Union. The brief covered both general news and the economic services. Not surprisingly, Long never forgave me.

Portugal was unusual for Reuters because, unlike most of Europe, it did not distribute through a national news agency but directly to newspapers and banks and brokers. In charge was a doctor, Luis Tieves. When he was studying for his medical degree he became the stringer for the British news agency, Exchange Telegraph, and was later taken on by Reuters. He decided to specialise in heart diseases, which he considered could best combine with his work for Reuters. One of the senior office staff was a great fan of the Benfica football club and I commented to Tieves that it was surprising that on the salary Reuters paid him he could afford to travel around Europe following the club. "Oh, he has a private income," he explained. When Nigel Judah later announced to me that there had been a major embezzlement in the Lisbon office, I realised the source of his private income. I flew out to Lisbon and the father of the embezzler offered me his fish restaurant in Cascais on the sea as a security for repayment if we would not prosecute. Unfortunately another more fungible security was found so Reuters did not go into the fish restaurant business.

The first international news agency to sign a distribution agreement with EFE, the news agency Franco set up in 1939, was Reuters in 1944. Reuters therefore had a privileged position in post-Republic Spain. After World War II it was not too difficult to get EFE in 1946 to form a joint company, Comtelsa, to distribute economic services. I was pleased that we eventually appointed as manager, Pepe Garcia Alegre, who had been a clerk in the Tangier office when I had been training there. He went far and eventually became business manager of EFE.

A great pleasure of visiting Madrid was to spend time with the Reuter correspondent, Henry Buckley. Buckley had been the correspondent of *The Daily Telegraph* on the Republican side in the Civil War. He had arrived in Spain in 1929, had been in the country for the whole of the life of the Republic and was recognised as the greatest authority on the period. All thought highly of his book *Life and Death of the Spanish Republic* (London: Hamish Hamilton, 1940). Unfortunately all unsold copies were destroyed in bombing in 1940, so it is now a rarity.

In *We Saw Spain Die: Foreign Correspondents in the Civil War* (London: Constable, 2008) Paul Preston devoted a whole chapter as a tribute to Buckley. William Forrest, who was in Spain during the war, representing first the *Daily Express* and later the *News Chronicle,* said in his obituary in *The Times*: "Buckley saw more of the Civil War than any foreign correspondent of any country and reported it with a scrupulous adherence to the truth that won the respect even of those who sometimes might have preferred the truth to remain uncovered."

The Spanish government forgave him for his Republican sympathies and when he retired in 1966 awarded him the Cruz de Caballero de la Orden de Isabel la Catolica.

Buckley covered many stories with Ernest Hemingway, who always came to see him after the War. Buckley said of Hemingway: "He was a terrific person, kindly, almost infantile at times. I think he almost loved the war, exactly like some of the characters in his own books."

In 1938 Buckley married a Catalan girl, Maria Planas, whose father owned the gasworks in Sitges. The Catholic Church was proscribed in Republican Spain, but Buckley got a dispensation and was married in the chapel in Barcelona used by the exiled Basques. One of the Buckley sons, Patrick, eventually worked for Reuters. Buckley joined Reuters in 1943 and was badly wounded on the Anzio beach-head. He suffered pain for the rest of his life.

I always stayed at the Ritz Hotel in Madrid, where Henry and I often had lunch. He was full of anecdotes about this most aristocratic of hotels. James Stewart arrived one day and signed in as "film actor." The receptionist told him that the hotel did not allow actors to stay there. So Stewart signed in as "Colonel, US Air Force." That was acceptable.

Reuters took little account of the fact that their man was renowned as the best informed and distinguished foreign correspondent in Spain. The big story for the British Press was no longer Franco. It was the latest rape or brawl of British tourists on the Costa Brava. And on that story Buckley was invariably beaten. The reason he was trounced was that as tourism developed the British tabloids posted reporters to the seaside resorts like Benidorm. The Spanish government had invested heavily in telephone communications on the coast to benefit tourism, but not in Madrid. So while Buckley was waiting hours for a telephone operator to put him through from Madrid to his stringers on the Costa Brava, the London newspaper reporters' stories that they had had dialled through to Fleet Street were already in print. Reuters budget did not run to staff correspondents on the coast.

The Spanish Minister of Tourism who had ensured that the tourists got their dial-out telephones, Manuel Fraga-Iribarne, was also Minister of Information. Soon after he took office in 1962 he visited EFE. Reuters rented an office in the EFE building and I happened to be there when he arrived. "Ah," he exclaimed. "This is EFE's Gibraltar." In December he announced that EFE was going to become an international news agency. Stuart Underhill flew out to Madrid to try to persuade Fraga that EFE should distribute its news through Reuters, particularly in Latin America. I attended the dinner Fraga gave for Underhill, which was one of the most embarrassing meals I ever attended. Underhill had started to take Spanish lessons a few months earlier and insisted on speaking Spanish to Fraga, a fluent English speaker and even author of a book on the British Parliament. Not surprisingly Fraga did not accept Underhill's proposal. I had learned some Spanish at evening classes when I first joined Reuters, but it had never occurred to me to try to speak Spanish to Fraga on our earlier meetings. I have always thought the decision of when to speak or not to speak a foreign language a nice judgment. Long spent a month in Madrid learning Spanish. I once attended a big dinner he gave for the President of Venezuela, Luis Herrera Campins, in Caracas. They sat next to each other, but did not exchange one word the whole evening.

Fraga was impressive and went out of his way to welcome me. One weekend he even gave me a lift up to the Escorial, where I was to spend the weekend. But he never did anything to help Reuters and refused my bid to get Garcia Alegre exempted from the law he introduced that all journalists had to be graduates. That meant he had not merely to take a degree, but also the qualifying school examinations, which he had never taken in Tangier.

EFE started distribution in Spanish in Latin America in 1966. They had great success. A survey conducted in 1992 showed that they were the most used international agency on the continent.

EASTERN EUROPE

I was flying from Belgrade to Bucharest on a Tarom plane in November 1961. It was my first visit to Eastern Europe and it was a revelation of how bizarre visits to that communist world could be. The pilot announced that we could not land in Bucharest because of fog and would have to stop in Sofia. I was sitting next to Dessa Trevisan, the Yugoslav correspondent of *The Times*. She was delighted by this news because she was *persona non grata* in Bulgaria. We landed in Sofia and hung around the airport for a few hours. The Tarom pilot explained that he could not find out if the fog over Bucharest had lifted because Tarom owed the Sofia airport money and they would not provide them any communications facilities with Bucharest. So an American woman of Romanian origin gave the pilot some dollars and he was able to telephone Bucharest. Bucharest airport was still closed. So we were moved by bus to the Balkan Hotel in Sofia for the night. Dessa Trevisan was allowed in.

When I turned on the shower in the morning it splayed all over the floor of the bathroom because it was bent. I straightened it and it came off in my hand. When I went to pay the bill the cashier said I had to pay for the repair of the shower. I summoned the manager and with great difficulty persuaded him that I had been doing him a great service in trying to straighten his shower. I did not pay for it.

We finally arrived in Romania. My task was to negotiate an increase in the subscription to the Reuter services paid by the Romanian news agency Agerpres. The increase barely covered the cost of the trip, but at that time Reuters did not see the business in that way. I asked my driver if he was a member of the party. "No. Are you?" he replied. "No," I explained. "I am a capitalist." "I have always wanted to be a capitalist," he whispered.

I later went back to Sofia to negotiate an increase in the subscription from the Bulgarian Telegraph Agency (BTA). The negotiations were with Madame Gavrilova, an old Stalinist known as the Iron Grandmother. She agreed an increase and for some reason I did not confirm it in writing until I got back to London. That was a mistake. She changed her mind and sent Cole a cable denying she had ever agreed an increase. "Mr Nelson is nothing but a merchant," she said.

I visited Moscow as a guest of TASS in August 1963. One of my hosts was the Editor, Gennady Shishkin, later to become Director-General of TASS. He had been the TASS correspondent in London at the time of the 20th Party Congress in 1956 when Nikita Khrushchev denounced Stalin. When he read the reports of the denunciation he went down to the Swan public house below Reuters, where TASS had its offices, and hurled beer bottles down the passageway. "They lied to us. They lied to us. They lied to us," he shouted as each bottle smashed against the wall of the Lutyens building. His time as correspondent in Washington was also unusual. He sent his children to the local grade school instead of to the Russian embassy school, and got away with it.

In London TASS took delivery of an economic news service from Reuters and relayed it to Moscow over their own communications. They sent everything twice because they needed two copies and teleprinter carbon paper did not exist in the Soviet Union. The man in charge of the relay was a Welshman, Gwynn Davis, who had once worked for Reuters. He was a communist who had been exposed as a member of a Reuter communist cell in the late forties and decided to leave. He hated his bosses in TASS and told me that joining the party had been the great mistake of his life.

When I arrived in Moscow my hosts said I could visit a provincial town of my choice. I chose Samarkand as Central Asia had always interested me. The next day they told me with great regret that Samarkand would not be possible. They explained: "You are a second class visitor, Gospodin Nelson. The budget for Samarkand is only for first class visitors. You can go to either Leningrad or Kiev." I chose Leningrad.

The TASS office in Leningrad was unusual because many of the journalists were former naval officers. Khrushchev had cut back the armed forces and did not know where to employ the redundant naval officers in Leningrad. So he put them in TASS. Journalists are renowned as heavy drinkers, but when that profession is combined with the navy the effect is shattering. The sailor journalists took me to dinner on the Saturday night at an enormous restaurant. Soon there was a crash at a nearby table and a guest staggered around with blood pouring from his face from a broken bottle. My host went to investigate. He soon returned. "It is all right. They are not Russians," he declared. They were Finnish sailors.

When the head of TASS, Dimitry Goryunov, visited England in 1963 I got the President of Magdalen, Thomas Boase, to entertain him together with Long, Bob Elphick, a former Reuter correspondent in Moscow, the TASS correspondent and myself. Goryunov was eager to visit Magdalen because Nikita Khrushchev, then Chairman of the Communist Party, and Nikolai Bulganin, then Soviet Prime Minister, had visited it in the course of a visit to Oxford on 21 April 1956. In the course of the leaders' visit strains of the spiritual *Poor Old Joe* could be heard coming from St. Swithun's Quad.

Khrushchev had recently denounced "Joe" Stalin. Goryunov, not surprisingly, did not refer to the joke.

Boase took us round the chapel. "How do intelligent scientists reconcile themselves with all this superstition," sneered Goryunov. "Oh! They have no problem," Boase brightly replied. "Some of our most distinguished scientists are our best attenders at chapel." Goryunov would have agreed with A.J.P. Taylor, who liked to argue that the college chapel should be turned into a swimming pool. Goryunov was not the easiest of guests. Against my advice, he had insisted on being taken to dinner at the *Talk of the Town* restaurant in London to hear Eartha Kitt. He pushed away the first course. "Mr Goryunov says this food it is shit," interpreted the TASS correspondent. I did not disagree.

LONG

Walton Cole died suddenly of a heart attack in his office on 25 January 1963. He was succeeded as General Manager and chief executive by Gerald Long, the Assistant General Manager in charge of Europe.

He promoted me to become a member of the Administration of Reuters, then the top management body, reporting directly to him, on 22 March 1963.

STOCKMASTER

It is hard to believe today how primitive the distribution of financial information was outside North America until the nineteen-sixties. Reuters sent news and data by radio or land-line teleprinter to its offices and agents throughout the world. There it was re-handled and sent to subscribers by dial-up telex or telephone, messenger and mail. Only in London, South Africa and Malaysia was it transmitted by fixed line teleprinter. Not surprisingly did continental European clients complain that London subscribers often received important news before they did. Not until 1963 was the business in Europe mini-revolutionised when Reuters connected clients in major European cities to London by teleprinter. Not until 1964 were they fed directly from New York. The reason for the primitive nature of the services was that for years the owners of Reuters were unwilling to invest in expensive communications and equipment.

If a broker in, say, Amsterdam, wanted the price of a stock from New York which was not in the Reuter service, the situation was even more bizarre. He telephoned the office of Reuters agents ANP. "Latest American Brake Shoe," he said. The ANP clerk typed a message and sent it on Reuters wire to London at 50 words a minute. A clerk in Reuters in London tore it off the teleprinter, retyped it, gave it to a teleprinter operator, who retyped it and sent it on Reuters wire to New York. There a clerk looked at a chalk board for the price, typed it and sent it on Reuters wire to London where the routine above was repeated and ten minutes after his original telephone call the broker got his price. Thus was financial information disseminated internationally until 1964.

A cheap and efficient long-standing method of disseminating commodity prices in London was from a switchboard in 85 Fleet Street which was connected to brokers by dozens of permanent telephone lines over which clerks read the latest quotations.

Internal communications were also primitive. In Brussels the Reuter office was on the top floor of the building of the Belga news agency, who handled the Reuter communications. The Reuter correspondent would punch his story onto perforated teleprinter tape, attach it to a bulldog clip and lower it down the well in the staircase on a piece of string to the hall lobby, where a Belga telepinter operator would retrieve it for transmission to London. In 1938 the German company Siemens had installed a vacuum tube communications system in the new Reuter and Press Association building in 85 Fleet Street but it had never worked because journalists fed beer bottles down the tubes. Siemens had not been paid for the system by the time war broke out and they never got their money after the war either. A more efficient system was overhead hoists as in old department stores.

International financial information was revolutionised when on 23 April 1963 I signed an agreement with Robert Sinn, President of Ultronic Systems Corporation, for Reuters to acquire rights outside North America to his corporation's Stockmaster.

Three years earlier Jack Scantlin, a clever engineer from Cal Tech, had invented Quotron, a desk unit that reproduced on thermo tape the last sale transaction of any stock on the New York Stock Exchange that was keyed into the desk unit. At that time stock market information was obtained from primitive systems that had not changed for 30 years like the famous stock ticker tape that cascaded down into Wall Street to celebrate elections. When I heard about Quotron I flew to New York to meet Scantlin to try to persuade him to give Reuters rights to his system outside North America. But I could never get him to make a decision.

In the autumn of 1961 Robert Sinn's Ultronic Systems Corporation brought out Stockmaster, which was similar to Quotron, but although Quotron's data was more comprehensive it was difficult to use. Sinn brought out an improved version and I invited him to London in early 1964 to discuss collaboration.

Ultronic had started to serve brokers in London, Geneva and Paris. But Reuters asset was that it leased what was then considered to be a wide-band circuit from New York to London via Montreal which was broken down into 24 teleprinter circuits by frequency division. Sinn proposed breaking the circuit down by time division multiplex to give a data stream in addition to the teleprinter circuits. It could then feed a computer in Reuters in London, which would serve Europe and eventually the world. Reuters problem was that it had no money. Its newspaper owners were unlikely to let it borrow any. So Sinn, a businessman of great imagination and creativity, offered to put up the money and proposed that would split the profits 50-50 in what we called a joint venture. It was a deal made in heaven. We started to serve clients on 1 July 1964.

Until 1964 Reuters had been in the news dissemination business: we dictated what information the client received. We were now in the news retrieval business: the client himself selected what he wanted. It was the greatest revolution in the information industry since the invention of the teleprinter.

On my recommendation, Glen Renfrew, the Australian who had walked into Reuters in London to be hired by Geiringer, who had joined Comtelburo shortly before me, was appointed manager of the Computer Division to run the Stockmaster joint venture as part of Reuters Economic Services. In 1969 he was made my deputy in Reuters Economic Services.

NORTH AMERICA

North America was a tough market. But sometimes we had a lucky break.

One day Cyril Smith, the North American Manager of Comtelburo, and I were surveying the market for a metal news service to be delivered by teleprinter on the West Coast. Our first cold call visit one Monday morning was to a metals firm down in the railyards of Los Angeles. I gave my card to the receptionist. "I think the president will see you," she said. She ushered us into his office. "Michael Nelson meet Michael Nelson," was her introduction. So the two Michael Nelsons signed the contract for the delivery of the Reuter service and Reuters was born on the West Coast of the United States. We never looked back.

One of the most important dates in Reuters history was 2 March 1964. On that date Reuters launched the Wall Street Printer in Europe. It fed news and prices, primarily from the United States, by teleprinter directly to brokers and banks. The date was important because it precipitated the rupture of Reuters relationship with Dow Jones and the AP.

Under an agreement dating from 1937 Reuters exchanged the City Ticker, the global financial news service it distributed by teleprinter in the United Kingdom, for the Dow Jones Broad Tape of United States financial news. Reuters exchanged the Press Association UK news, in which it had overseas rights, for the AP. A wire of domestic US news.

It took Dow Jones a year to wake up to the implications of the Reuter Wall Street Printer and on 2 March 1965 Dow Jones told Cyril Smith they planned to distribute the Broad Tape in the UK. I flew to New York and Smith and I met William Kerby, the Chairman of Dow Jones. He proposed that Reuters and Dow Jones operate a joint venture, with Reuters distributing the Broad Tape in the UK. I said I would report to my superiors and we agreed we would continue the discussions in London. I gave him lunch in London on 6 May and told him we were not interested in a joint venture. He was very surprised.

We decided to spend the princely sum of £14,000 (£200,000 at current values) in 1965 to improve our coverage of financial news from the United States against the day when we would lose the Broad Tape, our most important source of financial news. We then started to survey the market for our own wire in competition with Dow Jones. We were greatly encouraged by Merrill Lynch, the largest broker, who were eager to see the Dow Jones monopoly broken. Cyril Smith and I made a presentation to the top partners, which received a favourable response. The most important of the partners was clearly Donald Regan, who had travelled up from Philadelphia, where he was in charge of the office, for the meeting. He took over as Merrill Lynch's chairman and CEO in 1971, the year the company went public. He later became Ronald Reagan's Treasury Secretary and White House Chief of Staff. Such are the vagaries of business that in 2008 Merrill Lynch made a fourth quarter loss of $21 billion and was taken over by the Bank of America. Reuters made a profit and was taken over by Thomson.

Did the Merrill executives recall the limerick:

> In Wall Street a girl named Irene
> Made an offering somewhat obscene
> She stripped herself bare
> And offered a share
> To Merrill Lynch, Pearce, Fenner and Beane.

We were defeated by the Dow Jones rate structure. Brokers had to pay for the Broad Tape by "opportunity for use". They paid a subscription according to the number of offices, whether they took the service in them or not. That meant they were unwilling to pay anything more than a small subscription to Reuters. We calculated that we would need an investment of £500,000 (£7 million at current values) to launch the wire and that it would take five to six years to break even. I knew that Reuters owners would never agree to such an investment and with a heavy heart recommended that we abandon the project. On 11 May 1966 my recommendation was accepted.

Meantime, the Americans were preparing to gang up on the Brits. On 7 September 1966 the AP gave notice on the Reuter agreement. They wanted a differential payment by Reuters. On 8 September Wes Gallagher, the General Manager of AP, told Long in London that the AP planned to tie up with Dow Jones to operate an international economic news wire. Accompanied by John Lloyd, the AP boss in London, he elaborated his plans over lunch at Reuters with Long and myself.

In November Long and I, accompanied by George Cromarty Bloom, the General Manager of the Press Association, and D. Kimpton Rogers, Reuters North American Manager, met Gallagher and Stan Swinton, who was in charge of AP internationally, at the AP offices in New York. "We are trading mice for elephants," said Gallagher. Long had given Gallagher lunch in London but we received no hospitality in New York, an indication of how the relationship had deteriorated.

Only with great difficulty did Long persuade the Reuter board to let him break with Dow Jones and the AP. Particularly strong opposition came from Lord Drogheda, Chairman of the *Financial Times*. "Has Long gone mad? Does he know what he is doing?" were his questions as he telephoned round the other directors.

The Dow Jones agreement ended on 31 March 1967 and the AP on 7 September. On 1 April the AP-DJ economic news service started.

With no prospect of earning revenues from a financial wire in the United States to help finance the local reporting, the outlook looked bleak. But then Bob Sinn again came to Reuters rescue. When I told him of our predicament he said he would ask General Telephone and Electronics (GT&E), which had recently acquired Ultronic, to finance a financial wire. He and I negotiated an agreement whereby GT&E would finance the project, Reuters would produce the service and Ultronic sell it. Kerby threatened the President of GT&E that he would get no favourable coverage in the *Wall Street Journal* if he competed with Dow Jones, but GT&E stood their ground. The Reuter-Ultronic Report (RUR) started on 2 January 1968.

The Dow Jones Broad Tape was displayed in brokers' dealing rooms via a machine called Translux, which effectively produced a camera image of the tape on a cloth screen. We had to do something better. One day in 1965 I visited a computer exhibition at Olympia in London and for the first time saw a display of computer data numbers on a video screen. Until then I had only ever seen computer data displayed on nixie tubes or paper. It gave me an idea. A few days later I was having dinner at the Potinière du Soir restaurant in New York with Renfrew and George Hernan, a senior design engineer at Ultronic. I told them what I had seen at the Olympia. "Would it be possible to display words on a video display," I asked Hernan. "Sure," he said. And thus was borne Videoscan with which from 1968 we displayed the RUR. Was I the discoverer of the display of words on screens?

The RUR did not do well. The reasons were that the Dow Jones rate structure militated against a competitor and that the New York Stock Exchange handbook said that companies should release their news to Dow Jones. I met the President of the Exchange, but he refused to give equal treatment to Reuters. I met Manny Cohen, the Chairman of the Securities and Exchange Commission (SEC), in Washington who refused to help on the equal treatment front or the on the rate structure, although it was clearly anti-trust. Washington had not forgotten who had burnt the White House.

Dow Jones told its reporters to make it clear to companies by innuendo that if they failed to favour Dow Jones over Reuters in the release of news they would not get favourable coverage in the *Wall Street Journal.* The reporting problems were accentuated by the fact that Reuters was virtually unknown in the United States. In Washington our staff disliked going up on the Hill to report because they knew few Congressmen and few Congressmen were interested in talking to reporters from an organisation they had never heard of.

But then on 3 April 1968 things suddenly dramatically changed. On that day Reuters beat Dow Jones by 21 minutes with the news from Reuters Singapore radio monitoring that the Vietcong had announced in Hanoi that they were willing to talk peace. The brokers who subscribed to Reuters made a fortune from the surge in the market and Reuters were at last put on the map. I was sitting in the office in New York at the time and decided to take a full page advertisement in the *Wall Street Journal* with the headline "Vietcong willing to talk and it takes Wall Street 21 minutes to find out." In the two weeks following this success 40 new contracts for RUR were signed. That single story transformed Reuters fortunes in the United States.

The next time I saw the New York Stock Exchange they told me they were going to change the handbook to give equal treatment to Reuters with Dow Jones on the release of news.

Reuters were unhappy with Ultronic's selling effort on the RUR and ended the agreement at the beginning of 1972, renaming the service the Reuter Financial Report (RFR). On 22 June 1972 the Federal Trade Commission (FTC) agreed to investigate Dow Jones pricing policy at Reuters request. It took them three years to investigate and on 9 April 1975 the FTC told Reuters they were dropping it because it was too small, but said Reuters had a case.

FIRE!

On 18 May 1970 I was having dinner in the Intercontinental Hotel in Frankfurt with John Lawrenson, the European Manager of the Economic Services, when I was called to the telephone to speak to Long. Reuters headquarters at 85 Fleet Street was on fire, the building had been evacuated and no news was being distributed. He instructed me to go to the Frankfurt office, set up there an alternative headquarters and start again the distribution of the news service. Lawrenson said it would be a long night and that we should finish our sausages, which we did. Fortunately, soon after I began to try to restart the news services, Long phoned again. The fire was out and 85 Fleet Street was back in operation.

SWITZERLAND

Stockmaster and its sophisticated daughter Videomaster spread throughout the world in the late sixties, but the country that caused me sleepless nights was Switzerland. The Swiss banks, which were our most important market, cooperatively owned Telekurs, which processed historical stock market data. The banks decided Telekurs should go into the real-time business and invited Reuters and the American company Bunker Ramo to bid to supply a stock price data feed.

Competition from Telekurs could do immense damage to Reuters. So we needed alternative products. In early 1971 I therefore sent a young Reuter executive, André Villeneuve, to Switzerland to study the foreign exchange market and recommend a product to exploit it. I had been impressed by reports of his success in selling foreign exchange services in Buenos Aires and by his enthusiasm for our business. The reason we chose the foreign exchange market to study was that the fixed exchange rate structure set up at Bretton Woods in 1944 was breaking down. We could see that its collapse would present us with great opportunities.

Early in 1972 Long and I went to Switzerland to hear who Telekurs had chosen to supply their data feed. Max Siebenmann, our Swiss manager, went to Telekurs to hear the decision. He telephoned me at our hotel and I understood him to say, through his thick Swiss accent, that Reuters had been chosen. Long ordered the champagne. Siebenmann then arrived at the hotel. "No, no," he said. "We have not been chosen." How are the mighty fallen! That was a disaster and it was hard to see how Reuters could stand that loss of revenue when the banks subscribed to Telekurs, using Bunker Ramo data, instead of Reuters.

But nothing is ever as good or bad as it seems, and it took Telekurs more than three years to launch their service. By then we were deriving revenue from our new products and using them to counter Telekurs. So I could sleep easier.

DIVERSIFICATION

So uncertain was Long about the future of Reuters that in 1971 we commissioned American management consultants to do a study on what the development strategy of the company should be. Their report said there was no future in information and Reuters should develop a global business of the maintenance of communications equipment. We decided they were mad and went back to the development of information services.

Not long after the lunatic report, Gordon Moore, founder of Intel, the chip maker, must have decided that Reuters was doing something right because he took time out to come to see me when he was on a visit to London. I asked him about his famous law. In 1965 he had predicted that the number of components the industry would be able to place on a computer chip would double every year. I met him later at the Intel plant in California, but by then he had modified Moore's Law to once every two years.

Kenneth Olsen, founder of Digital Equipment Corporation, from which Reuters bought computers for the Reuter Monitor, was another imaginative engineer, whom I met and who admired what Reuters were doing. *Fortune* magazine described him in 1986 as the most successful entrepreneur in the history of American business.

CHINA

In October 1972 I accompanied Long on a visit to China. Brian Horton, the Editor-in-Chief, and Ian Capps, in charge of Asia for the Economic Services, were also in the team. The purpose of the visit was to restore relations between Reuters and Hsinhua, the New China News Agency, damaged by the arrest of the redoubtable Tony Grey, the Reuter correspondent, who had been placed under house arrest for 26 months – 807 days – on 21 July 1967 at the time of the Cultural Revolution.

The rather grim atmosphere which still obtained despite the ending of the Cultural Revolution was broken by some bizarre incidents. James Pringle, the Reuter correspondent, asked our Chinese minders if it would be possible to visit the underground shelters, which he understood had been built as a precaution against the Russians. One day they took us to a department store, pushed back the shoppers, rolled back a carpet and opened trap doors to reveal steps leading to vast cellars. We were led down steps to a virtual underground town and were the first westerners to be shown this labyrinth. Long was overcome with claustrophobia and the interpreter had to take him out into the fresh air. Our minder spoke no English, but he had been the Hsinhua correspondent in Chile, so we spoke Spanish. It felt most odd to be speaking Spanish in the Chinese anti-Russian air raid shelter in the capital of the People's Republic of China.

We were taken to a show-case farm called the Sino-Albanian Friendship Community. We saw ducks being force-fed to make the famous Peking duck. After each feed they ran off quacking down a corridor. I said they were obviously going to complain at a party struggle meeting. Long was furious and delivered a great lecture on how that joke showed I had no respect for the Chinese people and all their suffering over the centuries. But the story soon got round the diplomatic community, which thought it a good joke. We were impressed by the commune clinic where we saw demonstrations of the three schools of medicine: acupuncture, traditional herbalism and expensive western pharmaceuticals, which were used only when the others would not do. We later saw a harrowing film of acupuncture anaesthesia used in brain surgery.

Alec Douglas-Home, the British Foreign Secretary, was due to make a visit to restore good relations shortly after we were due to depart. The head of the Chinese Foreign Ministry Press Department, Mr Chi, who had dealt with Tony Grey in his house arrest, asked me if I could get some music to be played by the band on Douglas-Home's arrival at the airport. The official had been educated at Cambridge and remembered a piece of music from those days. It went, he said: "Dum dee dum, dum dee dum, dum dee dum dee dum." You don't mean *"Here we go, here we go, here we go again,"* I said. "Yes, that's it," he said with great delight. He could not understand my view that it was hardly suitable music for the restoration of good relations after the attacks on the British Embassy at the time of the Cultural Revolution. So I arranged for him to be sent the music.

Peter Gregson, who covered Douglas-Home's arrival at the airport for Reuters, confirmed to me later that as the Foreign Secretary stepped on to the tarmac the band indeed struck up with "Here we go, here we go, here we go again."

I went back to China in 1987, accompanied by Helga and Peter and Christine Job. Job was in charge of Asia. The purpose of the visit was primarily to inaugurate computerised Reuter services, unthinkable on the previous visit. Another great change was that the Reuter correspondent in Beijing, Mark O'Neill, spoke Chinese. For many years the Chinese would not let Reuters send staff to Beijing who spoke Mandarin. The most important interview was with Jiang Zemin, Mayor of Shanghai, who later became President of China. When I met him he spoke excellent English, but when he became President he found it politic to give the impression he did not speak it very well.

The most poignant engagement was at the café of the Peace Hotel in Shanghai to hear the jazz musicians, who had played there, apart from interruptions during the war and Cultural Revolution, since the 1930's. Their repertoire remained mostly pre-war.

On this visit to China I became interested in the figurines of the Han Dynasty (206BC-220AD). In the first millennium BC the Chinese buried servants and animals alive to accompany and serve their masters in the afterlife. They gradually replaced them with terracotta figures. I was taken by the vibrant dancers, musicians, clowns and jolly jugglers and started to collect entertainers. I mostly bought them in Hong Kong, London and Paris. My quests in Paris taught me to my surprise that there is no French equivalent to the English word "entertainer."

As with most antiques, there are many forged Han figurines and I became involved in the strange world of thermo-luminescence testing to determine age. One of the most important testing centres is the Research Laboratory for Archaeology and the History of Art at Oxford. So you either ensured that any object carried a certificate of age from the Laboratory, or made the sale conditional on your getting one yourself. But even so there was still a chance of fraud as the Laboratory showed with this caveat: "In making this report it is assumed that the sample has not been exposed to irradiation with X-rays or neutrons; this might cause the age as determined by thermo-luminescence to be greater than the true age."

JOBS

I was not inundated with job offers when I worked for Reuters, but looking back I am glad I declined those I received. The first in 1955 was to open a bureau for the Associated Press in Bangkok. To stay on in that sybaritic location was tempting, but when you looked around at the Europeans who had settled down there and married Thais and saw how many of them were alcoholics it was not too difficult to resist the temptation. The second was to become Assistant General Manager of the Press Association with a view to succeeding George Cromarty Bloom as General Manager in a few years. But what a boring organisation in comparison with Reuters. Quite attractive was to become Managing Director of London Broadcasting, the first all-news commercial radio in the UK. They got into a lot of financial difficulty so I was well out of that one.

In June 1974 David Leroy-Lewis, a Deputy Chairman of the London Stock Exchange, asked me if I would like to be considered for the job of Chief Executive of the London Stock Exchange. I said I would, met the head-hunters and had an interview with the Chairman and other members of the Exchange. But I did not like the city gent atmosphere and withdrew my application. They probably would not have offered me the job, anyway.

In 1971 I visited the Australian Associated Press (AAP) in Melbourne and Sydney. They were shareholders in Reuters and the agents for the sale of Reuter services in Australia. Duncan Hooper, the General Manager, decided it would be a good thing for the AAP if I were to accept the invitation of Malcolm Fraser, my old Oxford friend, the Minister of Defence, to spend the weekend with him and his wife Tamie at their property Nareen in the state of Victoria. He therefore chartered a plane from Melbourne to Hamilton and, since he believed I needed a minder, got Fraser to agree that I should be accompanied by Wally Parr, the manager of Reuters Economic Services in Australia. When we got to Melbourne airport the pilot refused to fly because of bad weather. I spoke to Malcolm on the phone. He was furious. He said he had invited the cream of the society of Victoria to meet me at dinner on the Friday night and many would be flying in to Hamilton for the occasion. "Give me the pilot," he barked. The pilot refused to budge. Malcolm clearly believed in Pompey's statement: "We have to sail. We do not have to live." We flew out the next day and Malcolm fielded the second eleven at a charming dinner on the Saturday night.

By the time the Reuter Board flew out to Australia for a visit in 1977 Malcolm was Prime Minister, which he had been since 1975. He was defeated in 1983. He and Tamie came to London and Helga and I took them to the opera at Glyndebourne. He was greatly cheered up in the interval as we walked over to our picnic when an Australian accosted him: "Good on yer Malcolm," he said. "We're right behind yer."

CHAPTER SIX

Internet's Precursor

REUTER MONITOR

On 4 June 1973 we launched the Reuter Monitor. It was the outcome of André Villeneuve's earlier visit to Switzerland. With the Reuter Monitor market makers contributed foreign exchange rates to a computer system which other dealers could retrieve on video terminals. Both the contributors and the recipients paid. It was the precursor of the Internet and proved to be the springboard for Reuters financial success. André Villeneuve had created one of the most inventive information products ever.

The Reuter Monitor and the Reuter Monitor Dealing Service, which followed in 1981, were designed by Reuter technicians led by Peter Benjamin. Benjamin, a renaissance man, contributed much. Patrick Mannix was the highly efficient project manager. The products followed the ARPANET, which had been launched in the United States in 1969 and which was the basis of the Internet.

A HOUSE IN FRANCE

After a good lunch on the last day of a holiday with the family in the Dordogne in 1971 I signed the *compromis* for a broken-down old farmhouse. British exchange controls prevented me from handing over a cheque for the deposit, which was as well, as it turned out. In the cold grey light of dawn back in England, I realised we could not afford it. So I offered what I described as an option on the property in the personal column of the *The Times* for £500 (£5000 at current values). I got 18 replies and sold it immediately. We spent the money on a Georgian clock.

Two years later our finances had improved a little and in April 1973 we bought a derelict old farmhouse called Préchaud in Chazeaux, Yssingeaux, Haute–Loire, France for FFrs 35,000 (£3500, £31,000 at current values). We chose this wild part of France because it was cheap. It was also beautiful. It was on one of the pilgrimage routes from Le Puy to Santiago de Compostella, marked by a stone *coquille St. Jacques.* We spent some money modernising the house and made the adjoining barn living quarters, but we could not afford to bring in town water, so suffered from the erratic behaviour of the spring. The whole family worked hard scraping the cow dung off the ground floor of the house where the peasants had kept their cattle.

NEWS DOES NOT PAY

A significant date for the future structure of Reuters was 1 July 1973 when Gerald Long, General Manager and Chief Executive, joined the Reuter board as Managing Director.

On 1 January 1974 Brian Stockwell became General Manager and I became a Deputy General Manager and took charge of Reuters Media Services outside North America in addition to Reuters Economic Services, but gave up responsibility for Reuters Economic Services in North America to Glen Renfrew, who was also appointed a Deputy General Manager.

The background to that change was an unsuccessful attempt by Long to make the provision of news to the media profitable. In October 1968 he had set up a General News Division (GND) as a profit centre alongside Reuters Economic Services (RES). Brian Horton, a New Zealander, was appointed to run it with the titles of Editor-in-Chief and Assistant General Manager. He was an able executive, but of extraordinary arrogance. I once sent him a note about Tokyo staffing. "Who or what is Satosan?" he asked of the most distinguished Reuter journalist in Japan. Bob Mauthner memorably described him as "The only living heart-transplant donor." A combination of inflation and competition meant that General News Division was never profitable, despite the fact that I set up a massive subsidy from RES to GND. Structurally it was crazy: it was like giving the production manager at Ford responsibility for selling the cars. Long had done it partly for political reasons. After five years GND was closed down and Horton resigned.

Helga and I very much liked his wife Sally, but she left him and in 1976 married Graham Carleton Greene, son of Hugh Carleton Greene, Director-General of the BBC and brother of the novelist Graham Greene. When I retired from Reuters Graham Carleton Greene, who was a Trustee of the British Museum, kindly asked me if I would be interested in becoming Chairman of the Friends of the British Museum, but I declined.

Horton married again and eventually moved to Spain. When Long became Managing Director of Times Newspapers in 1981, he called Horton back to London to become Foreign Editor of *The Times*. He subsequently took other jobs in News International, but did not last long after Murdoch eased Long out of the group and Horton returned to Spain where he spent his retirement. He died in 2009 aged 76.

LATIN AMERICA

Latin America was Reuters greatest burden for much of its history. In the time of the nineteenth century news agency cartels it was the bailiwick of the French news agency Havas. The British government paid for Reuters to take over the Havas operations when France fell during World War II. After the French returned under the name of Agence France-Presse (AFP), Reuters confined its general news distribution to Argentina, Chile, Uruguay and Brazil. But it could not compete with the American agencies and AFP, which was subsidised by the French government, and Reuters closed down its general news distribution in 1958.

Reuters returned to general news distribution in May 1960 with a contract with a new Buenos Aires newspaper *El Mundo*. Wider distribution started in 1961, but losses became intolerable despite a secret subsidy from the British government. In April 1968 Reuters persuaded a number of Latin American newspapers to take shares in a regional news agency to be run initially by Reuters. It was formed in 1970 and provided Reuters with its report from the region for the rest of the world. But the owners only paid their bills spasmodically and it soon got heavily into debt to Reuters.

In December 1974 I went for the first time to Latin America. We secured a substantial subscription from the Venezuelan government, which helped the finances, but Latin continued in deficit and closed in May 1981. Reuters then distributed news to the media under its own name again.

To go to a part of the world for the first time at the age of 45 was for me

1. BELOW. Grandmother Margaret Nelson, née Johnston, 1863-1950.

2. ABOVE. Grandfather Dr. Thomas Nelson, 1854-1935.

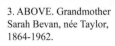

3. ABOVE. Grandmother Sarah Bevan, née Taylor, 1864-1962.

4. LEFT. Grandfather Reg. Sgt. Major William Bevan, 1864-1935.

5. A.J.P. Taylor by Marc. Taylor was my tutor for the nineteenth century. He was a left-winger and renowned as the first TV don.

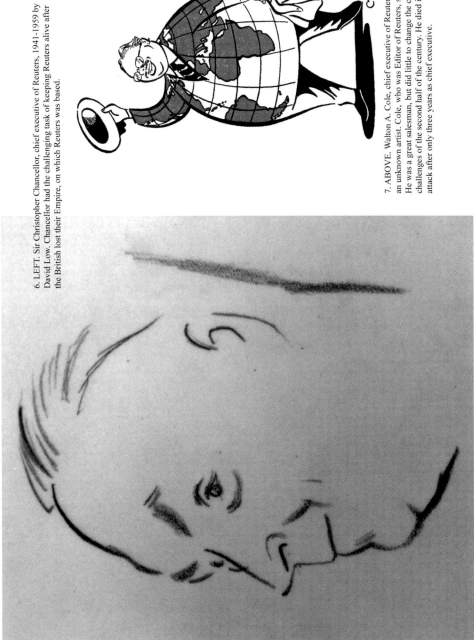

6. LEFT. Sir Christopher Chancellor, chief executive of Reuters, 1941-1959 by David Low. Chancellor had the challenging task of keeping Reuters alive after the British lost their Empire, on which Reuters was based.

7. ABOVE. Walton A. Cole, chief executive of Reuters, 1959-1963 by an unknown artist. Cole, who was Editor of Reuters, succeeded Chancellor. He was a great salesman, but did little to change the company to meet the challenges of the second half of the century. He died in his office of a heart attack after only three years as chief executive.

8. The Reuter House in Bangkok when Helga and I visited it in 1987, 32 years after I originally left. My flat was on the upper floor and the office on the ground floor. Some of the staff lived in huts in the compound. It was very Somerset Maugham.

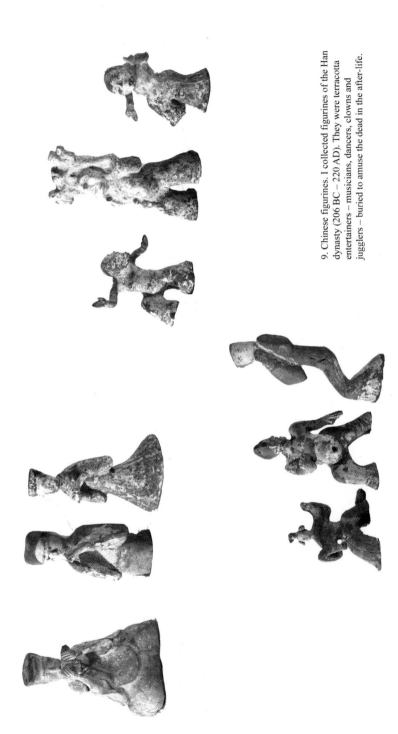

9. Chinese figurines. I collected figurines of the Han dynasty (206 BC – 220 AD). They were terracotta entertainers – musicians, dancers, clowns and jugglers – buried to amuse the dead in the after-life.

10. The SEATO Conference, Bangkok, 1955. (L to R) Michael Nelson, Denys Corley Smith, Saigon, Warren White, Singapore, Garth Roydhouse, Wellington, David Chipp, Rangoon.

11. Thirty-two years later in 1987 we staged a re-enactment at a dinner at the Nelson house in London.

12. Marriage to Helga den Ouden, de Beukenhof, Oegstgeest, Holland, 26 March 1960.

Gambling on success: Michael Nelson and his brainchild

13. *The Sunday Times*, 5 May 1985. It was not in fact my brainchild. Robert Sinn invented
the Stockmaster. But in 1964 I acquired from Ultronic Systems Corporation rights for
Reuters to market and operate it outside North America, which made Reuters a lot of money.

14. Gerald Long, chief executive of Reuters 1963-1981. Long succeeded Cole. Long's greatest achievement was to break with the American agencies, Associated Press and Dow Jones, and establish Reuters in the United States.

15. I had had a view of St Paul's from an office in 85 Fleet Street for nearly 20 years. When I became Long's deputy in London in 1976 I had to move to the other side of the building and lost the view. In a surprising act of generosity, Long commissioned Michael Harrison to draw this view to hang in my new office.

16. CENTRE. In Amsterdam, showing Lord Thomson, a trustee of Reuters, the balance sheet of the newspaper we were visiting. He did not buy the newspaper. The Reuter board visited Holland in 1967. Thomson died in 1976. His descendants acquired Reuters in 2008.

17. FAR RIGHT. André Villeneuve, inventor of the Reuter Monitor. It was one of the most important information services of the twentieth century and revolutionised foreign exchange trading.

18. ABOVE. A statue of Paul Julius Reuter was unveiled at Royal Exchange Buildings on 14 October 1976, the 125th anniversary of the founding of Reuters in London. Michael Black is here sculpting it in the De Lank quarry on Bodmin Moor in Cornwall.

19. LEFT. The Reuter flotation on the London Stock Exchange on 4 June 1984 was attended by Nigel Judah, Finance Director, Sir Denis Hamilton, Chairman, Glen Renfrew, Managing Director and myself.

20. ABOVE. Celebration of the Reuter flotation by Renfrew, Nelson and Judah by an unknown artist. The executive directors had been given stock options in the company in 1981. They became more valuable in the years following the flotation.

21. LEFT. Jiang Zemin, Mayor of Shanghai, 1985-88. President of China 1993-2003.

22. RIGHT. Tunku Abdul Rahman, Chief Minister of Malaya, 1955-57.

25. LEFT. Manuel Ulloa, Prime Minister of Peru, 1980-83.

26. RIGHT. Fidel Castro, President of Cuba, 1976-2008.

27. LEFT. Miguel de Madrid, President of Mexico, 1982-88.

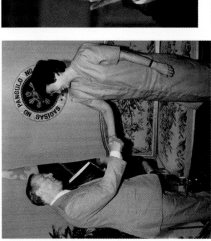

23. ABOVE. Corazon Aquino, President of the Philippines, 1986-92.

24. BELOW. Sheikh Isa bin Sulman Al-Khalifa, Emir of Bahrain, 1961-99.

28. Helga and I spent a night in an audience with Fidel Castro, President of Cuba, at his palace in Havana in 1985. He gave Helga a pamphlet he had written and in it wrote a dedication to her.

29. Gregorio Fuentes and Helga, Cuba, 1985. Fuentes was once captain of the Pilar, Ernest Hemingway's boat. Some claimed he was the inspiration for Hemingway's novel The Old Man and the Sea. He died in 2002 aged 104.

FIDEL CASTRO

HOW
LATIN AMERICA'S
AND THE THIRD
WORLD'S UNPAYABLE
FOREIGN DEBT CAN AND
SHOULD BE CANCELED
AND THE PRESSING
NEED FOR
THE NEW INTERNATIONAL
ECONOMIC ORDER

Para Helga,
afectuosamente.

Fidel Castro

Cuba, Abril 18, 85

FIDEL CASTRO

HOW
LATIN AMERICA'S
AND THE THIRD
WORLD'S UNPAYABLE
FOREIGN DEBT CAN AND
SHOULD BE CANCELED
AND THE PRESSING
NEED FOR
THE NEW INTERNATIONAL
ECONOMIC ORDER

INTERVIEW GRANTED
TO THE MEXICAN DAILY
EXCELSIOR

30. Family 1973: party to celebrate my parents' 50th wedding anniversary. (L to R) Helga, Patrick, Michael, Paul, Granny Nelson, Shivaun, Granddad Nelson, sister Denise, nephew John, brother-in-law Reginald.

31. Family 2011: (L to R) Patrick, Michael, Shivaun, Felix, Helga, Emilio, Alba, Mariana, Paul.

32. The Reuter Board in 1987. (Standing L to R) Alan Burnet, Sir Richard Storey, Rupert Murdoch, Glen Renfrew, Sir Christopher Hogg, Nigel Judah, Michael Nelson, Robert Maxwell, Donald Anderson, (Sitting L to R) Pehr Gyllenhammar, James Evans, Peter Gibbings, Lyle Turnbull.

a great experience, throwing open a new world of history, culture and people.

But the most stimulating encounter was getting to know two remarkable newspaper owners who were directors of Latin: Manuel Ulloa Elias of *Expreso* of Peru and Agustin Edwards Eastman of *El Mercurio* of Chile.

Ulloa was a wealthy businessman and banker and a politician. He rescued *Expreso* from bankruptcy and turned it into the largest circulation newspaper in the country. When I first met him he was in exile from Peru to escape unfounded charges of corruption from the then President General Juan Velasco Alvarado. Ulloa had been finance minister in the government of Fernando Belaunde Terry, which had been overthrown in a coup in October 1968. He had instituted wide-ranging tax reforms, which had infuriated the owners of land and capital and tried to control military spending, which enraged the army. Political scandals related to the IPC oil company brought the government down.

The exile spent most of his time in Madrid and New York. He reminded me of the refugees described in Macaulay's History of England. Inspired by the English refugees in Holland in the Seventeenth Century he wrote: "A politician driven into banishment by a hostile faction generally sees the society which he has quitted through a false medium. Every object is distorted and discoloured by his regrets, his longings and his resentments. Every little discontent appears to him to portend a revolution. Every riot is a rebellion."

Ulloa's seven years in exile meant that he had time to devote to Latin, of which he became chairman of the board. His acute intelligence and high profile were of great benefit.

In August 1975 the chiefs of the military regions deposed Velasco and appointed the minister of war, Francisco Morales Bermudez, head of state. Ulloa could return home. In the elections of 1980 Belaunde was again elected president and he appointed Ulloa prime minister and finance minister. Ulloa issued 240 decrees reorganizing the economy and dictated macro-economic measures in keeping with the Chicago school. But in 1982 the world recession sharpened the impact of the economic policy. Peru's export earnings were reduced to 50 per cent of the 1979 level. Ulloa was finally obliged to resign. His consolation prize was the presidency of the Senate.

I visited him in Lima and he invited me home for lunch. "That's my house," he said as he drove past a great mansion. "I don't live there. I have built a block of flats in the garden, which is safer." I asked him why he did not have a driver and a guard in the car. He said that was too dangerous – you never knew who was paying them off. "This is my protection," he said, uncovering an AK-47 assault rifle beside the gear shift and pointing to a hand grenade above the rear-view mirror. He had more than just his person to protect: a small Rembrandt hung above his bed in the flat.

I also paid a lot of attention to my own personal security and did not go to any country which our security staff advised against. They initially said I should not go to Colombia, but after a meeting with the government they said I could. I understood why. When we landed in Bogata no-one was allowed to leave the plane until the two security men who had boarded had escorted me off the plane and into a waiting car. They and their colleagues never left me while I was in Colombia, even sleeping outside my bedroom door.

On one occasion the Senderos Luminosos insurgents broke into the Reuter office in Lima, Peru, and at gunpoint made the staff send a message of their claims out on the teleprinter network. They thought it was going to the world. They did not know that the message only went to Buenos Aires, where the journalists threw it in the wastepaper basket.

Belatedly, we installed elaborate security in the Lima office. One day the intercom rang and the Senderos Luminosos announced themselves. They were refused admittance and a long argument ensued. Finally one of the girl insurgents asked if she could use the toilet. The gallant Peruvian Reuter journalist immediately opened the door and let her in. Out came her AK-47 and off again went the message to Buenos Aires and oblivion.

The most secure hotel I ever stayed in was the Granja Azul outside Lima. The guests stayed in cottages in the surrounding mountains and each one had its own funicular railway. The US Secret Service clearly liked the security because Rosalind Carter, the wife of the American president, was staying there. When my colleagues and I tried to go into one of the restaurants for dinner the Secret Service barred our way. "These gentlemen are staying in this hotel and have as much right to eat here as the wife of the American president," the head waiter said. So we had our dinner in the restaurant.

Protocol did not much concern Ulloa. He once flew down to see me in Buenos Aires when he was prime minister and when we sat down for lunch in the hotel he suddenly exclaimed "Oh God. That's the Peruvian ambassador sitting over there. And I haven't told him I was coming here. Let's go over and make amends."

Latin did not, curiously enough, have a shareholder in Argentina. Ulloa was able to arrange for the Latin Board, including myself, to have a meeting with General Jorge Videla, leader of the Junta. We soon had an Argentine newspaper shareholder. In 2010 Videla was sentenced to 25 years in prison for the torture and murder of 31 political prisoners in 1976.

In 1987 Ulloa came to London and asked if he could introduce Helga and me to his new bride. I invited them to lunch in the riverside restaurant of the Savoy. She was beautiful and self-assured. She ordered a beer as an aperitif, but sent it back because it was not cold enough. She talked about her daughter, Catherine Oxenberg, an actress, who appeared in the American soap *Dynasty*. "That was Princess Elizabeth of Yugoslavia," Helga told me afterwards. Ulloa died of cancer in Madrid in 1992 at the age of 69.

Sometime in the mid-seventies I had arranged to meet Ulloa and Edwards in Paris. Edwards was not at the Ritz hotel on the Sunday evening, as scheduled. He telephoned me at my hotel on the Monday morning and Ulloa and I went round to the Ritz. He was awaiting in the lobby with two large cases of wine. He explained:

When we met in Sao Paulo I told you about Chilean wine and the vineyards of Cousino Macul, which I owned. I promised to send you some. I could see you were thinking that I would never send the wine – I was a South American and they never kept their promises. So I decided to go one better and actually bring you the wine the next time I went to Europe.

I humped it through Customs in Caracas, New York and London. I took it to the Ritz in Piccadilly and then put it in a hire car to go down to Goudhurst in Kent where my mother is the governess at a girls' school. Then fog descended and Gatwick closed. So I drove to Dover and loaded the wine on to a ferry. I asked the purser to ask on the loud hailer if any lorry driver would like to take me from Calais to Paris and I did a good deal with one driver to take me right to the Ritz. The Transport and General Union representative in Calais started to cause some trouble, but I dealt with him.

So now you can wrestle through British customs with those two cases.

I bought Edwards and Ulloa a good lunch at the Bristol Hotel and we were all friends again.

The reason Edwards had been able to do a good deal with the lorry driver was that he had spent some time travelling on Pepsi Cola lorries in Spain, he told me. He was vice-president for Pepsi Cola small-eats for Spain. How could the richest man in Chile have descended to so lowly a job?

On 4 September 1970 the socialist Salvador Allende, who had been strongly opposed in Edwards' newspapers, won the presidential election. The day before, Edwards had told the US Amassador Edward Korry that he had ploughed all his profits for years into new industries and modernization and would be ruined if Allende won. Several days later Edwards again met Korry, who later recalled: "Edwards said that he wanted to ask me only one question: 'Will the U.S. do anything militarily – directly or indirectly?'" Korry responded: "My answer is no."

Edwards left Chile. He flew to the United States where he stayed with his friend Donald Kendall, chairman of PepsiCo, one of President Nixon's closest friends and largest campaign contributors. Edwards was a Pepsi Cola bottler in Chile. What happened during that visit is now known through an article in the *Colombia Journalism Review* of September/October 2003 by Peter Kornbluh of the National Security Archive following the declassification of the CIA Memorandum "Discussion of Chilean Political Situation." Edwards told Kendall of the threat Allende posed and Kendall told Nixon. Edwards met Henry Kissinger, the national security advisor, John Mitchell, the attorney general and Richard Helms, the director of the CIA. Nixon authorised Helms on 15 September to foment military action in Chile to prevent Allende assuming office and approved funding, much of which went to *El Mercurio*. Edwards did not return to Chile while Allende was in power and settled with his family in the United States. I had the impression that Kendall gave Edwards the job in Spain to give him something to do while he was in exile. In his memoirs David Rockefeller, the banker, said he helped Edwards and his family get settled in the United States. He also recalled that in March 1970 Edwards had warned him that the US had to prevent Allende's election.

Allende assumed office on 3 November 1970 and not until 11 September 1973 did a coup take place. Allende committed suicide.

In September 1971 Allende claimed Edwards deserved to be jailed for embezzlement. He put teams of inspectors into the newspaper but could never find any misdemeanour which stuck.

In September 1971 a representative of the Edwards media group requested covert support of $1 million ($5 million at current values) from the CIA, which Nixon himself authorised. In April 1972 Henry Kissinger's office approved a further $965,000. Other funds were paid through ITT, the communications giant. The funding continued after the coup, but ceased in July 1974, much to the concern of *El Mercurio*. We did not know it at the time, but Latin was benefiting in a small way from the CIA funding of *El Mercurio*.

I saw a great deal of Agustin and his lovely wife Manu in North and South America and in Europe. His family were English Chileans dating in Chile from the 1820's when his sailor ancestor jumped ship in Valparaiso. Agustin was the first member of his family to marry outside English stock. His wife's family came from Logrono in Rioja in Spain. He enjoyed the good things of life. I took Nigel Judah to dinner at his beautiful house in Connecticut where Nigel was staggered to be asked to choose a wine for dinner from all the first growth clarets. In Chile I stayed with him at the country house his grandmother had built in Valparaiso so that she had somewhere to go in the afternoons to play bridge. Edwards had planted the largest cactus garden in the southern hemisphere, complete with a resident German botanist. Edwards was highly intelligent, had wide interests and was great company.

When Helga and I visited him in Santiago just before I retired we had a disturbing security incident. When we went into the house Helga closed the front door behind her. "Never do that again," said Agustin. "The guards will think you are going to shoot me, and are likely to shoot you."

Latin American newspaper publishers attached great importance to the Inter-American Press Association (IAPA). The annual conference, which I went to on a number of occasions, was a great social event, attended by the rich newspaper publishers and their wives and sons and daughters. Agustin Edwards explained to me why it was not just social. It was also an insurance policy. If a newspaper publisher fell out with his government and was arrested, IAPA would protest and there was a good chance he would be released.

I got a taste of the atmosphere of Argentina in the course of my many visits. I was walking down the road one day with Anne Wright, wife of our Manager, David Wright, and their small son, Cornelius. He stopped to look at something in the gutter. "Come along, Cornelius," said Anne. "It's only a dead body."

JAPAN

Japan is probably the most important news market in the world and I went there often. My first visit was in January 1963. General MacArthur had decided that Japan needed a news agency structure as close a possible to that of the United States. He therefore set up two agencies, rather like the AP and UP called Kyodo and Jiji Press. Kyodo was a newspaper cooperative, owned by the provincial Press, whose job was to serve the Press. Jiji Press was owned by its staff and its job was to serve private subscribers. But they both invaded the other's territory and much of the task of any Reuter executive visiting Tokyo was to sort out the squabbles which arose from Reuters supply of the general news service to Kyodo and the economic services to Jiji Press.

In 1967 we negotiated a contract with Jiji Press for £81,000 a year (£1.1 million at current values), an increase of 125 per cent, the largest subscription and increase the Company had ever secured with a foreign news organisation.

Tokyo was regarded as one of the most important postings in Reuters. Distinguished bureau chiefs, who were a great support in my dealings there, included Lee Casey, Kevin Garry, Michael Neale and Vergil Berger.

Saiji Hasegawa, the President of Jiji Press, had been the correspondent of the Japanese news agency, Domei, in London before World War II and was interned when war broke out. He was a great nationalist and did not like the British. He was not only fierce in his dealings with the likes of me, but also with his own staff. He once bit a member of his staff during a labour dispute and the staff put a "Beware of the Dog" sign on his door. One of the greatest strains of visiting Japan was receiving hospitality, which was very liquid. I was mostly entertained by Hasegawa's lieutenants, Adachi and Bannai. Bannai's favourite saying was "I like drunk." The Reuter correspondent, Sid Brooks, an Australian, was also rather unusual. We went away to the country one week-end and he insisted on taking a lady interpreter with him. The only problem was that she did not speak English.

I always thought that one of the most bizarre experiences in Tokyo was to go to buy toys at the Kiddieland toyshop. The top floor was given over to pornography so that the fathers could occupy themselves while the children were choosing their presents.

ITALY

The news agency structure in Italy was rather similar to that of Japan. There were two news agencies, ANSA, a newspaper cooperative which had rights in the Reuter general news service, and Radiocor, privately owned, which had rights in the Reuter economic services. Radiocor was owned by Gianfranco Cobor, who had inherited it from his father, a Hungarian, who had set it up after World War I. He had left Italy when Mussolini concentrated news in the hands of the agency Stefani. He returned with the allies and stormed into the headquarters of Stefani in Rome, declaring, so the story goes: "I take over this agency in the name of liberty, equality and fraternity." The Stefani executives threw him down the stairs. Cobor always claimed they became the managers of ANSA and he never forgave them.

Cobor was the stringer for Italy for the economic services but as we grew we needed a staff correspondent in Milan and in 1967 we stopped using him. Just before the seven-year statute of limitations expired in 1974 Cobor sued us for wrongful dismissal. I flew to Milan for the court case, which was to start with mediation before a judge. I went with our lawyers to the court-house and we were shown into an ante-room, which had two chairs and a lot of cardboard boxes. A beautiful girl sat at a desk painting her nails. Cobor and his lawyers arrived. Cobor and I were allowed to sit. The lawyers stood around and started to chat to the girl. It eventually dawned on me that the girl was the judge and this was the mediation hearing. Our lawyers advised me to accept the judge's proposal for mediation and we paid Cobor a substantial sum, despite the fact that he had never been on our staff.

GERMANY

One of Reuters problems after World War II was the inadequacy and complexity of its distribution arrangements. Lack of money and a fear of the commitments involved in building up its own staff meant it mainly distributed through agents and sometimes bought into local companies. One such was Vereinigte Wirtshaftsdienste (VWD) in West Germany. It was owned one third by Deutsche Presse Agentur (DPA), a national news agency which distributed the Reuter general news service, one third by Reuters and one third by an industry grouping.

Once a month I went to Germany for a meeting of the VWD Board and battled to try to drag it out of its nineteenth century system of distribution, which was mostly mail.

DPA ended its relationship with Reuters in 1971 and Reuters set up its own German-language news service. It had excellent editors, including Manfred Pagel and Annette von Broecker. The relationship with VWD ended in 1978.

Our agent in East Germany was Allgemeiner Deutscher Nachrichtendienst (ADN). After German reunification I acquired my Stasi file through the German embassy in London to see what it said about my visits there. It only recorded my appointments and contained nothing of interest.

GAMPELL AND GLYNDEBOURNE

In 2009 a frisson of shock went through many Reuter journalists when Reuters confirmed its new commitment to commentary by buying a company called Breakingviews. But expressing opinion in a Reuter service was not new. In 1935 Reuters had started a weekly mailed bulletin called the *Economic X-Ray*. It was written by Sydney Gampell, who had joined the company two years earlier as a commodities statistician. It contained his opinion on markets (and also some good jokes) and had a wide following in the financial community. Gampell – known to many as "old blackface" – became Reuters Financial Editor in 1940, a position he held with great distinction until he retired at the age of 70 in 1974.

Gampell's other contribution to Reuters was to introduce us to the Glyndebourne opera in the country house in Sussex, of which he had been a member since opened in 1934. Reuters entertained many clients there, particularly from the Continent. An important feature was the picnic in the gardens provided by the Reuter chef. One of our guests once got lost in the labyrinthine buildings. So I hit on the idea of producing a bird's eye drawing and map, which could serve as the Reuter advertisement in the programme. We sent an artist, Paul Draper, up in a helicopter and in 1983 he produced a beautiful painting, which stood us in good stead for many years.

Some time before I retired, a painting of the Glyndebourne scene by Osbert Lancaster came up for auction. Lady Christie, wife of the owner of

Glyndebourne, was bidding for it against Nigel Judah for Reuters. Reuters won: Nigel was determined to secure it as my leaving present. Lady Christie regretted being outbid and tried to buy it from Reuters and later from me. We declined, but she borrowed it from me to reproduce on a notebook for sale in the Glyndebourne shop.

GARRICK

In 1974 David Chipp proposed me as a member of the Garrick Club. I immediately ran into an unprecedented row between the lawyers and journalists, who, with the all-important actors, made up the most significant groups of members. In June 1971 Bernard Levin had written in *The Times* a blistering attack on the late Lord Goddard, who had recently died. Levin said that as Lord Chief Justice Goddard was a calamity. He wrote:

> I see (PHS, last week)that a forthcoming book on the Craig-Bentley trial is to say that the late Lord Goddard who presided over it, subsequently claimed to have been "very unhappy" about the result of the case – which was that Derek Bentley, who had not fired the fatal shot was hanged, and Christopher Craig, who had, was not. If Goddard did indeed claim this, it was a breathtaking piece of hypocrisy, in view of his conduct of the case.

Lawyers rushed to the defence of Lord Goddard in the letters column of *The Times.*

When Bernard Levin's candidacy for the Garrick Club came up, the lawyers blackballed him, to the fury of the journalists. Relations between lawyers and journalists were the lowest they had ever been in the Club. "Don't ask me to sign the book for you," said John Metcalfe, a distinguished journalist whom I knew well. "You'll get blackballed." Never-the-less, in 1975 I was elected.

In 1970, before I was a member, I had been amazed to stand in the bar as a guest and hear the judge Melford Stevenson sounding off about the case he was trying. It was the Garden House riot trial in Cambridge. "They are as guilty as hell," he proclaimed. "I am going to send them down for a very long time."

I had first been to the Garrick Club in 1960 when the Chairman of Reuters, John Burgess, invited Helga and me to dinner. It was a bitterly cold night and Helga quickly went to warm herself in the members' lounge by the wood fire under the stairs. The porter rushed up: "Madam, do you realise that you are the first lady to have stood in front of that fireplace since 1864. Ladies are not permitted under the stairs." By coincidence the following night Walton Cole invited us to dinner at the Club. A lady had positioned herself in front of the fireplace. Inevitably, the porter rushed up: "Madam, do you realise that you are the first lady to have stood in front of that fireplace since 1864."

CHAPTER SEVEN

Enter Machiavelli

GENERAL MANAGER

On 1 January 1976 I succeeded Brian Stockwell as General Manager of Reuters. On 24 June I was appointed to the Board as a Joint Deputy Managing Director, along with Glen Renfrew, the other Joint Deputy General Manager.

Long often told me how much he admired Machiavelli. I believed him: *divide et impera* loomed large. He also agreed with Machiavelli that it was much safer to be feared than loved.

Since I returned to London in 1957 and until 1976 I had sat in offices on the east side of 85 Fleet Street with a view of St Paul's, one of the greatest city views in London, if not the world. I always puzzled why, when he designed the new headquarters of the Press Association and Reuters in the thirties, Lutyens had deprived the chief executive of Reuters of this view and sited his office on the south-west corner. John Entwisle, the erudite archivist of Reuters, explained it to me years later. Before World War II the view to the south of Fleet Street was open to the river, but the view of St Paul's to the east was obscured by buildings. They disappeared in the bombing.

When I became Long's deputy in London he insisted, despite my objections, that I abandon the view of Christopher Wren's masterpiece which I had enjoyed for nearly 20 years and move to an office next to his on the west side of the building. I went to South America for a long trip and returned to my new office. There, facing my desk, was a magnificent drawing of St Paul's which Long had commissioned for me from the artist Michael Harrison so that I still had a view of St Paul's. Long occasionally surprised with extraordinary acts of generosity. Reuters gave me the drawing of St Paul's when I retired and it hangs in our London house.

Tom Glocer, the last chief executive of Reuters to be housed in 85 Fleet Street, had the good taste to move to the site of my old office with the view of St Paul's when he was appointed.

Another human trait of Long was his willingness to make widely available his cooking skills. I had a letter about it published in the *Financial Times* years later:

> Rhymer Rigby's article on Office Haute Cuisine brings to mind the great attention Reuters has always paid to client lunches. "That was an excellent lunch," said a banker on one occasion. "Who is your chef?" "Today it was Gerry Long, our Chief Executive," was the reply. When he had heard that the French chef had fallen ill, Long, a famous gourmet, had donned his toque and stepped into the breach.

The Daily Telegraph followed up the next day:

> Current boss Tom Glocer fancies himself in the kitchen and once donated a dinner cooked by himself as a lot in a company auction. The winning bidder was one Herbie Skeete, who invited a tableful of friends whom Glocer had just sacked. Tasty.

The speciality of one distinguished chef was quenelles de brochet – pike dumplings. When guests admired them we used to explain that the chef had been trained in Paris under the famous fish chef, Madame Prunier. When he retired the kitchen eventually got a telephone call for him from a delicatessen in the Moscow Road in Bayswater. "We have been wondering where he has got to," they said. "He always used to come here to buy his quenelles."

MURDOCH AND MAXWELL

One of the most interesting experiences on the Reuter Board was to contrast two of its members: Rupert Murdoch and Robert Maxwell. Rupert Murdoch, Chairman of News Corporation, eventual owner of *The Times* and the *Wall Street Journal*, joined the Board as a representative of the Newspaper Publishers Association (NPA) in 1979. Robert Maxwell, Chairman of Mirror Group Newspapers, joined in 1986, also as a representative of the NPA.

Murdoch rarely missed a board meeting and always arrived on time. He rarely spoke, but occasionally asked a question on a subject which would be likely to benefit his own business, such as on international tax. He always attended the lunches with senior executives which followed the board meetings, which were a great morale-booster.

Maxwell did not attend many board meetings, but always arrived late with a noisy entry. He talked frequently and clearly had not read the papers under discussion. On one occasion he was reproved by the chairman for improper share dealing. He never attended the executive lunches. Once when we had a board meeting in New York each non-executive and executive director attended a dinner in a smart restaurant with senior executives and journalists. It was my luck to be twinned with Maxwell at the Cygne. He made it plain that he considered the occasion beneath him. When the soup was served he reversed his plate so that he could not be served. He ate a salad and without saying goodbye to me, the host, or anyone else, left the restaurant.

In 1985 Maxwell invited Helga and me to his fortieth wedding anniversary dinner at his mansion outside Oxford. It was a lavish black-tie affair which culminated in the host making a speech in praise of each of his five children, who had to stand and be toasted by all the guests. He was puzzled when Helga told him that she thought it extraordinary that he could make speeches in praise of all his five children. "Not many fathers could do that," she said.

I came across him again at the World Economic Forum at Davos in Switzerland. We were members of the media group. I was surprised to be invited to a party he gave in which he described himself on the copper-plated invitation as chairman of the media group. It was a self-appointment, but none of the officials of the Forum had the courage to dispute it.

On 5 November 1991 he drowned in the Atlantic, near the Canary Islands. It was soon discovered that he had been filching money from his companies' pension funds. There was much speculation that his money problems had caused him to commit suicide. Murdoch believed that. "He must have been terrified of going to prison – as he would have done," Murdoch told a biographer. I think suicide would have been out of character. More likely is that when he was urinating over the side of his yacht he succumbed to micturition syncope, the fainting during urination that often afflicts the elderly, and tipped over into the sea. After all, Conrad Black was prepared to face prison and seemed not to have found it too bad.

I asked Tom Bower, who wrote two biographies of Maxwell, for his verdict on the death. He said he agreed with the original verdict of the Spanish inquest that he was dead when he fell into the sea and that he had probably had a heart attack. The Israeli pathologist who carried out an autopsy just before the burial supported that view.

Murdoch took his Reuter responsibilities very seriously. He was the only director who thanked you for what you were doing for the company. He was also hospitable. On one visit by the board to New York he gave a black-tie dinner party in his Fifth Avenue apartment. He cleared the furniture out of the apartment and hired dining tables and chairs. When we got up from the dinner we saw that white paint stripes had appeared down the backs of all the dinner jackets, picked up from the hired chairs. The next day the secretary of Lord Rothermere telephoned Murdoch's secretary to say that her boss, the multi-millionaire owner of the *Daily Mail,* would be grateful if Murdoch would pay for him to have a replacement dinner jacket made. Murdoch declined but said he would pay for the jacket to be cleaned.

Over the years I posed a number of questions to Murdoch.

What do you think of banks? Don't trust them.

What do you make of Gerry Long? A bit mad.

Do you plan to introduce colour into your newspapers? Colour does not sell newspapers.

Why do you never sue for libel? Not worth the hassle.

What's your key to success? I have a knack of seeing opportunities.

The hacking scandal at the *News of the World* and the closure of the newspaper in 2011 reminded me of a discussion in the Reuter Board in 1979. I explained to the Board why we were not getting more revenue from sales of the Reuter Monitor in the United Kingdom. Lack of investment meant that there was a great shortage of telephone lines needed to connect our computers with potential clients. Some stockbrokers bribed engineers of Post Office Telecommunications with the gift of cars to get telephone lines. "If you decide to do that," Rupert Murdoch told me, "don't get found out."

We did not change our policy that we did not give bribes.

DROGHEDA

The non-executive director who best understood what we were trying to achieve with the economic services was Garrett Drogheda. The 11th Earl of Drogheda was Managing Director of the *Financial Times* when he joined the

Reuter Board in 1963. He went far beyond the bounds of duty when Bob Sinn, with whom I had just signed the lucrative joint-venture agreement, and his wife Betty came to London in the summer of 1964 and he invited them one weekend to his country seat in Englefield Green in Surrey. He was Chairman of Covent Garden and he then invited them to the opera there. Betty Sinn, a former Hollywood starlet, had never been to an opera performance before and was greatly taken by the experience. A few weeks later I had a telephone call from Lord Drogheda. Betty Sinn was back in London and had called him to ask for some opera tickets. "Reuters will have to pay for them," he said. "I cannot afford to pay for them."

Such was his contribution to the work of the Board that when he retired from the *Financial Times,* where he had become chairman, in 1975, he was asked to stay on the Reuter Board for a further three years. Oddly enough, his entry in *Who's Who* does not mention Reuters.

ROC DE CHERE

In 1978 we sold the house in Chazeaux and Reuters bought for our use the Roc de Chère, Menthon-St-Bernard, on Lake Annecy, Haute-Savoie, France. It was a fine gothic-style house built at the end of the nineteenth century situated on a rock dominating the lake. It had an annexe where the children and their friends enjoyed an independent life.

The reason Reuters bought the house was related to the possibility of Reuters moving its headquarters to nearby Geneva. That possibility had nothing to do with internationalism, but with British trade unionism. Relations with the unions had become so bad in the seventies that in 1979 I recommended that Reuters put up a building on the Continent to house a data centre, which could be an alternative to London if we could not get satisfactory deals with the unions. It could also be a new world headquarters. Helga and I spent some pleasant weeks surveying the possible locations. We narrowed the choice down to Brussels, Zurich and Geneva. We ruled out Brussels because the labour laws were too strict and Zurich because of difficulties in finding staff.

When the Geneva building was finished we left it empty but flew out to Geneva representatives of the unions on a number of occasions. We gave them a tour of the building and took them for a good lunch on Lake Geneva when we told them that if we could not get what we wanted in London, we would move to Geneva. The strategy worked and we did not need to move. However, by 1982 our business in Europe had so expanded that we opened the Geneva centre to serve continental clients and also made it the headquarters for Europe.

I had occasion to write about it to the *Financial Times* in 2009. Andrew Hill, the Lombard columnist, wrote:

> Unions are again threatening strikes and (erroneous) parallels are being drawn with the situation thirty years ago. But the story is a timely reminder of how much heavier the pressure was in the late seventies; of the lengths employers went to in order to hedge their bets; and of how Reuters, a media pioneer in so many other ways, came close to showing the way forward to Eddie Shah and Rupert Murdoch. As Mr Nelson points out: "Geneva was not Reuters Wapping, but might have been."

We were fortunate in the excellent staff who worked in Geneva, who we were able to entertain on Lake Annecy. They included Gerard Baverey, Bob Evans, Marcus Ferrar, Adam Kellett-Long, Jean-Claude Marchand and Hans Ouwerkerk.

TWELVE GOOD MEN AND TRUE

Jury Service always seemed to me to be a citizen's privilege. I was therefore pleased when I was ordered in the late seventies to serve on a jury at Croydon Crown Court. The first case was a woman accused of stealing a pair of shoes from Allders Department Store. When we retired to consider our verdict one of the jurors said it would be helpful to know if she had committed an offence before. I explained the important principle of the English judicial system that a jury was not allowed to know of previous convictions, which could prejudice their decision in the case before it. We found her guilty.

In the afternoon a young north-country man was accused of growing cannabis on his window-sill in his flat in Penge. He repeatedly accused a policeman of lying. "It weren't my stoof and I never said it was," he declared. Eventually the judge asked the jury temporarily to retire. The jury had been so impressed by my elucidation of the English legal system in the morning that they unanimously elected me foreman. When we were summoned back into court the judge proceeded to recount all the accused's previous offences in dealing in cannabis. He then adjourned until next day. The amazed jurors turned on me to explain this complete contradiction of what I had told them. I had no idea what the reason was, but told them it was a technical question, which I would explain the next morning. I rushed home and telephoned one of the Reuter lawyers, who explained all. The following morning the judge opened proceedings by saying "You must have wondered why I went against the usual principle of English law before we adjourned yesterday." The other jurors nodded emphatically. He explained that if an accused has brought the reputation of a witness into doubt, as the young man had done with the policeman, the judge could give his record in order to redress the balance. I was saved! We retired and found the accused guilty.

REUTER STATUE

The year 1976 was the 125th anniversary of the founding of Reuters. Reuters had decided to place a commemorative blue plaque on the London house of Paul Julius Reuter, the founder of the agency, in Kensington Palace Gardens, until we discovered it was now the Russian Embassy. At the height of the Cold War, such a commemoration would not have been appropriate, even if the Russians had allowed it. So Henry Manisty of our legal department and I went to see the Manager of the First National Bank of Chicago, the occupiers of 1 Royal Exchange Buildings in the City of London, which was the address of Reuter's first office. Not inappropriately it had been owned by Magdalen College. The Manager readily agreed that we could place a plaque on his building. But when we came out onto the vast courtyard and saw there was only one statue on the square and that at the far end, that of the American philanthropist George Peabody, I abandoned the idea of the plaque and decided to recommend that we place a statue there in a splendid site in the centre.

Manisty asked the City Corporation if we could put up a statue on the square. They said no-one had put up a statue in the City since the twenties and they liked the idea. The only problem was that the telephone switching centre of the London Stock Exchange was on the site where we wanted the statue and it would take two years to move it. So we built the statue over the switching centre and incorporated it in the base.

Two days before the statue was due to be unveiled Manisty came to my office ashen-faced. He had been talking to the Victorian Society, who told him that Reuter's first office was not where we had placed the statue. At the end of the nineteenth century the street names had been changed. His office was round the corner. Long, who wrote the caption had misspelled Cassel, the city of Reuter's birth, using the German Kassel. But he redeemed himself because by good fortune the caption said his office was "near this site." We sighed with relief that we had not gone ahead with the project for the plaque.

We asked Edmund de Rothschild, President of N.M. Rothschild and Sons, great-grandson of Reuter's first customer, Baron Lionel de Rothschild, to unveil the statue on 13 October 1976. He told the audience that he had also been looking in Rothschild's archives and had discovered the first invoice from Reuter. "Unfortunately, I cannot discover that we ever paid it," he confessed. At compound interest for 125 years he was concerned at how large the debt would now be.

Theo Crosby of Pentagram designed the monument, which consisted of a monolith and a head. The lettering was drawn by Alan Fletcher of Pentagram. The sculptor was Michael Black. He was well-known for having carved the heads of the Roman emperors round the Sheldonian Theatre in Oxford. They all look like him. When he was carving the Reuter statue he was at the same time working replacing the angels, which in friable Cotswold stone, had become worn, on Oxford Cathedral, which is in the college of Christ Church. One night he arrived at the Roc de Chère, the Reuter house in Menthon-St-Bernard on Lake Annecy, in a Volkswagen bus with one of the replaced angels in the back, a thank-you present for my having commissioned him to carve the statue of Paul Julius Reuter.

So a stone angel from Oxford Cathedral graced the gardens of our houses successively in Menthon-St-Bernard, Veyrier-du-Lac and Opio. Our French neighbours always claimed angels were a-sexual, but we believe the beautiful angel is feminine.

PLAYBOY

We had some fun with the American magazine *Playboy* in 1977. They published a story which alleged there was a relationship between Reuters and the Central Intelligence Agency (CIA).

The allegation was not new. In 1976 a draft report of the House of

Representatives committee on intelligence said the CIA had frequently manipulated stories by Reuters. Reuters protested and at a press conference William Colby, director of the CIA, said, "We have no manipulation and no management of Reuters news."

In 1977 *Rolling Stone* magazine said the Senate intelligence committee had deliberately misrepresented the extent to which the CIA used American journalists. The story, which was picked up by *The Times,* said it had used more than 400 in the previous two years. The article said Reuters, AP and UPI all cooperated with the CIA. Long wrote to *The Times* denying that Reuters had ever cooperated with the CIA.

The *Playboy* article read:

> ...you know Reuters, known affectionately in some circles as the CIA School of Journalism because so many of its stories, supposedly originating in Europe and supposedly uncovered in European journalism, coincide in peculiar fashion with our own government's propaganda.

I decided that Henry Manisty should tell our offices worldwide to contact the distributors and tell them that if they did not remove the offending paragraph we would sue for libel. I sent my son Patrick down to WHSmith in Beckenham and was delighted when he came back with a copy of *Playboy* with a sticker on the cover alongside a beautiful bunny: A PARAGRAPH ON PAGE 169 HAS BEEN EXCISED AS IT CONTAINS A POSSIBLE LIBELLOUS STATEMENT.

The managers at the magazine's headquarters in Chicago were thunderstruck to receive dozens of faxes from all over the world reporting Reuters threats of libel suits. They promptly agreed to publish a letter of apology in the next edition.

My view had always been that if there were no CIA employees working in Reuters, the CIA was not doing its job. What was important was that such were our checks and balances there was no way they could corrupt our news report.

DEATH OF MY FATHER

My father died on 23 September 1977, aged 81. He was a fine man who had had a tough life.

NEWS

In September 1977 Jonathan Fenby, Editor, Reuters World Service (RWS), resigned. His appointment by Long three years earlier had been foolish. He was an excellent journalist and later became Editor of the *Observer*, but lacked the experience to handle the demanding management tasks of the job. He was moved from the post and offered the assignment of Chief Correspondent in Johannesburg, which, not surprisingly, he declined. The *Financial Times* commented in the *Men and Matters* column:

> The resignation of Reuters editor Jonathan Fenby and a reorganisation of the top level executive committee has caused a stir in Fleet Street. Fenby, a 34-year-old former foreign correspondent only took up the job three years ago following the surprise resignation of former editor Brian Horton.
>
> His removal has revived fears that Reuter, which has expanded aggressively and successfully into supplying economic and financial news and market information through a sophisticated range of electronic devices was about to downgrade the general news service.
>
> Long himself is out of the country so I sought a comment from Michael Nelson, whom insiders regard as the real mastermind behind Reuter's leap into electronic financial services.

I said we had no intention of reducing our activities in the news business. The reporter was my old friend and Reuter colleague Bob Mauthner, who thought he was doing me a good turn by referring to me as the mastermind. In fact it was no good turn: it infuriated Long, who liked to claim the credit for the development.

While we did not want to cut back the news services to the media we clearly had a wasteful structure with two teams of correspondents, one for general news and one for economic, with reporters rarely wearing both hats. Long had often tried to merge the two teams, but I had always refused because the boss would have been a general news man and I did not want to dilute the specialisation of news for business. In 1979 Jack Henry, an old stager who had succeeded Fenby (although reporting to an Editor-in-Chief, the distinguished Michael Reupke), retired. Long at last agreed to the unthinkable: that a journalist who was an economic news specialist – the poor relation of yore – could head a combined editorial. The man selected to head this revolution was Manfred Pagel, a German of vast good judgement, who was Editor of Reuters Economic Services, although he had originally been hired in Bonn as a general news journalist. We set up a massive training programme for the general news journalists in Chicago, where there was a wide range of markets. Reuters news for business was immeasurably strengthened.

LONG'S DEPARTURE

One day early in 1981 Long came into my office. "Murdoch has just offered me the job of Managing Director of Times Newspapers," he proclaimed. "I took all of two minutes before I said yes." "Congratulations, Gerry. What is he going to pay you?" "I don't know, but more than I am getting here." It had been clear to Nigel Judah and me for some time that Reuters would soon move into considerable profit. We decided not to tell Long. We knew he was bored with Reuters and would accept almost any offer of another job. If we let him into our analysis of the profits to come, he might stay. Since we both loathed him, that would not be a good thing.

Long left Reuters on 1 March 1981. *The Power of News: The History of Reuters* by Donald Read says: "Gerald Long was succeeded as managing director not by Michael Nelson, as many in the company had expected, but by Glen Renfrew." I was appointed Renfrew's deputy with the title of Deputy Managing Director and General Manager.

Michael Reupke years later wrote me a note recording that in 1994 Long told him he wondered if he had been right to recommend Renfrew to the Board as his successor instead of Nelson.

The *Oxford Dictionary of National Biography* entry on Renfrew, written by Donald Read, said:

> Whether the selection of Renfrew to lead Reuters through the 1980s was the right choice will remain debatable, however. Nelson would have made many fewer acquisitions, preferring organic growth. John Jessop, who worked for both men, in retrospect favoured Nelson's balance of enterprise with caution.

Long quickly became a Murdoch lackey, as this story from the memoirs of Harold Evans, the new Editor of *The Times,* shows:

> …it soon enough became obvious that nothing less than unquestioning backing of Mrs Thatcher on every issue would satisfy Rupert.

His managing director, Gerald Long, wrote me a stream of memos asking me to downplay or suppress news that was bad for the government. In the spring the Chancellor of the Exchequer had said the recession was over and recovery would begin in the early summer. It didn't. Six months later the Central Statistical Office released figures showing that output had fallen for the sixth successive quarter. Gerald Long stood amazed at our temerity in printing a summary of this official report. Did I not understand that if the government said the recession was over, it was over? As far as I was concerned his rebuke was a red rag to a bull. I was not going to let anyone in management tell me to fix the news. (Output fell by 2.2 per cent in 1981.)

The warfare with Long escalated through the winter of 1981-2, with Murdoch himself giving instructions to editorial writers, and continually ducking the pledge to give me a budget. Of course, this came in handy later for the fiction that I had exceeded non-existent limits. In fact, by this time he'd blithely broken all the editorial pledges. Stories mysteriously appeared that I was thinking of resigning or being asked to resign. Murdoch denied them all. On 10 February 1982, hours after I'd been named Editor of the Year in the Granada press awards, he issued a statement saying there were absolutely no plans to replace Harold Evans whose outstanding qualities, etc. The reality was that on two occasions early in March he went to the national directors to ask them to dismiss me and install a new editor. They refused both times. They told him that if he himself dismissed me, I had a right of appeal to them and no pressure should be brought on me.

By 9 March 1982 Murdoch had demanded Evans' resignation, which, after initially refusing, Evans gave to Murdoch on 15 March.

On 6 February Evans had helped to cause Long's downfall by publishing a ridiculous correspondence between Long and Albert Roux, the owner of Le Gavroche restaurant, on cheese. It appeared just before Murdoch was due to tell the unions that 600 jobs had to go. He feared they might refer to Long's lifestyle. Murdoch kicked Long upstairs as Deputy Chairman of News International shortly after Evans left. He had lasted just a year as Managing Director. Long ceased to work for Murdoch on 31 August, 1984. "Murdoch ruined my life," he said.

CHAPTER EIGHT

Rewards at Last

STOCK OPTIONS GRANTED

In November 1981 Reuters made available to Renfrew, Judah (who in March 1981 had joined the Board as Finance Director), and me valuable stock options. We were each allowed to buy one year's salary-worth of shares. Renfrew ended up with 545, Judah 306 and I 361. Mine cost £53,037 (£152,000 at current values). By September 1983 mine were worth £2,328,450 (£6 million at current values). Reuters went public in 1984, which, combined with the continued growth of the Company, made the shares even more valuable.

The first public discussion of the possibility of floating Reuters came from Lord Matthews, a builder, who had acquired Express Newspapers. On 18 October 1982 the *UK Press Gazette* carried this story:

> It was ironic that last week's startling suggestion – that Reuters should float a public issue of shares on the stock market – should have come from Fleet Street's newest Press Baron.
>
> Lord Matthews – whose Fleet Holdings collected a spectacular £280,000 first dividend from Reuters earlier this year – told his shareholders about Reuters at his AGM on Wednesday.
>
> "For many years we've been helping to prop Reuters up ..." he said. The 'we' referred to members of the NPA (almost 42 per cent holding), the Press Association (the same), with the residue held by the Press in Australia and New Zealand.
>
> That 'prop' had been provided by PA since the General Strike year of 1926. It has been shared by the NPA without dividend since 1941, just into the third year of the 1939-45 War.
>
> Not surprising, therefore, that last week's disclosure from Lord Matthews – that he had been 'chivvying' Reuters towards a market quote – evoked something of a shock-horror rebuttal from Reuters deputy m.d. Mike Nelson. His board, he said, had not authorised any such action. Or even its exploration.

Lord Matthews told his shareholders that if his newspapers could substantially reduce overmanning, which "sticks out like a sore thumb," they too could make profits: at least 10 per cent on turnover instead of the present losses.

In contrast. Reuters last year made £16.4 million profits on £138.8 million turnover. That's almost 12 per cent. The idea of radical changes at Reuters might be better received when newspapers are enabled to match that.

Given the way the owners had starved Reuters of cash for so many years, with the resultant exiguous salaries, we were pretty mad at Matthews' suggestion that they had been helping to prop up Reuters.

THE MAN WHO LET £4M SLIP THROUGH HIS FINGERS

The headline in the *Daily Mail* on 19 May 1984 read "The man who let £4m slip through his fingers". "He is the man in the shade of one of the worst personal financial decisions in history," said Diana Hutchinson as she interviewed Long in the suite of the Deputy Chairman of News International. Her rather wicked article continued:

Long has a limitless well of personal eccentricity on which he is now drawing. He tries to tell me he refuses to look back on might-have-beens.

"I have always had the fairly fortunate characteristic of being able to roll up my life behind me like a carpet. You can't just stay somewhere to collect the jackpot. That is inadmissible behaviour. And besides there was no hint of an equity participation while I was at Reuters."

"Look," he says confidentially, "it's simply that I was 33 years at Reuters and that's a long time. I was travelling for six months of every year as far as Japan."

"I actively began to dislike the kind of life I was forced to lead. I hate airports and hotels. There are only three or four hotels in the world I would willingly stay at."

It is true, he reflects, a journalist is a poor man, who lives like a prince. "I lived the life of the rich and I didn't really enjoy it."

"Honestly, I can tell you when you actually get all the good things in life you find it is all Dead Sea Fruit."

It was a good try.

THE CHANCELLOR CAMPAIGN

There was much opposition to the idea of a flotation, including from Sir Christopher Chancellor and his son Alexander. I got to know Alexander well when he was Reuters Chief Correspondent in Rome. Our family and I spent a memorable and particularly happy day with him and his charming wife Suzie and their two daughters at their country house in Italy in the late sixties. He left Reuters in 1974 and, after a spell with ITN, became Editor of *The Spectator*. Alexander believed the Press barons had treated his father badly when he left in 1959. On 22 October 1983 *The Spectator* carried a three page article by Alexander and Geoffrey Robinson entitled "The Price of Greed", which attacked the possible flotation.

I was annoyed at the suggestion in the article that I, along with Renfrew and Judah, had a personal financial interest in the flotation. It said we stood to become millionaires if Reuters went public. I invited him to lunch at the Boulestin with Nigel Judah to explain that the three of us already had shares which were valuable whether or not the company went public. He apologised in the issue of 5 November 1983 and corrected the record. He also estimated what our shares would be worth if Reuters went public at around £1,000 million (although he said that estimate was now considered rather over-optimistic): Renfrew £5,450,000, Nelson £3,610,000, Judah £3,060,000.

Never-the-less, the contrast between our fortunes and the treatment of his father still rankled and when I invited Alexander to the house-warming party we gave when we moved into 44 Phillimore Gardens in Kensington, he rang me and regretted he could not come because he would be visiting his father, who was living in modest circumstances in Somerset. However, we still remained very good friends.

The House of Commons debated the flotation on 27 January 1984. The Board had asked me to brief Kenneth Baker, the minister for information technology, a Magdalen man. I also briefed Jonathan Aitken, who planned to take part in the debate on Reuters side. I went to his luxurious offices in Mayfair and remember thinking that I had never met a more arrogant man. He later went to gaol for perjury and seemed to be less arrogant when he came out of prison. Aitken and Alexander Chancellor had been contemporaries at Eton. Chancellor attacked him in his report on the debate in *The Spectator*. He particularly objected to his "horribly well-cut suit." Baker said in the debate that he was satisfied the board and trustees of Reuters would preserve its independence after flotation.

REUTERS FLOATED

The preparations for the flotation were immensely burdensome and I confess that I leaked to the historian of Reuters the one piece of light relief in the whole exercise. On 11 January 1984 the Board met to discuss the mechanics of the flotation. David Scholey of Warburgs, Reuters principal banker, said it was desirable to add some non-press directors to the Board. Rupert Murdoch asked him what sort of persons and Scholey suggested they might be bankers. "We don't want to fill the Board with a lot of City stiffs," replied Murdoch. Scholey, the banker, looked much discomforted. The dialogue did not go into the Board minutes. The minutes did note the decision that three directors would be appointed, one from the United Kingdom, one from the United States and one from continental Europe. Warburgs were deputed to recommend on the United Kingdom, Renfrew on the United States and I on continental Europe.

How do you pick a director from continental Europe? I asked all our managers to suggest speakers for our annual lunch, with an assessment of their characters, careers and speaking ability in English. Outstanding was Pehr Gyllenhammar, chairman of Volvo AB, recommended by the astute Gordon Hanson, Managing Director of the Northern Region of Europe. The Reuter board agreed I could offer him the vacancy. I asked Sven Gerentz, chief executive of the Swedish news agency, TT, who knew him well, to arrange a meeting and I flew to Gothenburg to meet him at the Volvo headquarters. Gyllenhammar, a towering personality, accepted immediately, but with one reservation. He was a director of S. Pearson and Son plc, which owned the *Financial Times,* and Reuters would have to change the dates of its board meetings to those of Pearsons so that he did not have to travel more frequently to London. When I told the Reuter board, Rupert Murdoch hit the roof. I told Gyllenhammar that his proposal was not acceptable. He immediately withdrew his reservation. Gyllenhammar served on the Reuter board with great effectiveness until 1997, when he became a trustee.

Warburgs recommendation for the director from the UK was Sir Christopher Hogg, Chairman of Courtaulds, who later became chairman of Reuters. The Latin tag "suaviter in modo, fortiter in re" could have been composed for him. He had a keen brain and was a good chairman, but, as I found in the board discussions on the acquisition of control of Visnews, he was more concerned with the niceties of price-earnings ratios, which he understood well, than the future of the media.

Renfrew's recommendation for the USA was Walter Wriston, chairman of Citicorp. Wriston had a good understanding of the financial information business and made good contributions to board meetings. One of his pet theses was that governments could not go bankrupt. He died before Argentina proved him wrong.

Reuters went public on 4 June 1984.

THE PRICE OF TRUTH

The first book to appear about the flotation was *The Price of Truth: The story of Reuters £££ millions* in 1985 by John Lawrenson and Lionel Barber, later to become Editor of the *Financial Times,* (Edinburgh: Mainstream Publishing, 1985). The blurb said:

> The Price of Truth is the dramatically true story of how a few worthless bits of paper turned into a billion pounds. It is a story of greed and intrigue surrounding Fleet Street and of how a small group of men broke a solemn undertaking in their efforts to unlock a treasure house. It tells how a handful of people, largely anonymous, have changed one of the best known British institutions and turned it into one of Britain's most valuable companies.

I was surprised that the extract in *The Sunday Times* on 5 May 1985 carried this box as its introduction:

> In 1952, Michael Nelson joined Reuters, one of a group of bright young men hired to revitalise it. The first extract from a new book, *The Price of Truth*, describes how his stubbornness transformed Reuters fortunes.

I did not know I was stubborn. They were referring to the survey we had commissioned in 1964 into the European market for Stockmaster. The extract from the book said:

> Reuters had spent £3000 on the survey, an exceptionally heavy cost at the time. But its conclusion was that for continental Europe and the United Kingdom, Reuters might be able to sell just three or four of the new devices.

Nelson disagreed and he won the backing of his chief executive at Reuters, Gerald Long. The decision to back the Stockmaster concept was, in retrospect, the single most important commercial judgment in the agency's history and an event which would have prolonged implications for the whole of Britain's national newspaper industry 20 years later.

BRIGHT YOUNG MEN

When I look back at the group of bright young men hired to revitalise Reuters in the early nineteen-fifties, referred to in the box in the newspaper serialisation, three names stand out. They are Glen Renfrew, Patrick Seale and James Wolfe.

Patrick Seale, Balliol College, Oxford, bilingual in French and English, was the first correspondent assigned abroad for the economic services when he went to Paris. He left Reuters in 1959 to study at St Antony's College, Oxford. For 12 years he worked for the *Observer,* succeeding Kim Philby as the newspaper's correspondent in Beirut when he defected to the Soviet Union. He wrote many books, the latest of which was *The Struggle for Arab Independence: Riad el-Solh and the Makers of the Modern Middle East* (Cambridge: Cambridge University Press, 2010). At one point in his career he was a literary agent and ran an art gallery in Belgravia. He married a young novelist Lamorna Heath who gave birth to two children, Orlando and Delilah. His wife died when Orlando was five and Delilah was two and he brought up the two children. When she was 18 Patrick told Delilah that her biological father was Martin Amis, the novelist.

In an interview in *The Sunday Times* on 6 January 2011 Delilah said she had thought it odd that she had blonde hair while her father and brother were dark. Helga and I wondered the same. Delilah commented on her father:

> He was suddenly left with these two children. For a man of his generation that was a huge undertaking. It's only when you have children yourself that you realise what an incredible thing he did. We had nannies, but even if you have help, you're still the one getting up in the night, you're still the one there on Sunday morning, but he never complained, he was just so strong and loving.

Patrick's second wife was a prominent Syrian scholar, Dr. Rana Kabbani, by whom he had two children, Alexander and Jasmine. Patrick has a house near us in Fayence in the South of France so I am glad to say we often see him and the children.

James Wolfe, Wadham College, Oxford, of Hungarian origin moved from the economic services to general news and became correspondent in Conakry. He later became news editor in Paris. Stephen Somerville, a senior Reuter executive, wrote a note for me about him:

When I was posted to Conakry I heard, from an Israeli friend, of one of James' best practical jokes. James had spread the word, through some Russian journalists, that CIA agents from the US Embassy used to meet their local informants at a particularly scruffy bar on the outskirts of Conakry. He then tipped off an American diplomat that the Soviets were using the same scruffy bar to run their local intelligence network. Having sown the seeds, James sat in a far corner of the bar and watched.

When he came back to Conakry, I asked James about the story. He did not deny it. "I was bored," he said. "What do you do for fun?"

His body was found in the river Seine in Paris on 25 September 1965, five days after he went missing between the Reuters Paris office and his flat in the neighbouring Marais district. He was 35 years old. As far as I am aware, I am the last known person to have seen him alive. Was it an accident, suicide or murder? I still don't know.

I was in London for pre-posting briefings when I heard the news that James' body had been found in the Seine. According to the preliminary evidence, it could have been in the water since the night he vanished. Suicide, perhaps, or a mugging? I did not have time to give the case much thought as I flew off to Saigon.

Some months later I received a message from the British Embassy in Saigon. Would I kindly give a statement under oath about the last time I saw a man called James Wolfe? It was a request from a Coroner in England who, they said, was making further inquiries into the cause of death. I gave my statement. Later I heard that the Coroner had refused to accept the French police conclusion of suicide. Mr Wolfe was a strong swimmer who would have been unlikely to commit suicide by jumping into a river, he said. A British Home Office pathologist gave evidence at the hearing, held in Horsham, Surrey, saying that a post mortem examination had shown no water in Mr Wolfe's lungs. Death was therefore not caused by drowning, he said, although it could have been due to the shock of immersion. The Coroner concluded: "I think it proper to return an open verdict although I may add that it may well have been an accident."

The Coroner's name, I noted, was Mr F Haddock. James would have enjoyed that. A fishy tale, I can hear him saying. That was the end of the Wolfe affair as far as I was concerned, apart from two footnotes.

A year or so later I re-based from Saigon to Paris, taking over James' old job of News Editor. In my spare time, out of curiosity, I made some inquiries about James' death. Shortly afterwards I received a telephone call warning me to stop asking questions about Monsieur Wolfe. The caller, French, sounded official, maybe police or security, but refused to give his name. He said something about the authorities having an interest in the matter. I continued to ask around, but drew a blank wherever I turned. Reluctantly, I gave up.

Sometime during the same assignment in Paris, James Wolfe's mother came to see me. She was an elderly lady with a strong Central European accent. She refused to believe that her son had committed suicide and was not convinced that his death had been accidental. She asked if I could help her investigate the case. I had to tell her that my amateur attempts to do so had already met a dead end.

So what do I really think, after all these years: accident, suicide or murder? I usually shy away from conspiracy theories, but in this case, I am inclined to make an exception. With no firm supporting evidence, I suspect foul play. But who? A random mugger? A cold war assassin? West African diamond smugglers?

It's still an open verdict.

Peter Wolfe, his older brother, was also an original. He successfully published books on bluff with titles like "Bluff your way in salesmanship".

James married Olga of St. Hugh's College, Oxford, whom I knew well. They split up when they were in Conakry and James married again; an architect, Santa. Olga married the well-known journalist and author, Michael Leapman. I met them from time to time at the Biographers' Club and in 2010 I plucked up the courage to ask Olga if she would be willing to talk about James. She agreed, but was only able to tell me that she did not believe his death was an accident because he was a strong swimmer.

SPYCATCHER

An old Oxford friend I helped to recruit as a Reuter trustee was Nicolas Browne-Wilkinson. The background to his appointment was the most extraordinary court case of the century involving newspapers and espionage. In 1986 Peter Wright, a former MI5 secret service officer, and Paul Greengrass fought a court case in Sydney, New South Wales against the British government, which tried to stop them publishing *Spycatcher: The Candid Autobiography of a Senior Intelligence Officer*. The book tells of the MI6 plot to assassinate President Nasser during the Suez crisis and of the MI5-CIA plot against Harold Wilson, who was suspected of being a KGB agent. The British government lost the case in a judgement given on 13 March 1987. The case had been avidly followed around the world and went down in history for the apology that Sir Robert Armstrong, the British cabinet secretary, made to the court for having been "economical with the truth."

The English courts had imposed gag orders on the *Observer* and *Guardian* in 1986 to stop them publishing extracts in England but the *Independent, Evening News* and *Daily News* later published. On 2 June Sir Nicolas Browne-Wilkinson, the Vice-Chancellor (senior judge of the Chancery Division), barred the Attorney-General from bringing contempt proceedings against the three newspapers.

Nicolas Browne-Wilkinson was, of course, the hero of the day to the British Press. Lord McGregor, Chairman of the Reuters Founder Share Company – the Reuter Trust – saw him as exactly the sort of person to protect the independence of Reuters. Knowing we were old friends, he asked me to help to persuade him to become a trustee. I invited him for a drink at the Garrick, I explained the workings of the trust and he agreed.

On 15 July the Court of Appeal overturned Nicolas' judgement. The *Daily Mirror* later published upside-down photographs of three Law Lords with the caption *YOU FOOLS*. They were fools because when they gave a further banning judgement the book was by then widely on sale. Nicolas was vindicated a year later when the Law Lords ruled that the Press was free to publish extracts.

Some years later Nicolas, by then Lord Browne-Wilkinson, resigned from the Board of Trustees on a point of principle. Pehr Gyllennhammar, by then Chairman of Trustees, proposed that Trustees should be paid. Nicolas said that would impugn their independence and he resigned.

HOUSES

We moved to 44 Phillimore Gardens, Kensington in London, in December 1984 and in the same year moved from Menthon-St-Bernard to a house we had built at 17 Route du Port, Veyrier-du-Lac, on Lake Annecy. The land stretched down to the lake where we had a jetty and a motor boat for water-skiing. Helga designed the layout, which provided for an annexe for the children.

One of our neighbours in Veyrier, who became a good friend, was Georges Salomon, the most impressive non-media businessman I ever met. His father manufactured saw blades, but Georges persuaded him to turn to the manufacture of ski parts and he revolutionised the industry. When he died in 2010 the obituary in the *Financial Times* summarised his achievement:

> In 1955, he designed and produced the first releasable binding for the toe-end of a boot, which he called the Skade. Two years later, he perfected and manufactured the first binding that released the heel of the boot depending on the pressure placed on it. In line with the English and American influences of the time, he called his new device le Lift. With his bindings that snapped before bones did, he revolutionised the ski industry, preventing countless injuries.

Salomon then went into the production of ski clothing and state of the art boots and skis.

I sat with him as he wrestled with the question of whether or not he should buy the rising US-based golf manufacturer Taylor Made, whose founder Gary Adams had invented the revolutionary metal wood. He bought it and sold his entire business to Adidas in 1997 for €1.2 billion. It was a wise move because growing competition and the growth of the ski rental market meant his brand had peaked. When Adidas sold it to the Finnish-based Amer Sports in 2005 they got only €485 million for it.

Salomon and his wife Perry, who spoke English, liked to invite us over for supper on Saturday evenings, where they served bread, local cold meats and cheese, together with a range of outstanding white burgundies and clarets. But you only got one glass: you had to rinse the glass between each tasting.

REUTER FOUNDATION

The Reuter Foundation was set up in 1982 on my recommendation to fund scholarships for mature third-world journalists at the universities of Bordeaux, Oxford and Stanford. I chaired the board of trustees. It later became a wide-ranging charity arm of Reuters and created the Reuters Institute for the Study of Journalism at Oxford.

The foundation was Reuters response to the UNESCO 1980 paper *Many Voices One World,* also known as *The MacBride Report,* after the chairman of the International Commission for the Study of Communication Problems. It attacked the western news agencies for maintaining a stranglehold over the coverage of news.

I chose Oxford as the British university for obvious reasons. The institution we selected there was Queen Elizabeth House. At the Board Meeting which discussed the establishment of the Foundation Rupert Murdoch, an alumnus of Worcester College, objected that it was not a proper college. It was a hybrid institution, part University and part independent, funded by the British government to introduce "persons of authority and influence" in the Commonwealth and third world to the University. I replied that the problem was that, such was the attitude of Oxford colleges to journalism, they would not be interested in our project. Attitudes to journalists changed and in 1992 Reuters moved the programme to Green College. We were fortunate to have as director of the programme Neville Maxwell, a former journalist. He was succeeded by two other excellent programme directors: Godfrey Hodgson and Paddy Coulter.

The Foundation at Oxford soon expanded beyond its third-world remit to embrace the developed world and eventually the number of fellows attending the programme reached 22 in a year.

I thought the natural home for the programme in the United States would be the Niemann Foundation at Harvard. I visited them, but was horrified to find that they spent 70% of their budget on administration and only 30% on the fellowships. So I flew to Stanford and chose the Knight Fellowship programme there, led by the splendid Lyle Nelson (no relation).

In France we chose the University of Bordeaux. We were influenced in our choice by the fact that the head of the school of journalism was Robert Escarpit, a distinguished journalist and a fluent English speaker. Escarpit was famous in France for his short pithy comments which appeared at the bottom of the left hand front page column of *Le Monde*. *Un escarpit* passed into the French language for such a comment and *un escarpito* even passed into Spanish.

The Hon. Alan Hare had been a Reuter director. He was Chairman and Chief Executive of the *Financial Times,* being a member of the family that owned it. Hare had a number of careers: during the war he had shared a cave in Albania with the future President Hoxha and later became a spy. He retired from the *Financial Times* in 1983 and was given the retirement present of the chairmanship of *Château Latour*, which was owned by the Pearsons, who also owned the *Financial Times*. He was the host at *Château Latour* at the most elegant and bizarre lunch I ever attended.

I had told Hare about Escarpit and he invited him to lunch at *Château Latour*. That afternoon I received an infuriated telephone call from the distinguished chatelain. "You never told me he was a communist. We first growths don't like communists, you know." "Come off it, Alan," I replied. "A communist representative in a French regional assembly is not like a communist in Soviet Russia." I sufficiently convinced him that he forgave Escarpit his communism and invited him to lunch again with trustees of the Foundation when we visited Bordeaux. Present at the lunch on 25 March 1986 in the beautiful round dining room of *Château Latour* were the hosts Alan and Jill Hare, Robert and Denise Escarpit, Michael Reupke, Editor-in-Chief of Reuters, and Elizabeth, Michael Cooling, Director of the Reuter Foundation, and Ann, and myself, Chairman of the Foundation, and Helga.

The first wine was, by tradition, not from *Château Latour*, but a white from another distinguished vineyard and the name did not appear on the crested menu. The first course was *Foie frais aux raisins*, accompanied by the modest second wine of *Château Latour, Les Forts de Latour 1970*. The four waitresses cleared the plates and Escarpit pulled out his pipe. Jill Hare was horrified. "Oh," she gasped. "Would you mind not smoking here. It is the staff, you see. It ruins their palate. But please go into the garden, if you wish." "That's all right," said Escarpit as he scattered tobacco over the tablecloth. "I can do without it." The next course was *Roti de Boeuf* with *Croquettes de pommes de terre*, accompanied by *Château Latour 1966*. (Robert Parker, the wine critic, described it as *the* wine of the vintage). When the butler served – in fresh glasses, of course – the second bottle, Escarpit opined: "You know, I think this bottle is better than the first. You realise," he told the ignorant English, "that even in the same year one bottle can differ from another." "We all know that," shot back Jill (who had done a course on wine). The cheese was accompanied by *Château Latour 1955* and the *Gâteau Belle Hélène* by *Château Sigalas Rabaud 1967*.

At half past three we retired to the comfortable arm chairs of the salon for coffee and brandy. Escarpit fell asleep.

To my surprise the *Daily Telegraph* thought the lunch was newsworthy, although they got the timing a bit wrong. On 14 October 1989 the newspaper ran this diary story about *Château Latour*:

Not everything at the vineyard's Bordeaux headquarters has been going swimmingly. Hare explains that last week the château's ban on smoking in the dining room – designed to protect the wine drunk by guests – was violated.

"It was the first time anybody had dared light up," says Hare. "A communist deputy decided to smoke over the cheese which is when we serve our best claret. I told him that he was not breaking my heart but the servants would be horrified."

I thought Alan Hare would never forgive me for the horrors of the lunch. But when I asked him where I could buy his wine *en primeur* he sent me to a broker in Bordeaux. The wine was unbelievably cheap so I bought six cases. I asked Hare why it was so cheap. He replied: "Oh, we own the broker and we use him to supply wines to our friends."

When the first of the trustees of the Reuter Foundation was about to retire I ordered a silver salver from Aspreys, engraved with his name and his wife's, to be presented in thanks at the farewell party. To keep the future cost down I ordered a job lot covering all the trustees, all suitably engraved. When we were about to go to Bordeaux to make the presentation to Escarpit we heard that he had just got divorced. Fortunately Aspreys could correct the engraving for the Escarpits' salver to delete Denise.

The last time I saw Escarpit was when he came to London accompanied by his new wife, whom I knew as his former secretary, and, to my surprise, their ten year-old son.

The Foundation developed Alertnet, a website devoted to humanitarian issues. It covered conflicts, natural disasters and health emergencies.

Reuters Institute for the Study of Journalism at Oxford opened in November 2006 with initial funding of £1.75 million from the Reuter Foundation. By then more than 400 fellows had attended the Foundation programme. The Institute's activities included short and long-term research projects, many of which were published, seminars, workshops, conferences and debates.

I was particularly pleased when Reuters appointed the clever and charming Monique Villa, a neighbour of ours in Lansdowne Road in London, and former London bureau chief of Agence France-Presse, to head the Foundation.

When Thomson took over Reuters the merged company Thomson Reuters expanded the work of the Foundation to establish Trustlaw to create an international hub for the practice of pro bono legal work.

VISNEWS: PART ONE

Visnews, the television news agency, was owned one-third by the BBC, one third by Reuters and the remaining third was split equally between the public service broadcasters of Australia, Canada and New Zealand. It had been founded in 1957 as the British Commonwealth International Newsfilm Agency (BCINA) to create a non-American source of television news and the name was later changed.

One of the prime movers in the foundation of BCINA was Lt-Gen Sir Ian Jacob, Director-General of the BBC, whom I once invited to lunch at Reuters. He was most impressive, with an extraordinary career, which included accompanying Churchill to the Yalta Conference. He skilfully handled Eden's attack on the BBC at the time of Suez in 1956.

The Managing Director of BCINA, Ronnie Waldman, was a household name because before World War II he had been the producer of one of the most famous BBC radio programmes *Monday Night at Eight*, which started with the refrain:

It's Monday night at eight o'clock;
Oh, can't you hear the chimes?
They're telling you to take an easy chair,
To settle by the fireside,
Look at your Radio Times,
For Monday Night at Eight is on the air

His voice was well known from his *Puzzle Corner.*

At the end of 1977 Waldman retired because of ill-health. Visnews had never had sparkling financial results. I had become a director in 1974 and, concerned at the meager profits, persuaded Long, who was Chairman, that Waldman's departure gave the opportunity to break away from the tradition of Visnews being run by a former BBC man and hire someone with a good commercial background to make us some profits. Visnews had great unexploited assets, including its library, the largest single collection of film and videotape of its kind in the world. It had more than 50 million feet of material covering international events since the turn of the century. Its earliest piece of film was coverage of the coronation of Czar Nicholas II of Russia in 1896.

Long told me to commission a head-hunter to find a new managing director with business background. But just as I was starting the search Long came into my office one day to say that Desmond Taylor, BBC Editor, News and Current Affairs, ("Enca" to the cognoscenti), and a director of Visnews, had telephoned him to say that Charles Curran, Director-General of the BBC, who was about to retire, wanted the job. "I cannot turn down the Director-General of the BBC," said Long. So to my disgust the commercialization of Visnews was put off for another day. Curran became Managing Director at the beginning of 1978.

By coincidence Curran was succeeded as Director-General of the BBC by Ian Trethowan, who in 1950 had married my cousin Pat, an actress, the daughter of my uncle Colonel Jack Nelson. They had no children and they divorced in 1963. In the same year he married his secretary Carolyn Reynolds, by whom he had three daughters. Ian was the son of Major James Trethowan, the best friend of Jack, whom he had known in the army. Jack recounted to me his dramatic encounter with his old friend when the marriage broke up. "I ran into him in the National Liberal Club. He put his arm round my shoulders and expressed his regrets. 'Get your hands off me. Your son has ruined my daughter's life,' I told him."

Ian and I continued to encounter each other socially after the divorce and he seemed to find our occasional meetings embarrassing. He was knighted in 1980 and died of motor neurone disease in 1990. In the Oxford Dictionary of National Biography Brian Wenham said: "He had a clear vision of the proper province of both commentators and those commented upon, and throughout his career this enabled him to defuse potentially explosive editorial challenges."

Long lived to regret Curran's Visnews appointment. Curran saw it as a two-day a week job, not full-time as did Long, and resented having to deal with Long. Curran showed his displeasure by always arriving late for meetings with Long. But Long only had to put up with him for two years. He died on 9 January 1980 following a heart attack.

So it was back to the head-hunters. I chaired a committee of directors of Visnews and we chose Brian Quinn, who had a good business background, and he served Visnews well for some six years. He was greatly supported for part of the time by Peter Marshall, the General Manager. When Quinn left we went back to the head-hunters and had a strange experience related to references, a subject which plays an important part in business life, but which receives little attention. We had chosen an impressive man and had been influenced by the excellent reference from a former employer, the then Sir John Cuckney, the Chairman of Thomas Cook. One Sunday evening I received a telephone call from the head-hunter. He had just heard that the candidate was a drinker, who had had a drink-driving conviction, so we obviously could not hire him. The candidate was due to meet Sir Christopher Hogg, the Chairman of Reuters, first thing the following morning. So when he arrived in the front hall a secretary had to tell him the meeting had been cancelled. He threatened to sue, but did not do so. In a fury I telephoned Sir John Cuckney to ask how he could have given such a reference. "I did not want to spoil his career," he said. I was not polite to him.

Disillusioned by the experience with the head-hunted candidate on 1 August 1986 we appointed Julian Kerr, a good Reuter manager, as Managing Director.

MI5 AND VETTING

Another experience related to references came about when one of the newspaper owners of Reuters gave us a good reference for one of the biggest trouble-makers in Fleet Street. Some years earlier we secretly got MI5 to vet our job applicants, but eventually we stopped it. That was a pity: if that trouble-maker had been vetted we would not have employed him.

The Reuter archives contain nothing about MI5 vetting, which must have been entirely verbal. We do not know when it started, but it may well have been after the discovery of the communist cell in Reuters in 1950 and the defection of John Peet, the West Berlin Reuter correspondent, to East Berlin. Peet himself filed the story of his defection to Reuters saying that he could "no longer serve the Anglo-American warmongers." Reuters was beaten on its own story by the Associated Press because the desk in London sat on it while the journalists awaited guidance from the bosses on how to handle it. From 1952 to 1975 Peet edited the fortnightly *Democratic German Report*. In it he attacked West German politicians, diplomats, industrialists, lawyers, police officials and generals for their alleged Nazi pasts.

MI5 vetting started in the BBC in 1937 on the initiative of Sir John (later Lord) Reith, the first director general. It was exposed in an article in the *Observer* on 18 August 1985 by David Leigh and Paul Lashmar under the headline *The Blacklist in Room 105*. Mark Hollingsworth and Richard

Norton-Taylor wrote about it in *Blacklist: The Inside Story of Political Vetting* (London: Hogarth Press, 1988). Neither the article nor the book mentioned Reuters.

BBC vetting, which was called "colleging" or "the formalities", was run from Room 105 in Broadcasting House. Suspect staff had a buff folder with a round red sticker, stamped "SECRET" and a symbol looking like a Christmas tree.

Curiously enough a director of documentaries who was prevented by MI5 from getting a BBC staff job was Stephen Peet. He was banned because of his brother John, whom he still saw, although Stephen was not a communist. Jerry Kuehl of the International Association for Media and History (IAMHIST) introduced me to Stephen at one of their meetings in the nineties and he gave me a copy of the film of the press conference his brother had given in Berlin on his defection, which Reuters did not have. I gave it to the Reuter archive. The Stephen Peet affair had a happy ending. He appealed to his MP, Kenneth Robinson, Minister for Health in Harold Wilson's Labour government, who took it up with the Home Office and the blacklisting disappeared. He made the much-acclaimed *Yesterday's Witness* series and won a Royal Television Society special award.

John Peet seemed to have retained a sentimental attachment to Reuters because he came to the reception when I inaugurated the new Reuter office in East Berlin in June 1987. The British Ambassador was Tim Everard, an old Magdalen friend, and he and his wife Josiane gave a dinner attended by journalists and diplomats for Helga and me. They did not invite Peet.

Peet died of cancer the following year. For some time he had been working on his memoirs. When he learned he had incurable cancer he added to the draft the information that when he was with the International Brigade in Spain in the thirties he had been recruited as a spy by the NKVD, the Soviet intelligence agency. The NKVD contacted him later in London and in East Berlin. He says that in East Berlin he fed them a certain amount of West Berlin journalistic scuttlebutt. They made various proposals of the work they would like him to do for them but he generally declined. The exception was when he went, at the suggestion of the NKVD, to the 1954 Geneva Conference on the Far East. There the Soviet contact suggested he should get on good terms with some of the female members of the various UN agencies stationed in Geneva. He declined to become a honeytrap and soon entirely ended the relationship with the NKVD. He tells us in his memoirs that since 1978 he had been very happy with his fourth wife, who was East German.

The memoirs were published after his death as *The Long Engagement: Memoirs of a Cold War Legend* with a foreword by Len Deighton (London: Fourth Estate, 1989). The book presents his quandary: "In the 1930s, when party members or fellow travellers were upset or mystified by inexplicable events in the Soviet Union, they were often assuaged by the glib phrase that you could not make an omelette without breaking eggs. But where is the omelette? I am still looking."

Peet did not mention in his memoirs the incident described below, which I came across in *Postcards from Abroad: Memories of PEN* by Elizabeth Paterson (London: Sinclair-Stevenson, 2001) when it was published:

> Peet had been appointed International Press Officer of the organisation PEN — an acronym for Poets, Playwrights, Editors, Essayists and Novelists. The appointment had raised some eyebrows, as some of the members regarded him as a traitor. A conference was held in Stockholm in 1978 at the Grand Hotel, which opened with a formal welcome party. Peet turned up to this rather informally dressed and explained that when he got to his hotel room and unpacked the smart suit, which he had brought with him for this occasion, to his horror he found that his wife (whom he was just about to abandon for another woman) had taken her revenge by slashing it to pieces.

It is unlikely that MI5 would have known of Peet's NKVD connection when he joined Reuters in August 1945 and anyway we do not know if they were then vetting Reuter applicants.

Manfred Pagel, Editor of Reuters, told me that Brian Heywood, an executive in what was then called Staff Department, handled the MI5 vetting. Phil Wardle, Assistant Managing Editor, recounted to me the story of the occasion when he wanted to hire a girl with good German at a time when we were short of German speakers. He put her name to the Staff Department for MI5 vetting, but after a couple of days the message came that he could not hire her.

Sir David Nicholas, former Editor-in-Chief of ITN, has confirmed to me that MI5 never vetted his applicants.

In *The Defence of the Realm: The Authorized History of MI5* (London: Allen Lane, 2009) Christopher Andrew writes at length about vetting, but strangely does not mention the BBC or Reuters. I wrote to Andrew and asked him why he had not mentioned the BBC or Reuters vetting. I did not receive a reply. I ran into him at a seminar in February 2011. He apologised for not replying to my letter: he had been ill. He said the subject had not been covered for space reasons, but he had dealt with the BBC in the paperback edition (London: Penguin, 2010). Interestingly, Andrews discloses in the paperback that pressure to increase vetting in the BBC came not from MI5, who resisted it, but from Sir Hugh Greene, the BBC director general. Sir Roger Hollis, the head of MI5, noted after a meeting with Greene that there was an irreconcilable difference between them over the purpose of vetting. "We were concerned with defence interests but they were really concerned with the avoidance of embarrassment," he wrote.

The paperback edition does not mention Reuters. We have to wonder who initiated vetting in Reuters and when.

Andrew discloses that among the 100 organisations whose applicants were vetted were the National Bus Company and the Sports Council, which is odd. MI5 had a million names for vetting on its files. In 1985 it handled 327,000 vetting enquiries. The total number of man-hours it devoted to the process came to 64 years. Only in 913 cases (0.28 per cent of those submitted to it) had MI5 found security concerns. It discontinued vetting in the old form in 1990 and concentrated on counter-terrorist checking. In 1992 it stopped keeping a record of rank and file members of subversive organisations. The proportion of subversives detected by MI5 during vetting had declined from 2.7 per cent of all applicants in 1971 to 0.06 per cent in 1990. Since the 1970s the number of organisations identified as subversive had fallen from over 70 to around 45 and their total membership from 55,000 to around 14,000.

Partly because of the outcry following the *Observer* article, the BBC stopped all security vetting in October 1985 except in two areas involving about 120 jobs. Firstly staff involved in the planning and operation of a wartime broadcasting service and secondly some jobs in External Services. We do not know when Reuters stopped vetting.

CHAPTER NINE

A Night with Fidel Castro

VISNEWS: PART TWO

In 1983 I recommended that Reuters buy out the other shareholders of Visnews. Reuters had had a chequered career in television, mainly because of problems with the Reuter board. In 1954 the Board had rejected a proposal from management that it should make the news programmes for commercial television, later performed by ITN. In 1955 the Board refused to allow it to join the planned British Commonwealth International Newsfilm Agency (BCINA), although it relented five years later. Indeed, as if he did not have enough to do as chief executive of Reuters, it allowed Walton Cole to become Managing Director of BCINA in 1961. No wonder he dropped down dead eighteen months later. By 1983 it was clear that its minority interest in Visnews meant that Reuters was missing out in a major media market.

In 1985 the BBC agreed to sell enough of its shares so that Reuters could get control with 55% of the equity. I became Chairman. We wanted to get more of the shares so that we could make NBC, our source for American news, a shareholder. I found it extraordinary that Visnews was dependent for its news from the most important news source in the world on a contract subject to three months' notice at any time and no other tie-in. The Canadians were willing to sell their shares. I flew out to Sydney and Auckland but the Australians and New Zealanders would not sell. Once a year the chief executives of the broadcasters flew to London with their wives for the annual general meeting of Visnews. They were duchessed (to use a good Australianism), with visits to Wimbledon and Glyndebourne and lavish lunches and dinners. The cynics suggested that the reason they would not sell was that if they sold their shares they would not get their trips to London. I was sure this could not be true. Fortunately, a trustee of Visnews was the very wise lawyer James Evans, who had master-minded the legal side of the famous thalidomide case for Harold Evans in *The Sunday Times*, and he gave me the clever idea of converting their shares into non-voting redeemable preference shares. Then they could still come to the annual general meeting and get their jollies in London. The deal was done in February 1988 and Reuters increased its shareholding to 88.75%, later to become 51% when in November 1988 NBC became a shareholder against a payment of $10 million ($18 million at current values). Reuters gained full control in 1992 when it bought out NBC and the BBC.

A curiosity of the relationship between Visnews and its broadcasting shareholders was that Visnews had exclusive rights to their television news outside their home territories. That meant that the BBC could not start a television news service for viewing outside the United Kingdom without the agreement of Visnews. Visnews therefore extracted a heavy price for that agreement when the BBC started its television world service.

The most important story that Visnews broke while I was involved with the company was in October 1984 when Mohammed Amin, the head of the Visnews Nairobi office got into Ethiopia and reported the famine.

The now historical pictures of the starving population triggered a massive global reaction within hours of being shown. The response still continues today with Band Aid, Live Aid and other programmes all triggered by that single event. Ethiopia's borders had been closed because of widespread rebel activity, but Amin, using local contacts, managed to get special permission to go in. His links locally with World Vision, an American charity undertaking aid in East Africa, enabled him to borrow a small light aircraft to fly in his equipment. At the last moment the BBC, hearing of the move, asked Amin to wait while they sent up an unknown reporter from their Johannesburg office to accompany him. Amin did not wish to delay and feared being hampered by someone inexperienced in what was a dangerous mission. He was persuaded, however, to do so and Michael Buerk arrived the next day and joined Amin on the expedition. The rest is media history and Amin was summoned to the White House to be congratulated on his achievement. He was also made cameraman of the year by the Royal Television Society.

SHAKESPEARE'S GLOBE THEATRE

I met Sam Wanamaker, the actor, when he was raising money to build

Shakespeare's Globe Theatre in London and undertook to help him. I had been introduced to him by Theo Crosby, Reuters design consultant, who was the architect for the Globe project. Reuters contribution was a promotional film made without charge by Visnews, which was a great success. I valued my acquaintanceship with Wanamaker, a man of imagination and determination, who succeeded in his project despite immense difficulties and scepticism from much of the British establishment. His daughter Zoe, the actress, whom I also knew and admired, was invaluable support to him.

Sam, who had been born in the United States, a son of Russian immigrants, had been a communist from 1944 to 1947 and had to move to England to escape the anti-communist witch hunt. In 2009 files were released which showed that the British government had planned to arrest him in the event of an emergency, such as war with the Soviet Union. He died aged 74 in 1993, sadly just four years before the opening of the Globe.

Theo Crosby wanted to develop a neglected part of the Thames riverscape and the plan for a footbridge was his brainchild and that of his wife, the artist Polly Hope. Unfortunately he died before he could compete for the commission to design it.

THE IMPORTANCE OF PAY TOILETS

Reuters had never had a news pictures service. This was a great competitive disadvantage in markets like Latin America, where textual news and pictures were sold as a package. The two major news picture agencies were United Press International (UPI), owned by Scripps-Howard, and the Associated Press (AP). So when in 1982 Scripps-Howard sold UPI to two entrepreneurs, Doug Ruhe and William Geissler, for $1 and they started to get into financial difficulties we decided to try to acquire their news pictures business outside the United States.

I might well have never been employed by Reuters had I not been recommended to Reuters following the day's work I did at British United Press. So I always followed the fortunes of UPI with particular interest.

United Press International (UPI) was formed of the merger of United Press (UP) and International News Service (INS) in 1958. UP had been founded in 1907 by the newspaper publisher E.W. Scripps to compete with the Associated Press (AP) after it refused to sell its service to several of his newspapers. The owning company eventually became Scripps-Howard Newspapers. William Randolph Hearst founded INS in 1909, but it never had the standing of UP.

UPI had a great reputation as a lively, hard-hitting wire service, often cutting corners, with immense staff devotion. Its most famous scoop was the assassination of President Kennedy in Dallas when Merriman Smith grabbed the telephone in the agency limousine at the sound of gunfire and beat the AP man to the draw.

In the seventies UPI began to run into financial difficulties as afternoon newspapers, where it was particularly strong, began to fail as a result of the rising popularity of television news. In 1981 UPI asked Reuters if it was interested in buying it from Scripps-Howard. I was against because I could never see Reuters competing successfully with a cooperative. Renfrew was initially inclined to favour buying, as was John Stephens, the very experienced executive who led the market survey. But Renfrew eventually came round to my point of view and we rejected the offer.

In March 1984 we decided the time was ripe for Reuters to talk to UPI about news pictures so I flew to New York to meet its new chairman, John Jay Hooker. He was a Nashville, Tennessee, First Amendment lawyer, who had twice lost a bid to become governor and once a senator. I had been told he was flamboyant, but was bowled over by his vested blue suit and bright red and blue striped tie and his folksy stories.

Down to the Wire: UPI's Fight for Survival by Gregory Gordon and Ronald E. Cohen (New York: McGraw-Hill, 1990) recounted Reuters approach to UPI with the following:

In March 1984 a four-member UPI contingent met with top Reuters executives Mike Nelson and Peter Holland at the Parker Meridien Hotel overlooking Central Park. Hooker seized the moment to describe, in flowery full-drawl, his vision for UPI. The Brits sat bemused. Never had they encountered his like.

"This is a $100 million company now, but it is going to be a billion dollar company," Hooker boasted.

Then, without warning, he launched into his story about the Greyhound Bus chairman, who, concluding that travelers with battered kidneys would leave the bus and head straight for the restroom, hatched the idea of pay toilets.

Nelson, a proper Englishman who might have come from straight from central casting in London, was baffled until Holland explained. "He means a loo, where you have to pay to get in."

> Not missing a beat, Hooker declared. "Well that's what we're looking for here. We're looking for UPI's pay toilet."
>
> If Hooker's down-home analogies precipitated a minor culture shock, the Brits were not dissuaded from offering $5 million for UPI's foreign picture service. Reuters was politely turned away – for now.

By June 1984 UPI had run out of cash and accepted Reuters offer for the foreign picture business. We paid $3,300,000 in cash ($7 million at current values) and contracted to pay £2,460,000 (£5.9 million at current values) over the first five years of a ten-year agreement. We exchanged international and US pictures. When I gave a celebratory dinner in London to Ruhe and Geissler, Ruhe told me that when they had received my message confirming the deal he and Geissler had stood up and sung "God Save the Queen".

But Mike Hughes, the vice-president in charge of the international division, saw it otherwise. He was reported as saying: "The sale to Reuters was the most idiotic deal that was ever made. Had Reuters worked 24/7 to organise its own service it would have taken them three years just to put all the transmitters in place. I'd say a conservative guess is that we saved them $20 million and five years."

Mark Getty showed that his figures were not far wrong when in 1995 he started a picture service from scratch, which cost $20 million of family money and the next year $50 million from the market.

Overnight the acquisition transformed Reuters service to the media. At last Reuters had a complete range of products. For 32 years the salesman had had to counter the potential client's statement: "We do not take Reuters because you have no pictures." No longer.

In 1984 UPI filed for Chapter 11 bankruptcy and at the end of 1985 Mario Vazquez Rana, a Mexican, bought it out of bankruptcy. I decided I should get to know the new owner of UPI so in May 1986 I flew to Mexico City to meet him. Vazquez Rana, one of Mexico's wealthiest men, had made his fortune in furniture and had bought the *El Sol* newspaper chain out of bankruptcy. He was president of Mexico's Olympic Committee. Pieter van Bennekom, his interpreter and principal UPI assistant, told me Vazquez had been wondering what he should talk to me about and had decided on sex. We did not talk about sex, but spent a lot of time touring his enormous office complex which consisted of a soccer field, indoor pool, gym, sauna, bedroom, private theatre, dining room, bar and kitchen. In the central courtyard was a fifty-foot waterfall, an enormous cage of exotic birds and two Russian black bears, Olympia and Nacho. By 1988 Vazquez had lost a lot of money through UPI and sold it to Infotechnology Inc., controlled by a Californian venture capitalist, Earl Brian.

In 1993 UPI closed most of its bureaus and fired most of its staff. It was the culmination of a decade of changes of ownership, product sell-offs, staff cutbacks and salary reductions. In 2000 it was acquired by News World Communications, a media company owned by the Sun Myung Moon's Unification Church. It produced a few specialised services, but was no longer a major news agency.

One has to wonder why Reuters did not approach UPI to get access to its United States news service when faced with AP's demands in 1966. The reason was probably that we regarded UPI as rather a wild-west outfit which we would not want to rely on. Equally one has to wonder if later there were ever talks about cooperation between UPI and Bloomberg.

The world of the media was diminished by the effective disappearance of UPI and the reduction of the major international news agencies from four to three.

One of the photographers we took over from UPI was Willy Vicoy in Manila. He died on 25 April 1986, aged 45, a day after being hit by shrapnel in a communist guerilla ambush in the northern Philippines. He was part of an army escorted press party. The most painful duty I had to perform in all my years in Reuters was to visit his young widow and children in Manila to express the condolences of Reuters on the death of her husband. In 1987 Reuters established a scholarship in his name at the University of Missouri.

FIDEL CASTRO GIVES AN INTERVIEW

The most exciting meeting I ever had with a Head of State was on 18 April 1985 when, in the middle of the night, Helga and I had a five and a half hour interview in Havana with Fidel Castro, President of Cuba. I had come to Havana to inaugurate the Reuter Monitor.

While I was launching the Reuter Monitor, Helga went with Lesley McSeveny, the correspondent's wife, to Cojimar, about 10 miles east of Havana, to visit Gregorio Fuentes, once captain of the *Pilar*, Ernest Hemingway's boat. Some claimed he was the inspiration for Hemingway's novel *The Old Man and the Sea*. He died in 2002 aged 104.

The government put at our disposal a vast house with swimming pool, staff and food and drink, where Reuters gave a large garden party. Towards midnight the Foreign Minister, who was at the party, took a telephone call and told us that Fidel Castro wished to see us.

At midnight the Reuter area manager, Michael Blair, photographer, correspondent, Colin McSeveny, Helga and I were ushered into Castro's presence in the Palace. He was dressed in his usual army fatigues. He dismissed the area manager and the photographer from his presence. On the arm of his chair sat a beautiful heavily pregnant girl, who translated simultaneously throughout the interview. Given that Castro had at least 10 children, there was much speculation afterwards that he was the father of the interpreter's forthcoming child. Here are some extracts from the note Colin McSeveny wrote on the discussions:

> The meeting began on a light-hearted note with Castro joking that so many journalists seemed more interested in how many girlfriends he had than on his views.
>
> The main body of the discussion started with a number of questions from Castro about the Reuter operation in Cuba – how many Monitor and media clients, what they were paying, how the cost was calculated, exactly what services they received.
>
> He then asked about how Reuters operated in the rest of the world, showing particular interest in the United States. He appeared greatly interested in the database of the Reuters financial network – who put in the information, how it was retrieved, what kind of communications systems were used, and so on.
>
> Castro also asked for details about the way in which different institutions and companies were charged and how these calculations were made. Did economies of scale apply in the sense that more clients per country allowed lower average prices, he asked.
>
> He also queried Nelson on the ways that Monitor enabled Cuba to save money through the greater speed and variety of the financial information offered.
>
> Castro listened intently as Nelson made the point that Reuters had no connection whatsoever with the British government but just happened to be based in London.
>
> The discussion then ranged over politics, economics and the media, in which he showed a keen understanding and interest.

At 5.30 in the morning, after no less than five and a half hours of talk, I broke the protocol of a visit to a Head of State when I told the President we had to go as we had a plane to catch to Kingston, Jamaica. He was reluctant to let us leave. "You must come back again for a proper meeting, not a short one like this," he said, and tried to fix a date, which I resisted. Castro was very taken by Helga, particularly because she had been born in the now communist city of Bucharest. Before we left he presented a booklet to her containing an interview he had given on world economics. He dedicated it: "Para Helga, afectuosamente, Fidel Castro." ("For Helga, affectionately, Fidel Castro"). I am giving it to Helga and not to you, he told me, because, he said, tongue in cheek, I had been rude to him. Castro would not allow the Reuter photographer to take photos, but used his own. We never received the photos.

We went back to the villa to collect our bags. When we arrived at the airport, the Foreign Ministry official there expressed his great regret that Helga would not be able to leave because the plane had been overbooked and had only one seat. Helga went back to the swimming pool at the house to await a plane due to leave the next day.

I boarded the plane: it was half empty.

When I arrived in San Francisco after the visit to Kingston, I was greatly relieved that Helga had indeed been allowed to catch a later plane and had already checked into the hotel.

BRASS

Part of the job of General Manager of Reuters was sometimes to call on Heads of State when travelling. In addition to Fidel Castro, those I met included Sheikh Isa bin Sulman Al-Khalifa, the Emir of Bahrain; Corazón Aquino, President of the Philippines and Miguel de la Madrid Hurtado, President of Mexico. Who has heard of them now? But they were very important at the time and the Reuter correspondents liked to use these visits to give them the opportunity to meet the Head of State, often for the first time.

Representational visits were not always sweetness and light. The President of Syria declined to see me when I visited Damascus. Dinner with the staff at a restaurant was interrupted by the crash of a bottle of wine landing on the table. We hid behind pillars and under tables as a woman on the other side of the restaurant rained bottles at us until the waiters wrestled her to the ground. The chief of police came to apologise. He said he was deporting her to Lebanon, but did not explain why we were attacked. We shall never know.

My visit to the widow of Willy Vicoy was followed by an audience with President Corazón Aquino. I was accompanied by Graham Lovell, an engaging but rather casual correspondent, who so protracted lunch that we were almost late for our appointment. Also in the party were Helga and the area manager, Geoffrey Weetman and his wife Christine. The charming housewifely President, in her signature yellow dress, impressed because of her history. Her husband Benigno Aquino, opponent of President Ferdinand Marcos and his famous wife of the shoes, Imelda, had been assassinated in 1983. Corazón Aquino was swept to power in 1986 by acclamation after a rigged election by Marcos. Sadly her regime was beset by troubles, but at least she had the satisfaction of transferring power democratically and without bloodshed at the end of her term in 1992.

I met Margaret Thatcher at a reception given by the Newspaper Press Fund shortly after the installation on 11 February 1983 of the Reuter Monitor in 10 Downing Street. "Your service is very expensive. Why do you not give it to us free as a public service?" she asked. I suggested that that would not fit well with the entrepreneurship which she was promoting. She was not pleased.

TED TURNER

In June 1980 Ted Turner had launched CNN, the world's first 24-hour television news service. Visnews and Reuters provided communications facilities to CNN, but Turner wanted the Visnews news feed. He could not have it because use of it in the United States would have conflicted with the Visnews contract with NBC. Turner invited me to dinner at the St. James' Club in London on 7 January 1986 to try to persuade me to give him the Visnews feed. Other executives present were Bob Wussler and Charles Bonan from CNN and Peter Smith, the Reuter executive in charge of strategic planning of communications facilities and a director of Visnews. Also standing at the bar when I arrived was a tall, elegant young lady. "We have not been introduced," I said to her when we sat down for dinner. "My name is Michael Nelson." "I have not been introduced either," said Turner. "Who is she?" "She is our social secretary," said Wussler. "We hired her this morning."

According to a senior CNN executive, he and Turner "used to lie awake at night worrying about whether Reuters would launch a satellite news channel." So much of the conversation was trying to probe our intentions. Then he bid for access to Visnews feeds. When I told him he could have them for use internationally, but not within the United States, he grabbed his glass of red wine, seized hold of the top of my trousers and made as to pour the wine down my trousers. He then leant over the table, kissed me on the forehead and said: "I love ya, Mike." Having thus made his position clear, and satisfied himself that he was not going to get the feed, he spent the rest of the evening recounting his problems with his current wife ("she is, after all, the mother of some of my children") and other ladies. It was therefore no surprise when we heard of his divorce and eventual marriage to Jane Fonda.

The evening was rounded off by a little man descending on the table. "Mr Turner. I'm Tony Bennett and I want to tell you how much I admire you." So we ended the evening with *"I Left My Heart in San Francisco"* ringing in our ears.

BRITISH SANG-FROID

On 19 October 1987 David Mayhew and Anthony Forbes, the heads of Cazenoves, stock broker to the Queen and Reuters, invited Nigel Judah and me to dinner at their elegant company flat in Cadogan Square. Just after the dessert had been served the butler came back into the dining room to tell David Mayhew he was wanted on the telephone in the kitchen. David returned, finished his dessert and only then announced that Wall Street had crashed, with the Dow falling over 500 points. That David would say nothing until he had finished his dessert was for me the best example of British *sang-froid* I had ever encountered. Nigel and I made our excuses and left.

SKY'S THE LIMIT

On 8 June 1988 Murdoch announced that he had decided to launch satellite television in the United Kingdom, including a news channel, on the Astra satellite. I had been to see him in Docklands on 26 April to sell him on the idea of using Visnews on the news channel. But I made no impact: he was obsessed by

Independent Television News (ITN), and rightly greatly admired David Nicholas, the Editor-in-Chief and Chief Executive. Clearly his dislike of the BBC, part-owners of Visnews, played a large role in his attitude. To my surprise he said he had not decided whether or not to carry advertising. I never believed that the television stations that owned ITN would ever let it supply Murdoch with a news service for one of a cluster of channels which would compete with them. And indeed the proposal ITN made to Murdoch was so hedged in with restraints as to be unacceptable in Murdoch's eyes. I tackled Murdoch again after a Reuter Board meeting in New York on 15 June. By then he had received the proposal from ITN which he regarded as unsatisfactory. He therefore invited me to come to Hollywood on 5 July to discuss a deal.

I flew there with Julian Kerr, the Managing Director of Visnews and Stephen Claypole, the Head of News. We waited in the Darryl F. Zanuck suite at the Twentieth Century Fox Studios. Murdoch arrived late, profusely apologising. He had just returned from the July 4th weekend at his holiday home in Aspen, Colorado.

The Visnews executives had prepared an excellent brief for me to present to Murdoch and Sir James Cruthers, Chairman of Satellite Television plc., a former member of Murdoch's staff in Australia. We had two proposals: Visnews would run the whole channel for £23 million a year (£46 million at current values) or supply news feeds for £7 million (£14 million at current values), including Reuter textual news and pictures. We agreed to meet in London three weeks later to receive the decision.

There was a contractual problem over material which Visnews received from NBC. Murdoch wasted no time. He and I flew to New York two days later to meet Bob Wright, President of NBC. The problem was settled and SKY got access to the NBC Nightly News and TODAY.

Murdoch was still excited by his acquisition of Twentieth Century Fox four years earlier and it was a delight to be shown round the studios by him after our meeting and catch something of his enthusiasm.

On the evening of our Hollywood negotiations we had drinks at Murdoch's large house high up on Misty Mountain in Beverly Hills and met Anna Murdoch and the sons, Lachlan and James. Little did we think that the teenager, James, would, in a few years, head with great skill the satellite project that we had been discussing with his father over lunch. Anna had been busy that day supervising the lowering of trees into the garden by helicopter.

I gave lunch at Reuters on 27 July. Again Murdoch arrived a little late, apologising profusely. On the Concorde flight over from New York to London he had won an onboard raffle for a Burberry gift voucher for £1000 and had gone down to Regent Street to cash it in for raincoats, which took longer than he had expected.

Accompanying Murdoch were Cruthers, Jim Styles, the SKY Managing Director, and John O'Loan, Head of News of SKY News. On our side were Kerr, Claypole and Barry MacDonald, the Secretary of Visnews. Murdoch told us he had gone for the feed option, a proposal to set-up five UK newsgathering bureaus and foreign coverage, circumventing the European Broadcasting Union, which, along with the BBC, was on his list of the loathsome.

The Visnews executives were disappointed not to have got the programme option, but I was secretly relieved. Murdoch tried to beat us down on price: "most of the material is already there, it doesn't cost you anything," he said. "That's what African news agency heads always say," I replied. "The news is all there up in the sky. Why can we not have it for free?" "I don't think you ought to compare me to an African news agency head, Mike," said the pained Murdoch. We did a five-year deal to start on 1 January 1989, initially worth £7 million a year and escalating in subsequent years. The Visnews subscription represented 20% of the SKY News budget of £35 million (£70 million at current values). Murdoch's parting shot was that he was immediately going to write to ITN to tell them there was no deal.

SKY nearly bankrupted News Corporation, but it put Visnews onto a new plane. It added the five news bureaus in Britain and Northern Ireland and moved into profit.

REUTER HISTORY

In 1951, the centenary of Reuters, Graham Storey, a Cambridge English don and friend of Chancellor, published *Reuters Century 1851-1951* (London: Max Parrish, 1951). It was a slim volume, clearly targeted at a middle market, adequate up to the end of World War I, but rather thin thereafter. I determined that before I left Reuters we would have commissioned a professional work on a scale appropriate to the history of the great company.

I first approached the American historian, Stephen Koss, Professor of

History at Columbia University, New York, author of *The Rise and Fall of the Political Press in Britain* (London: Hamish Hamilton 1981), but we could not agree terms. He was a young man, but shortly after our conversations he died. I then asked Norman Stone, a fellow of Trinity College, Cambridge, author of *Europe Transformed 1878-1919* (Oxford: Blackwell, 1999), if he would be interested. The morning he came to see me he had received a letter offering him the professorship of Modern History at Oxford. So he declined. I then asked Lord Briggs, the former provost of Worcester College, Oxford, author of the great five-volume *History of Broadcasting in the United Kingdom* (Oxford: Oxford University Press, 1961) for his advice. He recommended Donald Read, Professor of Modern History at the University of Kent at Canterbury, author of *Press and People, 1790-1850: opinion in three English cities* (London: Edward Arnold, 1961). "He will do a good job and finish it on time," he promised. And he did indeed do a good job and did almost finish it on time.

John Entwisle, the Corporate Records Manager and later Group Archivist and Justine Taylor, Research Assistant, made a great contribution to the success of the book.

David Ure took over responsibility for the Reuter history when I retired, supervised it with his keen intelligence, and chose the strong title *The Power of News: the History of Reuters*.

Oxford University Press published *The Power of News: The History of Reuters* in 1992. Reuters bought 20,000 copies and gave one to each of its clients throughout the world. A second edition was published in 1999.

Reviews were mixed:

> There is no seething humanity, blood on the streets, biting of nails or waiting for trains.
>
> Michael Fathers, The *Independent*
>
> … a fascinating, solidly researched, and well-written book.
>
> The *Scotsman*
>
> Reuters was to news what Rolls-Royce is to cars and Lords is to cricket … the biggest story to come out of Reuters is its own.
>
> *Daily Mail*
>
> … does not quite convey either the scale of the achievement or an adequate explanation for it.
>
> Ian Hargreaves, *Financial Times*

Alexander Chancellor disapproved of Read's treatment of his father, and described it in *The Spectator* as "somewhat naïve and shallow."

The reviews did not refer to Read's account of the sudden resignation in 1941 of Sir Roderick Jones, Chairman and Managing Director, who had headed the agency since 1915. The British Press clammed up at the time and neither Graham Storey nor Sir Roderick Jones in his autobiography *A Life in Reuters* (London: Hodder and Stoughton, 1951) told the true story. Read did so for the first time. It was the most telling exposure of an important era in Reuters history. The Board forced him out because he had kept from it elements of his negotiations with the British government. Moreover, the Board had lost confidence in him.

A skeleton in Reuters cupboard was its subsidy from the British government, the existence of which executives always denied. I determined that we should come clean. Read therefore described it exhaustively in its various forms. It ended in 1986. Since the publication of *The Power of News* two interesting sidebars have come to light.

The first is the disclosure in *British Propaganda and News Media in the Cold War* by John Jenks (Edinburgh: Edinburgh University Press, 2006) of a meeting between Christopher Warner of the Foreign Office and Christopher Chancellor in December 1948 in which they agreed any large subsidy would be too obvious but "an increased subscription on behalf of H.M.Embassy or reduced charges by Cable and Wireless" could be crucial. But Chancellor asked Warner to keep the arrangement highly confidential because of potential difficulties with the Reuter board.

The second is the disclosure in *MI6: The History of the Secret Intelligence Service 1909-1949* by Keith Jeffery (London: Bloomsbury, 2010) that an independent organisation might be necessary to run "news agencies, broadcasting stations, etc." after the war. This was contained in The Bland Report – "Future Organisation of the S.I.S." of October 1944. It led to the establishment of the Arab News Agency (ANA), one of the vehicles used to subsidise Reuters.

An unsolved mystery is why the Read history had no reviews in any academic publications. Donald Read thinks it may have simply been an oversight by the Oxford University Press, which failed to send review copies to the academic journals. They therefore missed some important revelations about the British government and the media in the twentieth century.

REUTER SOCIETY

In my contacts with UPI I had been impressed by the liveliness of their "Hold Down Club," their alumni society. Its name came from the inevitable end-year instructions to hold down on filing cables as the budget started to be exceeded.

I therefore suggested to the charming Aleco Joannides, the most social of all Reuter staff, that in his retirement he should start a similar club for Reuters, which he did with spectacular success.

The Baron, the alumni's website, later ran this story:

Aleco Joannides the Kingmaker

The influence of The Reuter Society was recognised by *The Times* as long ago as 2000.

Reuters was going through a change of command. Peter Job was retiring as chief executive and the search was on for a replacement. Four directors were in the running: Tom Glocer, Philip Green, David Grigson and Rob Rowley.

Michael Nelson, former general manager, suggested to Aleco Joannides, a veteran Reuters correspondent and manager who was then the Society's founding chairman, "as a joke" that he ask the Company for the four candidates for the top job to address the Society. "He did so and to my amazement the Company agreed," Nelson recalls.

Stephen Somerville, current chairman of the Society, remembers the 17 October 2000 meeting as a kind of "beauty contest" in which the four possible contenders for the top job all spoke to more than 100 members.

Nelson recalls: "By coincidence Raymond Snoddy, *The Times* media editor, telephoned me on December 6, the day of the announcement of the selection of Tom Glocer as chief executive. The reason for his call was to thank me for pointing out to him that he had misquoted John Milton's most famous statement on freedom of the Press which was in the Areopagitica of 1644: "Give me the liberty to know, to utter, and to argue freely according to conscience, above all liberties." We then talked about the Glocer appointment and I told him about the Reuter Society meeting. Thus the Reuter Society made *The Times* for the first time."

The following day *The Times* reported Glocer's appointment under the headline "Reuters appointment breaks with tradition" and said he impressed staff at a recent Reuter Society address. The break with tradition referred to Reuters appointment of its first non-journalist to the post of chief executive.

Snoddy wrote: "Tom Glocer, who is 41 and at present head of Reuters Information, is also the first American to take the top job. Mr Glocer's division currently generates close to half of total group revenues.

"Mr Glocer emerged as favourite to replace Peter Job, the current chief executive who retires next July, after impressing retired staff at a recent Reuters Society address."

The Baron, edited by the imaginative Barry May, a former correspondent, was greatly valued by the members of the Reuter Society.

RETIREMENT

I retired from Reuters on my sixtieth birthday on 30 April 1989, having spent 36 years with the Company.

CHAPTER TEN

The sky is filled with stars, invisible by day

BAUBLES FOR JOURNALISTS

Shortly after I retired Sir Christopher Hogg invited me to dinner at the Connaught Hotel to seek my advice on how to persuade Glen Renfrew to retire. Should he propose to him that he put his name forward for a knighthood? I told him I was sure he would refuse.

Some years later someone in the Cabinet Office leaked to *The Sunday Times* a list of those who had refused honours. The list, which was published on 21 December 2003, included Glen Renfrew, who had refused a knighthood in 1990, David Chipp, who had refused the award of Commander of the British Empire (CBE) in 1986 and Gerald Long, who had declined a CBE in 1974.

Long would have been furious that he had only been offered a CBE and not a knighthood, which is presumably why he did not mention it in a curious correspondence in *The Spectator* in 1992.

In the course of a Reuter Board visit to Rome in September 1973, the President of Italy conferred honours on the Reuter party, including, of course, Long. I was appointed a Cavaliere Ordine Merito.

Long did not have a British knighthood conferred on him. Why not? Cole was in the job too short a time to get one, but Roderick Jones and Christopher Chancellor were both knighted. Long told me that when Lord Barnetson was chairman of Reuters he had asked him if he would like him to put his name forward for a knighthood. Long told me he had declined and he told the same story to Michael Reupke. The reason he gave me was that it would lower him in the esteem of some of his friends and he gave as an example the writer Brian Inglis. He told Michael Reupke that it would be seen as a pat on the back for services to the government. He never addressed the illogicality of accepting an award from the Italian government and refusing one from the British.

The letter to *The Spectator,* which was published on 14 November 1992, reproved the Editor, Alexander Chancellor, for his review of Donald Read's history of Reuters. He wrote:

"I have not seen Professor Read's book, but I am told that it states that I let it be known that I would not accept a knighthood if one were offered. The emotive terms 'would spurn knighthoods' are Alexander Chancellor's gratuitous embroidery on what is in my case an untrue statement: I can speak only for myself. It would have been grossly improper for me to have indicated in any way that [sic] my attitude would be to the offer of a knighthood, and at no time did I do so."

The ethics of journalists accepting awards from governments is much debated by journalists. Perhaps the best comment is by John Cole, a former deputy editor of the *Guardian,* who rejected a CBE in 1993, who pointed to that newspaper's rule that only gifts that could be consumed within 24 hours were acceptable for journalists.

Rupert Murdoch always used to say that he was only interested in newspaper titles.

TWENTY-FIRST CENTURY

When Hogg persuaded Renfrew to resign in 1991, two years after our conversation, Renfrew recommended Peter Job as his successor. I found that appointment odd as I had had to fight hard to defend Job, who had a number of good qualities, against Renfrew's criticisms of him when Job worked for me.

Renfrew was not pleased when Job was manager for Asia, Australia and New Zealand, and without authority consulted Australian lawyers on how Reuters could take over the Australian Associated Press (AAP). AAP was the national news agency, Reuters agent in Australia and a shareholder. Unfortunately a secretary at the lawyers sent the opinion to the Australian Associated Press instead of to Reuters.

Job accepted a knighthood in 2001, shortly before he retired.

I would have chosen André Villeneuve to succeed Renfrew as chief executive. Another strong candidate would have been David Ure.

Tom Glocer will go down in history for negotiating the sale of Reuters to Thomson in 2007. Those of us who managed Reuters have to ask ourselves why Reuters was worth 24% less than Bloomberg, its main competitor, which started business in 1981, 26 years earlier. Reuters was worth $17.2 billion and Bloomberg's purchase of the 20% of the company owned by Merrill Lynch in 2008 put a value on Bloomberg of $22.5 billion.

Those who had participated in the decision to reject the Dow Jones proposal of a joint venture with Reuters some forty years earlier could take some satisfaction from the fact that in 2007 Dow Jones was sold to Rupert Murdoch's News Corporation for only $5.6 billion. Murdoch's write-down of the investment by $2.8 billion in 2009 showed it was in fact worth only half. Dow Jones' attempt to catch up with Reuters by the purchase of Telerate had been a failure and meant they had to take a write-down of almost $1 billion in the investment in 1997. It came as a surprise to many that in her book *War at the Wall Street Journal,* the history of the Murdoch takeover, Sarah Ellison, a former *Wall Street Journal* staffer, asserted that the Dow Jones newswires lagged in reputation behind Reuters and Bloomberg.

I posed the question about the differential between the value of Reuters and Bloomberg to André Villeneuve and David Ure. Villeneuve said that his experience as a director of the American giant, United Technologies, showed him that the most important quality a company needed was execution. I had ensured execution in Reuters, he said, but it was lacking in later years.

David Ure said it was because in the late nineties there was a lack of cohesion and lack of a clear goal beyond financial services. A further factor which was very important was lack of a sympathetic board in the best sense.

I believe one of the reasons for the differential between Reuters and Bloomberg is that Bloomberg resisted the temptation to make acquisitions, completing only three and they were small. Renfrew made many. I would have made only three for Reuters: Agence Cosmographique, Visnews and UPI news pictures.

If Reuter executives wanted to comfort themselves a little they could look at some comparisons from the half century from the end of World War II. In the fifty years from 1946 the revenues of AP had risen 20 times from $18,900,000 to $390,167,000. AFP's had risen 68 times from $3,300,000 to \$226,000,000. Reuters had risen 944 times from \$4,294,000 to \$4,054,000,000.

RETIREMENT JOBS

I agreed with Longfellow in his *Morituri Salutamus*:
>For age is opportunity no less
>Than youth itself, though in another dress
>And as the evening twilight fades away
>The sky is filled with stars, invisible by day.

Reuters asked me to continue for a time as Chairman of the Reuter Foundation and as a trustee of Visnews.

MERCI, LE QUAI

My first engagement outside Reuters on retirement was in September 1989 as rapporteur of the Information section of the European Community's *Assises Européennes de l'Audiovisuel*. Jean Dondelinger, of Luxembourg, who was the European Commissioner for Audiovisual and Cultural Affairs, invited me to fill this role. I thought it odd that he had that title since there is no mention of culture in the Treaty of Rome. The founding fathers were no doubt familiar with the reputed saying of Hermann Goering: "Whenever I hear the word culture, I reach for my pistol." Not until the Treaty of Maastricht in February 1992 did the European Community recognise culture by treaty.

The *Assises* were attended by no less than 300 delegates from 26 countries. It was the brainchild of the French President Mitterrand, who presided over the European Council at the time and was Chairman of the European Commission. He made the principal speech. The Conference had a strong anti-American flavour and its purpose seemed to be to promote the development of European audiovisual media through a project called Eureka based in Brussels.

I liked having my hotel bill in Paris paid for by the Quai d'Orsay.

The principal conclusion of my group was to support the establishment of Euronews, a satellite news channel, which was launched in January 1993. It was intended as a counter-weight to CNN. I tried without success to interest Reuters and the BBC in participating. The BBC had their own plans, but Reuters never got into 24-hour satellite news. It made a big mistake in rejecting the Euronews offer. ITN also said it was not interested, although in 1994 it bought a 31% stake. It sold it in 2003. Euronews was a success and by 2009 reached more than 179 million households in Europe, compared with 147 million for CNN, 88 million for BBC World News and 76 million for CNBC Europe.

IIC

Other voluntary work I undertook early in my retirement from Reuters included a trusteeship of the International Institute of Communications (IIC) from 1989 to 1995, and they appointed me Chairman of the UK Chapter from 1989 to 1992.

WORLD ECONOMIC FORUM

In October 1989 Klaus Schwab, the President of the World Economic Forum, asked me to create an Advisory Council of the great and the good for *World Link,* its magazine, and become chairman of the Council. I assembled an interesting body, ranging from Raymond Barre, the former prime minister of France, to Vitali Korotich, Editor-in-Chief of the liberal Russian news magazine *Ogonyok.* Korotich always had a glass of whisky by his side at our meetings, which shocked the Swiss.

The council meetings lasted until 1992 when the publication was sold to *Euromoney.* Klaus Schwab, a Swiss university professor, had created a unique forum, which became important. The year before I set up the Council the prime ministers of Turkey and Greece met at the Forum and signed a declaration which may have averted a war. Schwab must have met more Heads of State than anyone else in the world. In 2011 35 heads of state and government attended.

Kate Weinberg described it in an article in *The Daily Telegraph:*

Davos is, after all, the highest form of "wocial." For those who don't know – or don't have to go – the wocial is an event that is part work, part social. It is the brunch of the business world. People are casual, but nobody is entirely relaxed. There is drink, but it's unwise to get drunk. Conversations may be informal, but they are supposed to be important.

MONOPOLIES COMMISSION

The British government appointed me to be a member of the Newspaper Panel of the Monopolies and Mergers Commission from 1989 to 1995. I sat on the panel which decided The Guardian Media Group could buy the *Reading Post*. Little did I imagine that in 2010 it would sell all its regional media business, including the *Reading Post*.

A CONVERSATION WITH PRINCESS DIANA

My connection with St Bride's, the journalists' church in Fleet Street, of which I became a trustee in 1989, occasioned the only meeting Helga and I had with Princess Diana. She attended a service to inaugurate a new music room. When we were presented to her at the reception afterwards I told her how good it was to attend a service which was not a memorial service. "Do you have lots of memorial services?" she asked. I told her we did indeed and that journalists were dying all the time. "It must be the strain of reporting on our family," she replied.

NIGEL JUDAH

Nigel Judah died on 26 April 1991, aged 60.

The *Guardian* asked me to write an obituary, which it published with the rather over-the-top headline "Man who made Reuters":

Nigel Judah was the executive who masterminded Reuters finances in the news agency's explosive growth over the last three decades. When he became the company secretary and chief accountant in 1960 at the age of 29, Reuters revenues were £2.4 million and it made a loss of £18,000.

When he handed over his financial responsibilities last year, revenues were £1,369 million and profits £320 million.

One of Nigel Judah's great achievements was to negotiate the post-war Reuters first bank loan in 1967 with the Swiss bank, Credit Suisse. It called for all his considerable powers of persuasion given the company's miserable profit record and unattractive balance sheet. But it was essential for the investments which Reuters needed to survive in increasingly intense competition with the American news agencies and to expand into computerised financial information services. It also enabled Reuters to acquire a Swiss news agency which gave it a strong base on which to develop in the lucrative Swiss market.

Nigel Judah was appointed to the board of Reuters as finance director in 1981, and in 1984 he directed the immensely complicated administration of the company's flotation – the first initial public offering to take place simultaneously in London and New York. He established Reuters first budgeting procedures and showed rigour in controlling costs, but reacted creatively to the revolutionary products in the financial field.

He was a man of great elegance, in manners and tastes. Many bankers will remember lunches at Reuters where he served the wines he had bought at Christie's – always at the bottom of the market.

Reuters invited me to a meeting at St. Bride's Church to discuss Nigel Judah's memorial service, a service which almost did not take place. Present were Canon John Oates, the distinguished rector, Stephen Somerville from Reuters, Nigel's daughter, Henrietta, his sister, Cynthia Kee, and myself. Canon Oates opened the proceedings by suggesting that we first had to select a date.

"Not at all," said Cynthia. "We first have to decide if we are going to have a memorial service here at all. We are a good Jewish family and I do not think we want a service in a Christian church." Steve Somerville and I were aghast. But the clever John Oates explained at length how Nigel had supported St. Bride's, including providing the central heating and flood-lighting as a leak off the Reuter facilities. "Oh, all right then," said Cynthia. "But no Christology."

We discussed the hymns. "I think we must have 'Jerusalem' said the Canon. "You cannot have 'Jerusalem'," I protested. "Whose feet do you think in ancient time walked across England's mountains green?" "I never thought of that," he said.

Felicity Lott sang at the memorial service and Joseph Lapid, former Director-General of the Israel Broadcasting Authority and Managing Director of the newspaper *Maariv*, gave an address. He had had to get the permission

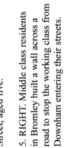

1. BELOW LEFT. Downham council estate, Bromley, where I spent my infancy. My parents were fortunate that the local authority allocated them a charming semi-detached house (2. LEFT) with a garden.

3. RIGHT. Burnt Ash elementary school.

4. ABOVE. Me preparing for Fleet Street, aged five.

5. RIGHT. Middle class residents in Bromley built a wall across a road to stop the working class from Downham entering their streets.

6. Furniture made by my father. His parents could not afford to educate him after the age of 14 so they apprenticed him as a ship's joiner in the Londonderry dockyards.

7. Magdalen College, Oxford, where I read Modern History. The College was founded by William of Waynflete in 1458. The deer park is top centre. To the right is Addison's Walk, one of the few meadows in England where fritillary flowers grow.

8. Reuters gift on my retirement: a painting of the Glyndebourne opera house by Osbert Lancaster for the programme of 1960. Lady Christie, wife of the owner of Glyndebourne, asked me to sell it to her, but I declined. She liked the depiction of her father-in-law with his pug dog (left foreground). To his right the General Administrator, Moran Caplat, is talking to the conductor, Vittorio Gui. On the far right are Jack Gough, the Head Carpenter, and Frank Harvey, the Head Gardener, although they rarely spoke to each other.

9. The Coffee Room at the Garrick Club, which I joined in 1975. Members of the Club, which was founded in 1831, are mostly actors, journalists and lawyers.

10. The European Sales Conference in Madrid in 1978. When I joined Reuters in 1952 the company had only one salesman, Joe Daffin (INSET). We eventually hired more women than the lonely two here.

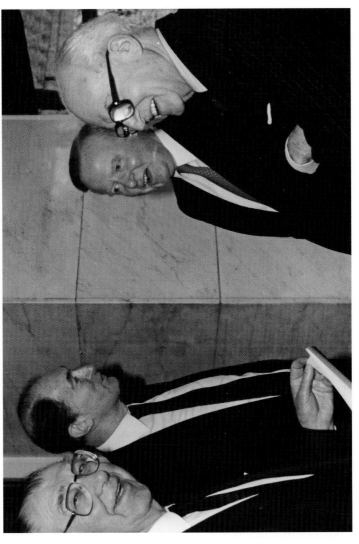

11. A retirement party in 1989 with my first two bosses, Alfred Geiringer (left) and George Bloom (right). Geiringer recruited young men from the universities who eventually ran Reuters. Ian Yates, General Manager of the Press Association, is on Geiringer's right.

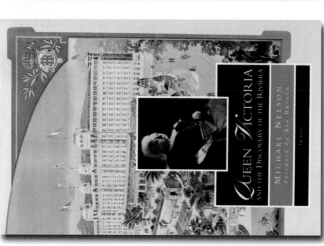

14. *Americans and the Making of the Riviera,*
McFarland, 2008.

13. *Queen Victoria and the Discovery of the Riviera,*
I.B. Tauris, 2001.

12. *War of the Black Heavens: The Battles of
Western Broadcasting in the Cold War,* Syracuse
University Press and Brasseys, 1997.

of his rabbi to attend the service. He gave the most moving address I have heard at a memorial service:

It is symbolic that Reuters and Nigel's sister invited me from Israel to speak in Nigel's memory – here in a church. Not your usual parish church, a Fleet Street institution, but still a church. For Nigel was a Jew. Not your usual God-fearing Jew, but a Jew. And his entire life was a quest to bridge, what he conceived as a gap, between his Jewishness and his aspiration to be the embodiment of a British gentleman.

Indeed, in the 25 years of our friendship, I never met a more perfect British gentleman. He was a loving father, gentle soul, impeccable in his manners, unerring in his style, unnerving in his reserve. He was also a financial genius, which some might have thought to be his most Jewish trait.

But I, his friend from the Holy Land, wanted him to be a proud Jew. I never really succeeded in this attempt but I did influence his perception of himself. You might have known little of this side of Nigel's personality.

It was years ago, in an Irish pub, that we had a good dinner and a long and particularly convoluted discussion. I spoke to him about the Biblical origins of his family name, Judah – Yehuda; the name of the fourth tribe; of David's Kingdom; and the source of the word Yehudi, which means a Jew. And I also told him about the importance of his mother's family, the Belilius tribe in modern Jerusalem. And then I pulled out of my pocket my ultimate weapon, prepared in advance, right out of Bartlett's, and read it to him.

It was Disraeli's answer to Daniel O'Connell, who taunted him in parliament for being a Jew.

"Yes, I'm a Jew, and when the ancestors of the Right Honourable Gentleman were brutal savages in an unknown island, mine were priests in the Temple of Solomon."

When I finished reading these sentences I looked at Nigel and realised that they made a difference to him. Perhaps, for the first time in his life, he understood that he already belonged to a great aristocracy, the aristocracy of the Book, of the spirit, of Western civilisation.

I thought it was my duty to illuminate to you this side of Nigel, hidden from the world, but as important as anything that he cared to show. Nigel was a British gentleman, a Jewish aristocrat and one of the finest human beings it was my privilege to know.

BOB MAUTHNER

Bob Mauthner died on 18 May 1994, aged 65. He was one of my closest friends. He was Austrian by nationality and could have avoided British national service by waiting until he was 28 before taking out British nationality. But with an admirable sense of the correct he took out British nationality and was called up in the British army.

He joined the *Wakefield Express*. David Nicholas, who also worked on the newspaper, loved to tell the story of running into Bob reading a letter at the time of the Bangkok Seato conference in February 1955. "Ah! A despatch from our Bangkok correspondent, I suppose," he joked. "Yes. It's from Michael Nelson, Reuters correspondent," he replied, to the amazement of David Nicholas.

Bob introduced me to the Thursday soirées given by the beautiful Marlene Schwarz whose family were refugees from Vienna. They were elegant occasions, redolent of a lost life in Austria, staged in her parents' house in Golders Green.

Marlene invited me to escort her to the Queen Charlotte's Ball in May 1953. The ball was part of the London season, which for debutantes had, as its peak, presentation to the Queen in Buckingham Palace. In 1953 more than 450 were presented. Reflecting the attempts to move to a more classless society, the presentations were abolished in 1959.

The 1953 ball was held in the Great Room of the Grosvenor House hotel in the presence of the Duchess of Gloucester, who was Dame d'Honneur. Tickets were four guineas each, including dinner, but excluding wine. So with the cost of the programmes and the wine, it cost me more than a week's wages. Marlene paid for herself. Much as I appreciated Marlene's invitation, I was glad I was not often a debs' delight.

The ball in 1958, a carbon-copy of 1953, was well-described by Fiona MacCarthy in her book *The Last Curtsey: The End of the Debutantes* (London: Faber and Faber, 2006):

"The first spectacular ball of the Season," as the social diarists described it, was held on the 6th May in the Great Room at Grosvenor House. Four hundred debutantes assembled with their parents and their partners, all of us in long white ballgowns and white gloves. We dined and danced. At 10.30 a signal was given for the hundred and fifty chosen maids of honour to gather in the upper gallery. From there they made a slow descent of the curved stairway like the maidens in a Burne-Jones painting and processed down the vast ballroom trundling in a huge white cake to the March from Handel's Judas Maccabeus.

This Historic Ceremony of the Birthday Cake was a re-enactment – some might say a travesty – of the annual birthday celebration of Queen Charlotte, wife of George III, held at St James' Palace. When the cake, with its flickering candles, was brought to a halt in front of the guest of honour, the Dowager Duchess of Northumberland, a mass curtsey was performed by the serried ranks of debutantes. They curtsied very low and rose simultaneously, having undergone a rigorous rehearsal in the morning. Though the curtsey was intended for the Duchess of

Northumberland, representing the long defunct Queen Charlotte, the effect was a surreal one of hundreds of debutantes worshipping a cake. Queen Charlotte's Ball, strangely combining the solemn and the mawkish, appeared to one later commentator as a mixture of the Nuremberg Rallies and the Dance of the Fairies in the Hall of the Mountain King.

The ball had first been held in 1925 with 181 electric candles representing the years since Queen Charlotte's birth.

Queen Charlotte's Ball ended in 1976. Asked in 1977 if she would want her daughter to be a deb today, the Marchioness of Tavistock, who as Henrietta Tiarks had been Deb of the Year in 1957, said: "The answer is that it would not work anymore, it would be meaningless. You cannot go to disco parties, wear make-up, smoke and go out with boyfriends before the age of seventeen and *then* be a deb."

In the context of the ball I went to with Marlene, I thought it odd that in 1962 Marlene should marry Eric Hobsbawm, the most distinguished English communist historian. He continued to espouse his communist beliefs even after communism had disappeared from most of the world.

Bob Mauthner worked for a period for Reuters in London and then joined the English service of French Radio in Paris. When Britain's entry to the Common Market became a hot story in 1961 I arranged for him to re-join Reuters as Common Market correspondent in Brussels. On 27 November 1961 he got a remarkable scoop with a copy of the confidential statement made earlier by Edward Heath, Lord Privy Seal, to Common Market ministers in Paris. His Dutch had stood him in good stead: he had been given the text by a Dutch journalist. Doon Campbell, the News Manager, wrote to him: "I cannot recall a single story from overseas for a long time which has made such impact on the British Press." Bob later left Reuters and joined the *Financial Times*, where he had a distinguished career, shown by the tributes in the obituaries in the Press.

He was exceptionally respected as the professional journalist, the heart, soul and mind of so much of our foreign coverage for a generation. Douglas Hurd, the UK Foreign Secretary, said: "I was always impressed by his grasp of foreign policy and his ability to explain the issues clearly and objectively."

Financial Times

The presence of Robert Mauthner in Paris contributed much to opening this newspaper [the Financial Times] to Europe.

Le Monde

Robert Mauthner was deservedly considered the doyen of the diplomatic writers for national newspapers: a man of sharp intelligence, long experience overseas and proven professional dedication, whose columns, reports, analyses and editorials for the Financial Times were among the most authoritative in British journalism today.

The Times

After a NATO meeting, where the press facilities were particularly disastrous, Douglas Hurd had to sign a "treaty of Turnberry" with Bob, undertaking that the Foreign Office would never again make journalists work under swaying tents with broken-down telephones on a storm-bound Scottish heath.

Hella Pick, *Guardian*

Some of his colleagues enjoyed provoking his acerbic retorts. One long-winded correspondent was interrupted with: "Do you want the copytakers or Jonathan Cape?"

Nor did his irascibility diminish his appeal to the opposite sex; a group of young female staff once voted him the most attractive man on the newspaper, comfortably ahead of men half his age. But for nearly 20 years he loved only one woman, Anne Freyer.

The Daily Telegraph

I first met Bob Mauthner in 1971, at the ramshackle old Continental Daily Mail building in Paris. Both the FT and the Reuters news agency, for whom I was then a trainee, had their offices there. Mauthner was a wonderful mentor, a source of encouragement and advice.

Rupert Cornwell, *Independent*

I helped Bob's widow Anne to organise the service of thanksgiving and we arranged for the Rabbi John Rayner to participate and say prayers; an unusual event in the history of St. Bride's church. Lord Howe, the former Foreign Secretary, read the lesson.

The service was distinctive in its content, which reflected Bob's eclectic tastes. David Sells, an old Reuter friend, read "We must have speech from a minister" by Noel Coward:

We must have a speech from a minister.
It's what we've been trained to expect.
We're faced with defeat and despair and disaster,
We couldn't be losing our Colonies faster,
We know that we haven't the guns to defend
The 'Mermaid' at Rye, or the pier at Southend;
You have no idea how we've grown to depend
In hours of crisis
On whacking great slices
Of verbal evasion and dissimulation,
A nice Governmental appeal to the Nation
We'd listen to gladly with awe and respect,

We know that the moment is sinister
And what we've been earnestly trained to expect,
When such moments we reach,
Is a lovely long speech
(Not a comment or chat
About this, about that)
An extremely long speech,
But a really long speech,
An ambiguous speech from a minister.
We must have a speech from a minister,
We don't mind a bit who it is
As long as we get that drab lack of conviction,
That dismal, self-conscious, inadequate diction.
We find Mr. Churchill a trifle uncouth;
His ill-repressed passion for telling the truth.
His 'Eye for an Eye' and his 'Tooth for a Tooth'
Is violent, too snappy,
We'd be far more happy
With some old Appeaser's inert peroration,
We'd give ourselves up to complete resignation,
Refusing to worry or get in a fizz
We know that the moment is sinister,
We've already said we don't mind who it is,
We'd fight on the beach,
For a really long speech,
(Not a breezy address,
Or a postscript on Hess)
But a lovely long speech,
A supremely long speech,
An embarrassing speech from a minister.

HOUSES

We felt the house in Kensington was too ambassadorial when I retired from
Reuters so in March 1994 we moved to Lansdowne Road, Holland Park,
London. At about the same time we also moved from Veyrier to Domaine de
la Rose, Chemin des Restanques in Opio in the Alpes-Maritimes, France.
The French move was a great wrench, particularly as we had made so many
good French friends in the locality, but we wanted more quiet and better
weather.

An attraction of the Opio house was that many former Reuter colleagues had retired nearby and we were able to entertain them and their children and grandchildren there in the summer. They included Bob and Eve Elphick, Jack and Beatrice Gee, Patrick and Rana Seale and Michael and Robyn Weigall.

CHAPTER 11

Broadcasters and Spies

WAR OF THE BLACK HEAVENS

Early one morning in December 1989 the phone rang with a call from New Zealand. It was Alan Burnet, Chairman of Independent Newspapers in Wellington, a onetime alternate director of Reuters. "Would I be willing to come out to New Zealand to give a lecture to the Institute of Directors at the conference to celebrate the 150ᵗʰ anniversary of the Treaty of Waitangi?" The Treaty between the British Crown and the Maori chiefs was New Zealand's founding document. Helga could come too. We would, of course, fly first class and have a suite in the best hotels. After the conference he and his wife Loraine would take us on a tour of New Zealand. Independent Newspapers would bear all the costs. We were welcome to break the journey in Los Angeles. The subject of the lecture would be "Communications in Europe." What that meant was up to me. I accepted.

The Berlin Wall had come down a month earlier and communism was collapsing all over Europe. I thought I had better find out about "Communications in Europe" on the spot. So in January I went for a week to Warsaw and Budapest, where the Reuter correspondents introduced me to key media personalities. I was struck that everyone I spoke to talked of the importance of western radios in the downfall of communism, particularly Radio Free Europe (RFE). I decided to write a book about it.

When I started work on the book I thought it would take three years, but in fact it took seven. Anne Mauthner, Bob's wife, an editor at Editions Seuil, suggested I ask Andrew Nurnberg if he would be my agent because he also represented Boris Yeltsin, who was a friend of Nurnberg. He agreed. My jumping off point for my researches was John Tusa, Managing Director of the World Service of the BBC, whom I had known for many years. He introduced me to his key staff and to the heads of the two other principal international broadcasters, Richard Carlson, Director of the VOA, and Gene Pell, President of RFE/RL. I flew to Washington and Munich to meet them and they introduced me to their staff.

In Washington the Reuter name was a good entrée. Cord Meyer, who had been the chief of the International Organisations Division of the CIA from September 1954 and therefore in charge of oversight of RFE and RL at a critical time in their history, invited me to lunch. He was an excellent source and gave me a valuable introduction to Richard Helms, the former head of the CIA.

SOURCES

I made an agreement with Malcolm Byrne, Director of Analysis at the non-government National Security Archive, whereby I would make my researches available to him in exchange for his filing applications for me with the US government under the Freedom of Information Act. I hired as a part-time researcher one of his staff, Marjorie Robertson and later Jon Elliston. In London I took on as a researcher Pat Spencer, who had worked with Asa Briggs on his History of Broadcasting in the United Kingdom, and as a Russian translator Mary Seton-Watson, former Head of the Russian Service of the BBC.

In Moscow Reuters hired for me Ludmilla Bonushkina and Dasha Lotareva, two excellent researchers. The material I acquired from the archives of the Central Committee of the Communist Party of the Soviet Union was invaluable because shortly after I received it much of the archives was closed and mine were the only copies. The best story was one of the most extraordinary snafus of the cold war. Despite an order of the Council of Ministers of 1953 banning the production of short wave radios, production had sharply increased and, by 1958, 20 million were in use. And 85% of them were in the European part of the USSR where the Russians' own short wave broadcasts could not be heard and where it was possible to listen only to Western radios.

In Munich my best source was Ralph Walter, former Director of RFE, who gave me a copy of the secret memorandum of William Griffith, political adviser of RFE, on what had happened in the RFE broadcasts to Hungary in

1956, which drew the charge that RFE had incited the continuation of the Revolution.

Pat Spencer knew the BBC Written Archives at Caversham backwards and was able to trace an invaluable document that I could not find. Professor Michael Tracey, the author of *A Variety of Lives, A Biography of Sir Hugh Greene* (London: Bodley Head, 1983), had tipped me off that there was a BBC document which exposed the fact that it was passing all letters from Eastern Europe (with the original envelopes) to a secret department of the Foreign Office. The letter was indicative of the nature of the relationship between the BBC and the Foreign Office

The array of aides I employed was essential for the complex subject I had chosen. It cost money, but I was able to charge it against tax. I was also fortunate that I could draw on the invaluable contacts of the Reuter correspondents around Europe.

LECH WALESA

The staff of the Warsaw Reuter bureau staged a great coup by getting Lech Walesa to write the foreword.

LITVINOV AND LADY PHILLIMORE

In June 1991 I flew to Moscow where Bob Evans, an old Moscow hand and distinguished Reuter correspondent, opened many doors.

David Morton, Head of the Russian and Ukrainian Services at the BBC, had given me an introduction to Maria (known as Masha) Slonim, a BBC stringer. Bob Evans and I took her to lunch at my hotel, which ominously looked out over the Lubyanka prison, seat of an unknown number of torturings and executions. After an hour of chat about the state of the nation over vodka and caviar, Bob Evans suddenly tapped on the table: "Now I remember you! You are one of the people who used to keep us in touch with what the dissidents were doing. I remember talking to you on the phone. You are Litvinov's grand-daughter." She was indeed the dissident grand-daughter of the former Soviet foreign minister, Maxim Litvinov. Her father was Ilya Slonim and her mother Tatiana Litvinov. Her cousin Pavel Litvinov was also a dissident and was banished to Siberia because he demonstrated against the Russian invasion of Czechoslovakia in 1968. Masha had been persuaded to leave the country for the United States. She later settled in England and worked for the Russian service of the BBC. She returned to Russia when the atmosphere improved after the accession of Gorbachev.

But Masha's identity was not the only surprise. When we said our goodbyes I gave her my card. "Phillimore Gardens," she mused. "You know I am Lady Phillimore." She had married Robert Godfrey Phillimore, the third baron, in 1983 when she was in exile in England. He died on 26 February 1990 aged 50. Only a few days before I had left for Moscow I had received a letter dated 31 May 1991 from Chestertons, the managers of the Phillimore estate, asking if we would like to extend the lease of our house at 44 Phillimore Gardens. The family needed the money to pay inheritance tax liabilities, following the death of the Baron, the letter said. Our answer had been negative. The beneficiary would have been Masha Slonim.

Maxim Litvinov, a Bolshevik, settled in London in 1906. In 1916 he married Ivy Low, who was British, and their children were born in 1917 and 1918. In 1930 Stalin appointed him Minister of Foreign Affairs, but he was removed from the post in 1939 because Stalin did not want a Jew to deal with Hitler. From 1941 to 1943 he was Ambassador in Washington and on his return to Moscow was a Deputy Commissar for Foreign Affairs under Molotov until his retirement in 1946. After World War II he spoke out bluntly, criticising Stalin's foreign policy, although only off the record. He was fortunate that Stalin left him alone.

When I went back to Moscow for a meeting of the International Press Institute in 1998 Masha was in a different world, producing "Fourth Estate", a TV Magazine. We had lunch in a different world too: the trendiest restaurant in town was a mock Ukrainian farm with cows and donkeys munching their hay alongside the tables.

Old eating habits died hard even seven years after the fall of communism. When the Western guests ambled into the buffet dinner at the first reception at the IPI conference almost all the food had gone. The Russian guests had armed themselves with plastic bags, which they filled with food and then rushed off home with their booty. The next night was a ballet performance followed by a buffet supper. So I sat at the back of the auditorium and was the first guest into the buffet. I loaded a grand piano in the corner with delicacies and refused to let the Russians near it. So that night the British delegation splendidly made up for the hunger of the previous evening.

When I was looking up the background to Masha's famous grandfather I found a story in Wikipedia which I had never heard before which amazed me, and which I hope is true. In 1933 he successfully persuaded the United States to recognise officially the Soviet government. Wikipedia says: "Franklin D. Roosevelt sent comedian Harpo Marx to the Soviet Union as a goodwill ambassador and Litvinov and Marx became friends and even performed a routine on stage together."

Another dissident I counted myself privileged to meet was Elena Bonner, widow of the Russian nuclear scientist, Andrei Sakharov. I interviewed her at the Conference of the International Institute of Communications (IIC) in Montreal in 1992. She was a fount of stories about the terrible life she and her husband had latterly led in Russia. They had been isolated from family and friends. They had no mail, no telephone and a twenty-four hour police guard outside their apartment. Their car was vandalised, with slashed tires and glue smeared over the windscreen. I thought her best anecdote was of the taxi driver who was convinced Czechoslovakia had invaded Russia in 1968.

On the 1991 visit Bob Evans and I had lunch with Vitali Korotich, Editor-in-Chief of *Ogonyok.* He worried me by saying a coup was imminent. Would I be able to get back to London, I worried. He was right about the coup even if he was wrong about the timing: it came two months later. Although he had been told his journalists could write what they liked, he had his doubts about how sincere Gorbachev was about glasnost. "Gorbachev had in mind giving an old trollop a sponge bath and putting clean clothes on her, assuming this would restore her virginity," he said. Korotich had taken over the editorship of *Ogonyok* about four years earlier and had trebled its circulation to over three million. My friend Rupert Cornwell of *The Independent* said it was "the most outspoken press defender of liberalism and reform in the land." Not all Russians approved of it, however. A letter to *Pravda* described it as "the scum bubbling on the crust of the mighty stream of renewal."

Gorbachev telephoned Leonid Kravchenko, Chairman of the All-Union State Television and Radio Broadcasting Company, when Bob Evans and I were interviewing him. He did not ask us to leave the room, but was pretty upset when he realised we had left the tape recorder on. We assured him we would not divulge anything of the conversation.

Gennady Shishkin, who had been Editor of TASS when I had visited Moscow in 1963, was now Kravchenko's first deputy in television and radio. He invited Bob Evans and me to dinner with his wife and children in his apartment. That would have been unthinkable in 1963. It was the first time in all his years in Moscow that Bob Evans had ever been invited to the home of a senior official. Shishkin's son, a sergeant in the army, was there, speaking perfect English with a strong American accent, the result of his time at an American grade school in Washington. The conversation turned to hazeing in the army. "They never hazed me," he said. Understandably: he was enormous.

We were pleased to be able to correct a little footnote of history. Historians, at least in the West, have always said Lenin's voice was heard when a message was broadcast from the cruiser *Aurora* in St Petersburg on the morning of 7 November 1917. We interviewed Vsevolod N. Ruzhnikov, lecturer in the history of Soviet Radio, Moscow University, and he was adamant that the message was in morse code. Not until 8 December 1922 was Lenin's voice heard on the radio.

CIA

I imagined I would mainly be talking to broadcasters when I researched for my book. In fact I talked a great deal to spies, particularly former operatives of the Central Intelligence Agency (CIA), who had been behind the founding of Radio Free Europe and Radio Liberty. A friend in the CIA gave me an introduction to the bravest spy I met. He was Oleg Gordievsky, who worked for the KGB, but became a double agent for the British Secret Intelligence Service (SIS or MI6). After he worked clandestinely for the British for some years in Copenhagen and London, where he was the head of the KGB as resident designate, in 1985 the KGB summoned him back to Moscow. He knew the Russians must have become suspicious about his activities, but he went nevertheless, despite the danger of trial and execution. He was betrayed by the American CIA operative, Aldrich Ames. Others Ames betrayed were executed. When Gordievsky thought arrest was imminent, the British exfiltrated him to Finland in the boot of a car.

My first contact with him was weird. My CIA friend had given me a telephone number which started with a London prefix 835. When I phoned him and invited him to lunch in the Garrick Club he said he would be coming up from the country. His telephone number was evidently in the SIS. I invited Tim Everard to joins us, who had known him when he was in the Foreign Office, and Stuart Parrott, who had worked for RFE. I was amused that "C," the head of SIS, who had welcomed him to London, was Sir Christopher Curwen, whom I had known in Bangkok in 1954, when he was a humble third secretary in the British Embassy and I was a humble Reuter representative. Christopher Andrew, the historian of MI5, said Gordievsky was "the most important British agent of the later cold war." "The remarkable quality of the intelligence he supplied marked one of the high points of British intelligence during the cold war," he wrote.

Gordievsky, who was still under sentence of death, recounted to us at length over lunch the important role Western radios had played in his decision to work for the British. By coincidence he heard one of the first broadcasts of Radio Liberty, which happened to be on the day of the announcement of the death of Stalin. He also listened to the Voice of America and the BBC World Service.

I met the Czech journalist Jiri Dienstbier through the IPI. He had been one of the leading figures in the Civic Forum dissident group. He told me how, when he was fired from Czech Radio in 1968, he got a job as a janitor. He had to leave meetings of the Magic Lantern dissidents to stoke the boiler at the building where he worked. He became Foreign Minister in 1989.

BANNED BY THE BBC

On 20 October 1997 *The Times* splashed a story with this headline: "MI6 fed Cold War propaganda to BBC." This was the story by Michael Evans, the Defence Correspondent:

BBC correspondents in Eastern Europe in the 1950s, including the veteran broadcaster Charles Wheeler, were fed classified material gleaned from covert intercepts of Soviet bloc communications in a secret government operation to generate anti-communist propaganda broadcasts during the Cold War.

In another private arrangement between the BBC and the Foreign Office, confidential letters written to BBC correspondents by people living in the communist bloc at the start of the Cold War were passed on to MI6.

The extent of the secret collaboration between the BBC and the Government in transmitting propaganda into Eastern Europe in the 1950s is disclosed by Michael Nelson, formerly of the news agency Reuters, who has been allowed full access to BBC archives. "The Foreign Office regarded the BBC as by far the most important propaganda weapon it had in Eastern Europe," he says.

He discloses that a Foreign Office unit called the Information Research Department (IRD), which was linked to MI6 and funded from the secret vote, used to give details of clandestine intercepts of East German and Russian communications to Wheeler when he was based in Berlin in the early 1950s.

Wheeler would send the material, selected to cast East Germany in a bad light, to London for the BBC's German Service programmes, Mr Nelson says in *War of the Black Heavens: The Battles of Western Broadcasting in the Cold War*, published by Brassey's next month.

The Cabinet approved the creation of the IRD for propaganda operations that would "emphasise the weakness of communism." The BBC agreed to co-operate. A Foreign Office telegram sent to all British Embassies said that the new policy was "of particular secrecy." In fact, the Russians were fully aware of it. Kim Philby was the MI6 representative on the Russia Committee of the Foreign Office and Guy Burgess worked, briefly, for the IRD.

Ernest Bevin, then Foreign Secretary, wrote a secret memo in April 1948 in which he said that the Government's views should be made clear in Iron Curtain countries principally through the BBC. Mr Nelson says: "The correspondent of the BBC External Services in Berlin was an important channel." The post had been established with the title BBC European Service liaison officer. Wheeler was assigned to the Berlin post in 1949. Mr Nelson says: "One of the two IRD men in Berlin would visit him in his office armed with cyclostyled sheets of information. He was not allowed to look at them, but the IRD man paraphrased the contents."

They were mostly "gossipy news items" about East Germany which Wheeler sent to the German Service in London. "The IRD had access to the clandestine British intercepts of domestic East German communications, so it was not too difficult to find items that put the regime in a bad light or stories that made it look foolish," Mr Nelson says.

From the end of 1954 the BBC also agreed to pass letters from East European countries "to a secret department of the Foreign Office" (MI6).

Wheeler, who left Berlin in 1953, knowingly gave information to MI6 on only one occasion. This was at the request of a young West German engineer who had been advised to contact Wheeler by a BBC engineer. He gave Wheeler information and asked to be put in touch with MI6.

Mr Nelson says: "Wheeler discouraged this idea, but agreed to pass on to British Intelligence what the engineer told him."

Evans also published an interview with Wheeler, which confirmed what I had said.

I had appeared on Melvyn Bragg's *Start the Week* on BBC Radio 4 on 24

February 1997 to curtain-raise the inaugural Annual Reuters Lecture at the University of Kent at Canterbury later that day. Michael Evans asked me for the story, but agreed to hold off until nearer the delayed publication date in exchange for my giving him a draft of the book.

The story in *The Times* created a considerable stir, with a number of broadcasts about it, and helped the sales.

The University appointed me an Honorary Research Fellow.

This is a synopsis of the book:

Why did the West win the Cold War? Not by use of arms. Weapons did not breach the Iron Curtain. The Western invasion and ultimate victory was by Radio, which was mightier than the sword.

War of the Black Heavens tells for the first time the full story of Western Broadcasting to Eastern Europe and the Soviet Union during the Cold War.

Radio, it will be seen, proved to be the major factor in the defeat of Communism. The broadcasters who fought against the Communist regimes, were the same who also had to fight political opposition in their own home countries, which in some cases wanted to shut down the stations. The victory was a triumph of the American and British peoples, their broadcasters and their Intelligence communities.

The Radios were an unequalled force for good in the fight against totalitarianism and changed the history of the twentieth century.

The three principal broadcasters were Radio Free Europe (RFE) and Radio Liberty (RL), eventually merged as RFE/RL, the British Broadcasting Corporation (BBC) and the Voice of America (VOA). Their characters were very different. RFE and RL were founded by the CIA as surrogate domestic broadcasters, designed to be like local radio stations of the target countries, with lots of local news. The BBC and VOA did not pretend to be local radio stations. They were national broadcasters, speaking for their home countries, but with strong international content. The international services of the BBC were provided by the independent Corporation, but paid for by the British Foreign Office. The Voice of America was part of the American government and for most of the Cold War was a section of the United States Information Agency (USIA).

Reuters gave a reception in London on 27 November 1997 to launch *War of the Black Heavens* in Britain and Mark Wood, the Editor-in-Chief, made the speech.

In the United States Peter Pritchard, the chief executive of the *Newseum* of the Freedom Forum in Arlington, invited me to hold the launch there. It took place on 23 November 1997 and Gene Mater, with whom I had negotiated a Reuter contract when he was editor of RFE in Munich, interviewed me. I met Brian Lamb, the founding CEO of C-Span and the host of its *Booknotes* series, at a book fair in Washington just before the launch and persuaded him to send a television crew to cover the event. It was broadcast on the C-Span book show on cable television in the United States on 20 December 1997, just in time for the Christmas book trade. I could not have asked for better publicity.

In Washington I was particularly pleased to see Mohsin Ali, one of Reuters most lovable characters, and his charming wife Dolores. Mohsin, a Pakistani, had been Reuters diplomatic correspondent for many years, but resigned to be with Dolores, an American, when they married. He then worked for *The Times* in Washington. When we went for dinner with him at his house in Sheen he always had the television on. "Mao might die," he explained.

When the BBC bookshop in Broadcasting House banned *War of the Black Heavens* the manager said it was because it was anti-BBC. However, the BBC bookshop in Bush House, the headquarters of the BBC World Service, stocked it and it sold well.

Here are extracts from some of the reviews:

Your Reviewer, who spent more than a quarter of a century at the heart of the Soviet state apparatus, has no doubt: Western radio played the central part in the exposure and undermining of the Communist empire.

Oleg Gordievsky, *Literary Review*

This volume adds the missing Soviet dimension that earlier studies have avoided so fastidiously, and it is this which makes it a compelling read.

Gary D. Rawnsley, *Intelligence and National Security*

Once Cold War succeeded World War, radio became one of its fiercest battlefields, the subject of Michael Nelson's informative and absorbing book.

Geoffrey Wheatcroft, *The Times Literary Supplement*

With a fine sense of irony, he is at his best in discussing the behind the scenes policy debates, bureaucratic maneuverings, and occasional blunders that involved the four main broadcasters.

James Critchlow, *Journal of Cold War Studies*

His encyclopaedic account displays the discernment and balance that one would expect from a good newsman located nearby but not within the institutions whose story he tells.

Edward E. Ericson Jr., *Books and Culture*

An engaging, scholarly and elegantly written work, written by a man who, as general manager of Reuters news agency, had a unique insight into the unfolding events of the Cold War.

Nicholas J. Cull, *The Historical Journal of Film, Radio and Television*

The author never describes what the Radios actually transmitted from day to day and how they went about understanding and reaching their audiences.

Michael Redley, *Intermedia*

Truth to tell, Western radio reporters never started the East-bloc revolutions, nor gave them fuel to run on. Western reporters there, like myself, watched and informed and maintained some level of public interest abroad. But I was always struck by the underground communications networks in Eastern Europe that beat Western radio broadcasts time and time again. They were better informed, quicker and often more reliable.

It's time to give them some credit, Mr Nelson, before you pat the Western broadcasters too hard on the back.

Tim Sebastian, *Reuters World*

Perhaps the most glaring problem with the book is that Nelson never probes the issues in any depth.

Jaclyn Stanke, *H-Net Reviews in the Humanities and Social Sciences*

A GRAHAM GREENE MYSTERY

I met Nicholas Scheetz, director of the Special Collections at Georgetown University, in the course of my research and he opened many doors to me in Washington, including to Norman Sherry, the major biographer of Graham Greene. When Bob Elphick heard I had met Norman Sherry, he asked me to send him this note, which I did:

I spotted Graham Greene in the Prague Alcron Hotel's dining room, a big gloomy place in the half dark. It was just after the Soviet-led invasion in August 1968, and most of the staff were afraid to return to the city centre. At the time the manager just produced sandwiches to cater for the few residents still there. The atmosphere was Greene-land to a T.

I introduced myself and he seemed happy to find someone to whom to confide his problem. This was that he had lost his passport. I told him that would be easy to fix; I knew the British Ambassador well, Bill Barker at the time. He told me he wasn't concerned about getting a new UK passport; what really worried him was getting a visa for living in France. He wanted to be sure he could get back to his life (and mistress) in Antibes whenever he wished.

Amused at what I thought was pretence of naiveté about the workings of international life, I informed him that I was sure the French Ambassador also would be only too happy to oblige.

As we sat over a drink or two, the conversation naturally led to discussion about the invasion and the sight of tanks guarding all the newspaper offices in the city as well as the Ceteka (official news agency) offices just round the corner in Wenceslas Square.

He expressed himself in bitter words about the iniquities of the Soviet action in snuffing out freedoms in Czechoslovakia as well as the bankruptcy he believed it revealed in the Kremlin's policies.

Greene mentioned the large sums of roubles he had accumulated in the State Bank in Moscow, royalties from his books the Soviets pirated. He couldn't spend them anywhere outside Russia. But this was the time of the trials and persecutions of Soviet writers and other dissidents.

He startled me by stating that he had just written to the Moscow Bankers ordering them to transfer his entire account to the dissidents Yuri Daniel and Andrei Sinyavsky.

Greene apparently got his passport and visa and I didn't see him again on that visit. But I have often wondered whether there was any evidence that the money was indeed transferred and whether Daniel and Sinyavsky could ever have received even a kopek of it.

———————

Since reading extracts of Norman Sherry's biography of the man and the emergence of a Doppelgänger, I worry whether I had in the event actually met Graham Greene number two. There is no mention of a trip to Prague in the diaries, as I am informed. There is also the possibility that my memory as to timing may be at fault. The meeting could also have occurred in January 1969 about the time of Jan Palach's self-immolation. But I would put money on August/September 1968. If it was 1969, then the Ambassador would have been Howard Smith.

I never heard from Norman Sherry. In 2010 Bob Elphick asked the British Ambassador in Prague if she could throw any light on the affair. She was fascinated by it but the Embassy records did not go back that far. The mystery is still unsolved.

NEWSEUM

The *Newseum*, where I had launched *War of the Black Heavens,* had been set up by the Freedom Forum, the charity arm of the Knight Ridder publishing group in Arlington, Virginia, in 1997 as a museum of news and journalism. Peter Pritchard had been the editor of Knight Ridder's *USA Today.* "Has Reuters got any artefacts it can give to the *Newseum?*" he asked me. "You know, like old teleprinters." I told him we did not, but that something might be available from St. Bride's, the journalists' church, of which I was a trustee. He was most intrigued by the idea that journalists had a church.

I talked to Canon John Oates, rector of St.Bride's, and he said the *Newseum* could have a piece of the Anglo-Saxon wall. When I told Peter Pritchard, he was so delighted that he sent one of his senior editors to London to meet Canon Oates. When he toured the church he saw the Roman pavement, which took his fancy. So it was agreed the *Newseum* would also be given a piece of the Roman pavement. To crown it all, Peter Pritchard invited Canon Oates to bring the artefacts to Arlington and lead the prayers at the ceremony inaugurating the *Newseum's* Journalists Memorial, a glass sculpture, where the address was given by Hillary Clinton. They flew him over first class and put him up at a smart hotel. Peter Pritchard also invited me to the ceremony, but did not pay my fare. John Oates became, in effect, the unofficial rector of the *Newseum*.

The *Newseum* moved to a new building, which cost $450 million, at 555 Pennsylvania Avenue in Washington DC in 2008 and became one of Washington's most popular tourist destinations.

CHAPTER TWELVE

The Palace Would Not Like It

QUEEN VICTORIA AND THE DISCOVERY OF THE RIVIERA

I.B. Tauris published my *Queen Victoria and the Discovery of the Riviera* in 2001. The foreword was by Lord Briggs. He and his wife Susan, Lady Briggs, were long-standing friends. In 1997, in a bookshop in Cannes, I came across a centenary history of the hotel which had been built in Nice with the needs of Queen Victoria in mind. It was *Le Regina: De la Reine Victoria à Nos Jours, Splendeurs et Métamorphoses d'un Palace, Nice 1897-1997* by Guy-Junien and Catherine Moreau (Nice, Serre Editeur, 1997). I had been looking for a subject for a book to occupy me when I was at our house on the Riviera. I was surprised that no-one had written a book on the Queen's visits to the Riviera, particularly since she had gone there no less than nine times. This was an ideal subject. However, London still demanded my presence because most of the source documents were in the Royal Archives at Windsor Castle.

TROUBLE IN THE ROUND TOWER

On 27 January 1998 I climbed the spiral stone staircase of the 12th Century Round Tower at Windsor Castle for my first meeting with the elegant Sheila, Lady de Bellaigue, the Registrar of the Royal Archives, one of the most extraordinary institutions I had ever dealt with. In order to be allowed access to the Royal Archives I had to sign an agreement, not without some misgivings, which contained this clause:

> All quotations from papers in the Royal Archives, and all passages based on information obtained from those papers, must be submitted to the Assistant

Keeper of the Royal Archives for approval before publication, and before the text is sent to the publisher. Quotations must be shown in context.

The agreement pointed out that the Royal Archives were the property of the Queen.

In the Royal Archives there are 500 to 600 volumes of Queen Victoria's letters and Journal extracts, some of which have been published. No-one has ever been allowed to publish them in their entirety. Queen Victoria left the manuscripts to Princess Beatrice with instructions to modify or destroy any portions which appeared to be unsuitable for preservation. I dipped into those parts that Beatrice had transcribed in her crabbed handwriting which related to the time the Queen was on the Riviera. Faced with the prospect of weeks of tedious work at Windsor, I soon went to see Lady de Bellaigue to tell her that I would need to get a researcher to work on the Journals and transcribe the passages which would be relevant to my book. "Oh Mr Nelson, that will not be possible. Access to the archives is personal to you." So I appealed to her superior, Oliver Everett, the Librarian and Assistant Keeper of the Archives, (the Keeper was the Queen's Private Secretary) and he finally over-ruled Lady de Bellaigue and agreed that Alison Adams, a trained librarian, could come and work in the Archives.

Two years went by and I submitted the extracts I had taken from the Archives. Lady de Bellaigue demanded to see the whole manuscript of the book, which I duly sent her. Such was the negative reaction of Lady de Bellaigue to the manuscript, I could see that my two years' work might have been for nothing and the book might never be published. I anticipated that I might have to conduct a campaign in the Press to expose the outrageous censorship of the Palace, so I made careful note of the conversations:

Telephone conversation with Lady de Bellaigue, Registrar, the Royal Archives, on 23 February 2000.

Lady de Bellaigue telephoned. She said she had not been able to speak freely when I called her on 21 February, but she wanted to discuss her disappointment with the book.

When we had first discussed it I had said it would be like Arengo-Jones' book on Queen Victoria in Switzerland. Later I had explained that the publisher did not want that sort of book and wanted something serious and academic, which was what she had been expecting. The sources on the opening up of the Riviera were fascinating, but there was much less about the original theme than she had expected. There were lots of spicy stories which seemed to be there for their entertainment and titillation value. The sources were uneven and she doubted the veracity of some of the stories. Some of the memoirs were probably ghost-written and therefore unreliable.

The story about Princess Beatrice never having been alone in a room with a man before had no doubt come from David Duff's book on her, and he was clearly unreliable. How could he know that? I said I had avoided many dubious secondary sources. She doubted the stories about the wedding nights of the Princesses Louise and Stephanie. I said they were both in their memoirs. Why was there so much unsavoury material about the Belgian royal family? I replied that it was clear that Leopold was a dreadful man, not only in sexual matters but also for his record in the Congo. She said I had said Edward Prince of Wales had had an affair with Sarah Bernhardt. When I categorically denied this she said I had implied it.

The references to the British monarchy of today would not go down well at Buckingham Palace, she said. She cited the reference to the present Prince of Wales taking a descendant of Mrs Keppel as his mistress. The reference to the Duke of Kent attending the Boer War commemoration last year was irrelevant, she said. I countered that it brought an historical event alive in contemporary terms.

I explained that the publisher and editor had already suggested I took out many of the contemporary references, including the story of the daughter of the present King of the Belgians, which I had done. The references to the present British royal family were not very important and I would have no problem in removing them.

Why had I written so much about the disreputable people whom the Queen met on the Riviera? I said biographies of the Queen usually concentrated on such as Lord Melbourne. They did not, as I had done, go to the Court Circulars to see who all the other people were whom she entertained. My book was very complimentary about Queen Victoria, I said; she was a good woman and a good queen.

I said a number of people, including Professor Donald Read, Elizabeth Longford, Mr Iradj Bagherzade, the publisher, and Dr Lester Crook, the editor, had read all or part of the book and had not reacted as she had. I was awaiting the comments of Lord Briggs, who had agreed to read it.

Lady de Bellaigue said she had a responsibility to see the Royal Archives were used in a responsible way and that they were not brought into disrepute. The Archives gave authority to a work. She would now have to discuss it with the Librarian, Oliver Everett. It was a great pity I had broken the rule about not giving a book to a publisher until they had seen it. I said it had not formally gone to the publisher. They had had a look at a draft.

She was concerned that the colourful stories dominated the rest. They had to be seen in harness with the authenticity given by the Royal Archives. I said the publisher and editor had already asked for more serious material on, for example, Lord Salisbury. I would send her what had already been deleted and what added so that she could now see what the balance was. She said she would telephone me when she had studied it.

GO AHEAD AND PUBLISH

Fortunately Gerry Ratzin, an old Reuter colleague, had known Oliver Everett well in India, where Ratzin was a correspondent and Everett was at the British High Commission. Ratzin advised me to go directly to Oliver Everett above the head of Lady de Bellaigue, which I did. This was the result:

Telephone conversation with Oliver Everett, Librarian and Assistant Keeper of the Royal Archives, on 28 February 2000.

Oliver Everett returned my call and thanked me for the deletions I had sent to Lady de Bellaigue. He said I did not need to delete all the references to the present royalty. He would be happy with deletion of the reference to Prince Charles and Camilla Parker Bowles and to the illegitimate daughter of the present King of the Belgians. He was also glad to see that I had deleted the reference to Beatrice never having been alone with a man until she met her husband.

When we had first discussed the terms for my access to the Archives he had said there would be a charge, but he had now decided not to make a charge as the character of the book had changed so much.

I asked him if it was now in order for me to give the text to the publishers and he said it was.

I thanked him for his intervention.

Lady de Bellaigue partly redeemed herself in my eyes by sending me two invaluable detailed letters containing 52 corrections and suggestions, which only an expert on the royal family could possibly have produced.

When James Lees-Milne (qv) in the eighties submitted to the Windsor Librarian those parts of his biography of Lord Esher, *The Enigmatic Edwardian,* which derived from the Royal Archives, to his amazement the Queen herself read the extracts. She was rather shocked by some of the things they contained, such as that Lord Esher had had a crush on her uncle Edward, Prince of Wales, the future Duke of Windsor, though she requested no changes.

My good friend Tim Everard arranged for the Queen to be given a copy of my book. The Queen said it looked most interesting and took it to Balmoral for her summer holiday in 2001.

OH, IF ONLY I WERE AT NICE

The blurb summarised the book:

'Oh, if only I were at Nice, I should recover,' said Queen Victoria as she was dying. The Queen fell in love with the Riviera when she discovered it on her first visit to Menton in 1882 and her enchantment with this 'paradise of nature' endured for almost twenty years. Victoria's visits helped to transform the French Riviera, by paving the way for other European royalty, the aristocracy and the very rich, who were to turn it into their pleasure garden.

Her visits, during the high noon of British imperial self-confidence, were never far from affairs of state, while her domestic affairs, whether handling the moodiness of the dour John Brown, the presumptuousness of her Indian Secretary the Munshi Abdul Karim or the premature deaths of her younger relatives, never dimmed the childlike pleasure she derived from the region's natural charms.

The book paints a fascinating portrait of Victoria and her dealings with local people of all classes, statesmen and the constant stream of visiting crown heads, from the beautiful Empress Eugenie of France to the monstrous Leopold II, King of the Belgians. It describes the conduct of British diplomacy and domestic politics from Victoria's holiday retreats, as well as the vagaries of Anglo-French relations, as the Queen's visits and the national interests of Britain and France all impacted on each other. In the process we see an unexpected side to Victoria; not the imperious, petulant, mourning widow but rather an exuberant girlish old lady thrilled by her surroundings.

Queen Victoria and the Discovery of the Riviera is based on much original research in the Royal Archives at Windsor Castle, which has enabled the publication here for the first time of many entries from the Queen's own journals. It makes an important contribution to our understanding of Victoria's character and personality and our view of the late Victorian period and its history.

We launched the book in London, New York and Paris. At the London launch at the Garrick Club, Lord Briggs gave the address. In New York Mrs Thomas M. Evans, a friend of Nicholas Scheetz, with great generosity made her splendid apartment at the River House on the East River available and Nicholas made a speech. In Paris we gave a reception at the WHSmith bookshop on the Rue de Rivoli where I gave a talk. We also had launches at the English bookshops in Monte Carlo, Nice and Cannes.

The previous year Bob Elphick had arranged for Sir Paul Lever, the British Ambassador to Germany, to invite Bob, Michael Reupke and me to dinner at the embassy in Berlin when we were there for a conference.

Knowing of my forthcoming book on Queen Victoria, the Ambassador kindly served Hochheimer Koenigin Victoriaberg Rheingau Riesling Kabinett. Queen Victoria and Prince Albert had visited the vineyard on the River Main in 1845 and the Queen agreed that the vineyard could be renamed after her. The label today carries an illustration of the statue of the Queen which was unveiled at the vineyard on her thirty-fifth birthday on 24 May 1854. We served the wine at all the launches.

My book was included in the *History Today* commended list in 2001. Here are some extracts from some of the reviews:

Of all the huge outpouring of Victoriana commemorating last month's centenary of the Queen-Empress' death, the most delightful study is this short and very well researched book by the former General Manager of Reuters, Michael Nelson.

Andrew Roberts, *The Sunday Telegraph*

One of the most fascinating books of the year ... Queen Vic helped invent international tourism – Britain's gift to the world.

Peter Preston, *Guardian*

Victorian scholar Nelson has uncovered a rich store of information on Queen Victoria's many trips to the Riviera. These trips, beginning in 1882, popularised an area that had seen only slowly developing tourism in the 19th century. Following suit, crowned heads and European high flyers transformed the Riviera into a major vacation venue. Nelson had access to the queen's journals, which are housed at Windsor. The result could have made for dreary reading, but Nelson chose just the right entries from Victoria's journals and sprinkled the text with letters from other aristocrats, making this a lively read. Nelson's own style allows the reader to vividly imagine being in the hotel drawing rooms right alongside Victoria's entourage. In the introduction, a gem of succinctness and anecdotal charm, Nelson outlines the development of tourism in southern France. One would hardly expect yet another book on Queen Victoria to be amusing, but this one's a rare treat.

Gail Benjafield, *Library Journal*

The fascinating story of Queen Victoria's love affair with the Riviera is beautifully recounted.

Ron Kentish, *Isle of Wight County Press*

Vastly researched and highly entertaining.

Brian Case, *Time Out*

As a detailed monograph on one specific aspect of Victoria's life, it is difficult to see how it could have been better done.

Paul Minet, *Royalty Digest*

There is no lack of diverting sidelights. On her first visit, the Queen's train lacked a restaurant car, and she brought some of the food from Windsor, rather like a tripper taking sandwiches to Paris.

E.S. Turner, *The Times Literary Supplement*

Do not be misled by the carefully-phrased foreword by Lord Briggs: this is emphatically not a suitable purchase for academic libraries.

John K. Walton, *Albion*

THE QUEEN IS DEAD: WHERE'S OUR REPORTER

I sold extracts of the book to the *Guardian* and the *Daily Mail*, which they ran as double-page colour spreads in week-end supplements. I sold a story about the Queen's death to *The Times*, which they erroneously said I had covered in my book. The headline was "The Queen is dead: where's our reporter."

It is a story to bring any news reporter out in a cold sweat. There was the foremost descriptive writer of the world's most august newspaper, sent by his venerable Editor to cover the imminent death of the great Queen Empress at her beloved home at Osborne.

Hotels and boarding houses all over the Isle of Wight were crammed with competitors from newspapers across the world. The Post Office had moved its newfangled telegraphic equipment into East Cowes, together with 40 emergency staff standing by round the clock.

Then came the terrible moment for which they had all been waiting; the chief of the Queen's police strode portentously down the steps of Osborne bearing a piece of paper. The press pack stood ready for his announcement, pencils and notebooks in trembling hands, ready to speed the news to the farthest corners of empire.

And James Vincent, special correspondent of *The Times*, was. . . nowhere to be seen.

The story of the hapless Vincent and his unexplained absence at the greatest story of his life was breaking 100 years ago is told in a new book on Queen Victoria which throws an intriguing light on her relationship with the royal ratpack and which has contemporary resonances in the hysterical coverage of the death of Diana, Princess of Wales, and the relentless pursuit of her two sons.

Vincent never satisfactorily explained where he was on that fateful night. My story concluded:

There is no record of any reproof from his bosses. Indeed, a couple of months later *The Times* sent him to accompany the Duke of Cornwall, later to be King George V, on a tour to Australia, New Zealand, South Africa and Canada.

But the newspaper was clearly getting fed up with him. Charles Moberly Bell, the manager, exploded when he received his expenses claim of £170 (£9,000 at today's values) for clothes for the trip, including 102 shirts. "I presume you do not suggest that you will have worn out this number in the 210 days of your trip," Bell berated him. Vincent received several cables criticising his coverage and eventually he was put out to grass as a part-time motoring correspondent.

DEATH OF MY MOTHER

My mother died on 28 May 1998, aged 97. She was a woman of great determination to whom I owe much.

MISCELLANIES

In 1998 Donald Trelford, former Editor of the *Observer* and Professor of Journalism at Sheffield University, asked me to become the external examiner for the MA journalism degree at the University. I filled the post from 1999 to 2001.

I often gave lectures related to my books and in 1997 gave a paper related to western broadcasting in the Cold War at a conference of the International Association for Media and History (IAMHIST) on *Knaves, Fools and Heroes: film and television representations of the cold war* at Salisbury State University, Maryland. The majority of the members of IAMHIST were university professors and no journalists were members when I decided to join. I persuaded Michael Reupke and Bob Elphick also to join and they made valuable contributions as media practitioners to the debates at the biennial international meetings.

IAMHIST elected me to their Council in 2001 and I served on it until 2009. The society produced a highly regarded journal, *The Historical Journal of Film, Radio and Television,* which was edited by the talented David Culbert, a professor of history at the Louisiana State University at Baton Rouge. It was published by Routledge, part of the Taylor and Francis Group, and generated good revenues for IAMHIST. I proposed that the society award a biennial prize and, when I retired from the Council in 2009, the President, Nicholas Cull, kindly announced that in future the prize would be called the IAMHIST-Michael Nelson Prize for a Work in Media and History. The first winner had been Professor Wendy Webster of the University of Central Lancashire with the imaginative *Englishness and Empire, 1939-1965.*

AMERICANS AND THE MAKING OF THE RIVIERA

In 2001 I started work on a third book: *Americans and the Making of the Riviera*. It was published by McFarland of Jefferson, North Carolina in 2008.

The preface gave the background:

> I had just finished my book *Queen Victoria and the Discovery of the Riviera* in the year 2000 and, strolling through the Riviera seaside resort of Juan-les-Pins, came across the Sidney Bechet square, dominated by a large statue of the American jazz musician. I walked down to the sea through a square named after another American, Frank Jay Gould, heir to the railroad fortune, and a few yards along the front was the Franklin Roosevelt square. Clearly I had found my next book. If the nineteenth century was the age of the British on the Riviera, the twentieth was that of the Americans.
>
> In fact the first American of note to visit the Riviera was Thomas Jefferson in the eighteenth century when he was minister in Paris. He took with him a portable copying machine, so I found a wealth of information from the copies of the letters he wrote, which are in *The Papers of Thomas Jefferson* edited by Julian P. Boyd and others and published by the Princeton University Press in 29 volumes to date.
>
> Many Americans visited the Riviera in the nineteenth century, including the eccentric James Gordon Bennett Jr., founder of the Paris *Herald*, but only in the winter. The revolution was wrought by Cole Porter and his wife Linda in 1921 when they came in the summer. Writers like Scott Fitzgerald followed in his footsteps and his novel *Tender is the Night* is one of the most important sources for life on the Riviera in the twenties. But, as I worked on my book in the villa my wife and I have in the Riviera village of Opio, I discovered many other important novels about the region by such as Willa Cather, Edith Wharton and Ernest Hemingway. The letters of Gerald and Sara Murphy, who were the center of American artistic life, were an important source.
>
> The most striking proof, which is evident today, of the role of the Americans in the making of the Riviera is the hotel Palais de la Méditerranée. It was built by Frank Jay Gould with American railroad money in 1928 and was recently refurbished as the most luxurious hotel in Nice.

My greatest pleasure in researching the book was to discover, in the Nice archives, the yellowed copies of the Riviera Supplement of the Paris edition of *The Chicago Tribune,* on which James Thurber and his wife Althea, who was society editor, had worked.

The newspaper was hilarious, as was its editing, as described by Thurber:

We went to work after dinner and usually had the last chronicle of the diverting day written and ready for the linotypers well before midnight. It was then our custom to sit around for half an hour, making up items for the society editor's column. She was too pretty, we thought, to waste the soft southern days tracking down the arrival of prominent persons on the Azure Coast. So all she had to do was stop at the Ruhl and Negresco each day and pick up the list of guests who had just registered. The rest of us invented enough items to fill up the last of her column, and a gay and romantic cavalcade, indeed, infested the littoral of our imagination. "Lieutenant General and Mrs. Pendelton Gray Winslow," we would write, "have arrived at their villa, Heart's Desire, on Cap d'Antibes, bringing with them their prize Burmese monkey, Thibault …"

In this manner we turned out, in no time at all, and with the expenditure of very little mental energy, the most glittering column of social notes in the history of the American newspaper, either here or abroad.

One of the most intriguing puzzles about Americans on the Riviera is the relationship between Sara Murphy, the doyenne of the twenties, and Picasso. I quoted John Richardson, the leading biographer of Picasso, on whether Sara and Picasso had an affair. He said in an interview published in 1998: "I would have thought nothing was more likely. Picasso was tremendously attractive and charismatic, and very physical, and it would have been hard for her to resist." Imagine my surprise when Richardson published the third volume of his biography of Picasso in 2007 and I read: "Sara adored her adoring and albeit far from heterosexual husband and was famously faithful to him."

I wrote to Richardson and said it appeared he had changed his mind. If that was so, I said I would be most interested to know why. He did not reply.

When I had finished the book I managed to track down, with some difficulty, the location on the Cap d'Antibes of the *Villa America* where the Murphys had lived. It was at 112, chemin des Mougins. A feature writer on the French newspaper *Libération* heard that I had been there and ran this piece:

Bought first of all by a Swiss industrialist, the Villa America was then acquired by Tissot, the watch manufacturer, who destroyed it to build a new house. Then the Russians bought it, Michael Nelson explained. He had a lively recollection of his pilgrimage to 112 chemin des Mougins. "The muscular Russian servants were pretty menacing and I very much had to watch out for the dog."

It was indeed a frightening visit which I did not repeat.

We launched the book at the Garrick Club where Jonathan Fenby, former Editor of Reuters and of the *Observer* gave the speech, and at the Hotel Negresco in Nice, where I gave a talk.

Here are extracts from some of the reviews:

Mr Nelson, well-known for his excellent book, Queen Victoria and the Discovery of the Riviera, here reminds us that Thomas Jefferson visited what became known as the Riviera in the late eighteenth century when the first English patients were going there for their consumption. This is an enjoyable book that reminds us of the role America played in the development of this distinctive and largely pleasant part of France.

Contemporary Review

This is a story that deserves to be told and it is recounted clearly and with a light touch by a writer well-equipped to disentangle the interlocking lives and life-styles of a large cast.

Martin Hills, *AMB-Côte d'Azur*

This is an entertaining book about a niche subject, a light way of gathering further intelligence on great American writers and artists with a Francophile penchant.

Sylvie Wheatley, *France*

Americans were one of the most influential groups in the shaping of tourism on the Riviera in the 20th Century, yet their achievements for the economy in the south of France are little documented.

Let's Go Riviera

The 'beautiful people' who gave the Riviera much of its glamour in the heady days before the '29 Wall Street crash – and left their names on dozens of Riviera streets and squares – are all here; millionaires, heiresses, impecunious geniuses who swam like a little shoal of fish among the rich."

Michael Taylor, *French News*

Nelson has had his head in a lot of books (and his walking boots on) and offers a fascinating account of this aspect of the Riviera's past. This is a plumcake of a book, full of tasty morsels.

Nelson offers few nits to pick though I'm pretty sure that Henry Clews dropped out of Amherst, not Amhurst, and it's not true that "the Anglo-American School in Mougins later moved to Sophia Antipolis." It's still in Mougins.

Patrick Middleton, *The Riviera Reporter*

Son Patrick designed a website michaelnelsonbooks.com, which helped sales of my books. It also led to London Weekend Television (LWT) getting me to research and front pieces for two films they made for the Discovery Channel in 2001. One was *The Man Who Broke the Bank at Monte Carlo* for "Millionaires Monte Carlo" and the other *Americans on the Riviera* for "Red Hot Riviera." We shot them outside the Casino in Monte Carlo.

I had known Harold Evans since he had been Editor of the *Northern Echo* in the early sixties. He eventually became Editor of *The Times* as I have described above. I saw him in New York, where he had lived since soon after he left *The Times,* just after I had published *Queen Victoria and the Discovery of the Riviera.* His wife, Tina Brown, who had been Editor of the *New Yorker,* was publishing a new magazine called *Talk* and, in the garden of his lovely apartment on Sutton Place, we discussed publishing an abstract of *Queen Victoria* in *Talk,* which would have been marvellous promotion. He introduced me to the commissioning editor there but nothing came of it: 9/11 struck and the consequent decline in advertising meant *Talk* folded. But I greatly appreciated that he had not forgotten our long friendship.

CHAPTER THIRTEEN

Dear Sir

LETTERS TO THE EDITOR

Retirement gives the opportunity to indulge in writing letters to the editors of newspapers. Mine were mainly about Reuters, *War of the Black Heavens* and my other books, which the letters were designed to promote. My old friends Sir David Nicholas and Bob Elphick and I competed to see who could get the most letters published. Here is a selection of mine and one of each of theirs, to which I replied.

COLD WAR

"Prophetic Levin"
The Times 22 July 1993
Bernard Levin's modesty forbade him to mention in his article, "How was the cruel lie perpetrated?" (July 16), the most interesting item in the special issue of The National Interest, "The strange death of Soviet communism", to which he refers.

The item is headed "One who got it right" and it is the article by Mr Levin that you published in August 1977 predicting the fall of communism. The prescience about why and how it would happen is remarkable, as is his forecast of the date July 14, 1989.

"Cold War propaganda"
The Times 24 October 1997
From Mr Robert Elphick
Your report (October 20) of Michael Nelson's book about broadcasting in the Cold War, headlined "MI6 fed Cold War propaganda to BBC",

seems to give the impression that there was something reprehensible in the activities of the Foreign Office's Information Research Department (IRD).

As a correspondent in the late 1950s in Moscow, and later in Vienna, trying to make sense of the communist dictatorships, I often made use of IRD's output. The stuff they produced was reasonably factual and far from the kind of propaganda we had to deal with from all the official media in these countries.

It was offered as a service. We did not regard it as propaganda and I could take what I liked from the supply. As such it was a necessary and welcome counterpart to the flood of lies and half-lies produced by the regimes in question, which were concerned to make us believe in the scientific inevitability of the triumph of communism over capitalism.

Far from having their achievement called into question now that the Cold War is safely over, the IRD ought to be given due recognition for their sterling service.

The Times 27 October 1997
From Mr Michael Nelson
I agree with Robert Elphick (letter, October 24), that the Information Research Department (IRD) ought to be given due recognition for its sterling service in counteracting communist propaganda.

One of the reasons the IRD has not received the recognition it deserves is the common view that propaganda is a pejorative term. This view is held today by many in the BBC. But at the height of the Cold War the BBC well understood that there was nothing reprehensible in drawing on IRD material for use in the propaganda war the BBC was itself engaged in.

In the late 1940s Sir Ian Jacob, then Director of the Overseas Service of the BBC and later to become Director-General, wrote: "It is evident that any country deciding to embark on a service of broadcasts to foreign audiences does so because it wants to influence those audiences in its favour. All such broadcasting is therefore propaganda."

Ten years later, shortly before he became Director-General, Sir Hugh Greene devoted much of an address to the Nato Defence College in Paris on psychological warfare to a description of the BBC and propaganda. He did not hesitate to use the word propaganda frequently.

As we celebrate the BBC's 75th birthday we should not fail to recognise the BBC's outstanding service in helping to bring down communism through propaganda.

"Dick Helms; Lives remembered"
The Times 30 October 2002
One of the greatest unsung achievements of Dick Helms [director of the Central Intelligence Agency (CIA) from June 1966 to February 1973](obituary, October 24) was winning the fight for the continued existence of Radio Free Europe and Radio Liberty. I interviewed him in Washington in 1993 when I was researching for my book *War of the Black Heavens: The Battles of Western Broadcasting in the Cold War* and he recounted for the first time how President Johnson had told him he was going to close down the stations. "But you can't do that," Helms replied, and explained how the Radios, which were run and financed by the CIA, were playing such an important role in Eastern Europe and the Soviet Union in the fight against communism.

"All right," President Johnson said, "if you think they're so important, you go up to Capitol Hill and get them financed. But you must tell those senators and congressmen that you do not have my support."

Helms prepared his brief well and was finally able to convince the appropriate senators and congressmen to support the continuation of the stations. President Johnson conceded defeat and they were saved.

The importance of Helms' victory is exemplified by the interview that Jerzy Urban, the Polish Government spokesman, gave to an American journalist in 1984. "If you would close your Radio Free Europe, the underground would completely cease to exist," he said.

"Reagan and the communist collapse"
The Times 16 June 2004
Mikhail Gorbachev also denied that Ronald Reagan's military build-up led to the collapse of the Soviet Union. He told Margaret Thatcher that the first impulses for reform were in the Soviet Union itself, in a society that could no longer tolerate the lack of freedom.

That knowledge of freedom came principally from Western radio stations. Reagan said in 1983: "The truth is mankind's best hope for a better world. That's why in times like these few assets are more important than the Voice of America and Radio Liberty as our primary means of getting truth to the Russian people."

One of Reagan's first acts when he became President had been to increase the appropriations for international broadcasting. Mrs Thatcher also increased spending on the BBC's External Services.

The irony was that Gorbachev, the target of the failed coup of August 1991 that finally toppled communism, when under house arrest in the Crimea depended on Western radio for the information on which he staged his comeback. It was Gorbachev who, in January 1987, had started to decrease the amount of jamming of Western radio, which finally ceased on 29 November, 1988.

"Jacek Kuron; Lives remembered."
   The Times 25 June 2004
   Jacek Kuron [activist of the Polish Committee for Social Defense (KOR)](obituary, June 18) was a master at handling communications. In the eighties in Poland, whenever anyone in the dissident movement was arrested, his friends could call Kuron. He, in turn, would notify Radio Free Europe (RFE), the BBC, or other news organisations and the information would be broadcast back to Poland. From 1980 Solidarity used RFE to announce times and places of meetings. It was easier to telephone internationally than domestically. One day Kuron was on the telephone giving a live interview to RFE when there was a knock at the door. He opened up and it was the police. "Excuse me," he told the interviewer, "I have to go to prison."

"Sir Charles Wheeler; Lives remembered."
   The Times 10 July 2008
   I interviewed Sir Charles Wheeler [BBC correspondent](obituary, July 5) for my book *War of the Black Heavens: The Battles of Western Broadcasting in the Cold War*. He disclosed that not only did he give information to British Intelligence when he was correspondent for the External Services of the BBC in Berlin, but also received material from them, which he sent to the BBC in London. When *The Times* carried the story on October 20, 1997, that I was going to reveal this in my book, there was great concern in the BBC. No-one had admitted that such a relationship existed between the BBC and British Intelligence. It was typical of the honesty of Charles Wheeler that he should acknowledge that such a give-and-take relationship existed as an essential part of the work of a BBC correspondent at the height of the Cold War.

"Russian translation"

The Economist 12 February 2011

Mikhail Gorbachev's quote that "the BBC sounded the best" while he was under house arrest in 1991 is not exactly right ("*Dosvidaniya, London*", January 29th). That was the BBC's take from the Russian. This is the translation used by Reuters: "We got BBC, best of all… they were the clearest signal." Mr Gorbachev was referring to the technical quality of the radio transmission, not to the content. However, he did pay this tribute to the BBC at a press conference when he could not see its correspondent: "The BBC knows everything already."

NEWS

"Rudolf Hell; Lives remembered."

The Times 21 March 2002

In the Sixties I visited Rudolf Hell [the German inventor](obituary, 18 March) in Kiel and thanked him on behalf of Reuters, for whom I worked, for the great contribution he had made through the Hellschreiber to making Reuters a leading news agency.

Reuters pioneered the use of broadcast radio for news dissemination by morse in 1923. It started to use the Hellschreiber in 1935 and it soon became the agency's principal means of news transmission by radio. It was this German invention which enabled Reuters during the Second World War to transmit from London an accurate and objective news service, by the best means possible, which had the effect of countering the lies of German propaganda.

The reason the Hellschreiber was the best system for many years was that each character was a miniature facsimile made up of 49 impulses, compared with up to six in other codes such as Morse or Baudot used in Teletype. So even if a few of the impulses were lost through radio interference, the character on the paper tape could still be deciphered, which was not the case with the other techniques.

Only in the latter part of the last century, when communications were improved by the use of cable and satellite, did Reuters finally stop using the Hellschreiber, which it replaced with Teletype.

"Single Source"
The Times 20 February 2004
From Sir David Nicholas

The BBC is about to produce new guidelines for its journalists about the use of single sources for news stories (The Sunday Times, February 15). It is worth recalling that in the postwar years, before ITN came on the scene, BBC News laid down that all items broadcast must be supported by two sources.

Some wily BBC foreign correspondents, aware that there was no broadcast competition in the UK, would give their exclusive stories to Reuters first and then file their own version to the BBC a little later. BBC executives back home were happy to go with the story because it had been confirmed by an agency.

The use of a single source is a matter of commonsense judgment of the sort made all the time in a sharp newsroom. It all depends on the quality of the source.

The Times 26 February 2004
From Mr Michael Nelson

Sir David Nicholas (letter, 20 February) says that some wily BBC foreign correspondents would get round the BBC's two-sources rule for news stories in the postwar years by giving their exclusive stories to Reuters first and then filing their version to the BBC a little later, thus satisfying corporation executives that the story "had been confirmed by an agency."

However, the Reuters correspondent would not have used the BBC tip-off without first checking that the story was true. The BBC did therefore receive the story from two valid sources.

"Radio days"
The Spectator 22 November 2008

Kate Chisholm is wrong (Arts, 15 November) when she says financing of the BBC World Service by the Foreign & Commonwealth Office is a hangover from the days when it was known as the Empire Service. The Empire Service, which was started on 19 December 1932 was financed by the BBC. Not until the Arabic Service started on 3 January 1938 did the Foreign Office provide any finance to overseas services of the BBC.

Not only did the British government refuse the BBC's request for finance for the Empire Service, but, because of the economic crisis, it asked the BBC for a voluntary contribution to the National Exchequer. Amazingly, the BBC agreed to contribute £50,000 by March 1932 and £150,000 in the course of the financial year 1932/3. It was as part of that deal that the BBC agreed 'to carry the cost of Empire broadcasting'.

"A brilliant design, despite my qualms"
Financial Times 20 February 2010
In his article about Alan Fletcher ("Persuasion with a smile," February 5), Edwin Heathcote says that the dot-matrix typeface Fletcher designed for Reuters evoked the ticker tape of the newswires. That is not correct.

Ticker tape carried stock market prices. The Reuter typeface evoked the holes in teleprinter tape that was used to drive teleprinters.

I attended the Reuter management meeting with Fletcher to discuss his design in the mid-60s and expressed reservations about it. I said that the technology on which it was based would be obsolescent in 20 years and the Reuter logo needed a longer life than that. I was right about the timing of the obsolescence, but am glad we adopted it because it was a brilliant design, which lasted Reuters in modified form for more than 40 years until the company was acquired by Thomson in 2008.

(The letter was preceded by a shot of Buster Keaton studying a ticker tape in the silent comedy "Seven changes." I had decided not to include in my letter that I had told the meeting that we might as well have a logo made out of pigeon droppings.)

"Wisdom of Libya's philosopher king"
Financial Times 11 March 2011
John Kiddell's letter "Memories are made of this"(March 7) reminded me of the conversation I had in 1968, when I worked for Reuters, with Major General Arundell Leakey, who had just retired as General Officer Commanding Malta and Libya.

Leakey first met King Idris when he took over the command in 1967. He told the king that he was going to make his army the most efficient in the Middle East.

"Don't do that, general," the king said. "They'll overthrow me."

They did so in 1969.

EDITH WHARTON

"Missing Wharton"
The Times Literary Supplement 19 March 2010

Laura Rattray should have omitted the definite article from the title of *The unpublished writings of Edith Wharton,* reviewed by Michele Gemelos on March 12. There are many other manuscripts which she has not included. As she says in her introduction, some are very substantial writings.

I came across one of them in the course of my research for my book *Americans and the Making of the Riviera* (McFarland, 2008). The unfinished novel *Tradition* is about an American family, the Graysons, who live in Valbonne in the South of France. My wife and I have a house in Opio, the neighbouring village to Valbonne, and I decided I would like to publish *Tradition* in English and French. The Beinicke Library at Yale sent me copies of three documents. They were:

1. A hand-written manuscript in pencil.
2. A typescript of 59 pages, edited in pencil (Missing is another edition between these two documents).
3. A typewritten synopsis, edited in pencil, and called a "sketch."

To my surprise I found Edith Wharton had moved Valbonne, which is eight miles from the Mediterranean, to the sea. Internal evidence indicates that she attached the Grayson family to St. Raphael. Edith Wharton had a house in Hyères, which is 53 miles from St.Raphael.

I was disappointed that the trustees of the Edith Wharton estate declined to give me permission to publish *Tradition.*

GENERAL DE GAULLE

"De Gaulle's Bad Timing"
History Today July 2010

In his memoirs Charles de Gaulle is wrong when he says he read his famous speech over the BBC to the French people, rallying them to his cause, at 6 pm on June 18th 1940. It was broadcast live at 10 pm. It is therefore not surprising that Jonathan Fenby (The Man Who Said 'NON', June 2010) and many other authors have not correctly recorded the occasion.

What happened was set out by the late Leonard Miall, who looked after de Gaulle at the BBC, in a letter to the *Independent* magazine on July 7th 1990:

> [The broadcast] was not produced by Patrick Smith, the distinguished BBC foreign correspondent, but by the late Elizabeth Barker. In 1940 they were both assistants in European News Talks, a BBC section I headed. Elizabeth Barker was on late duty the evening of June 18th when she received a message from the Ministry of Information saying that General de Gaulle had arrived in England and asking us to put him on the air in the 10 pm French news, not 6 pm as given in ...... de Gaulle's own memoirs. Because of the very short notice, she was unable to get the programme recorded.
>
> General de Gaulle announced at the end of his first broadcast that he would be speaking again at the same time the next day, which was the first that we in the BBC had heard about it. The Director-General [Frederick Ogilvie] sent me a message asking us to take General de Gaulle to his office after this second broadcast so that he might congratulate him on the courageous stand he was taking.
>
> Over our drinks General de Gaulle asked me whether we had recorded his appeal of the day before, and I had to tell him we had not. I then became one of the first British recipients of the famous de Gaulle temper. This imposing figure, in full military uniform, glared down from his enormous height and castigated the BBC in general, and me in particular, for failing to appreciate the historical significance of his broadcast. In poor French I tried to explain the technical difficulties, but I don't think he was mollified. De Gaulle was soon given a short daily programme slot to continue his call for resistance, and his next talk was on June 24th. The BBC suggested that he should repeat the essence of his June 18th appeal. That time it was recorded, and this is the version which was heavily used during the recent [50th anniversary] celebrations. Patrick Smith was the producer on this occasion. Writing his memoirs 34 years later it is readily understandable that he thought he produced the original appeal, just as General de Gaulle thought he broadcast at 6 pm.

Leonard Miall told me that the reason the speech was not recorded was that the BBC were short of recording equipment.

QUEEN VICTORIA

"Victoria's travels"
  The Times 14 April 2007
  Giles Coren (12 April) describes Queen Victoria as "famously stay-at home."

In the last two decades of her life she stayed on the French Riviera nine times, eight of those occasions in hotels, albeit accompanied by 100 staff.

"A royal visit – are you dead certain?"
Financial Mail on Sunday 31 December 2006

OK, so Philip Green is one of the richest men in Britain. But perhaps he should still check his bill from the luxury hotel on the French Riviera where he has just staged a £4 million bar mitzvah party for son Brandon.

Not that the swanky Grand Hotel du Cap Ferrat would stoop deliberately to overcharge the owner of Bhs and the Arcadia Group – or anybody else.

But we fear the prestigious hostelry is mathematically challenged.

Michael Nelson, author of the book Queen Victoria And The Discovery Of The Riviera, was surprised to learn of the hotel's claim that, pre-Green, distinguished guests had included Queen Victoria, who stayed there in 1908.

Nelson pointed out that the Queen would have had trouble making the visit, given that she died in 1901.

Undaunted by this minor detail, the hotel continues to advertise the Royal 'stay' on its website.

CHAPTER FOURTEEN

Making the Twenty-first Century

MEDIA SOCIETY AWARD TO REUTERS

In 2001, the 150th anniversary of the founding of Reuters, I proposed to Donald Trelford, then President of the Media Society, that the Society give its annual award to Reuters. The Society accepted the proposal and made the award at a dinner at the Savoy Hotel on 12 March 2002. Previous winners had included Alistair Cooke, the Anglo-American broadcaster, but it was the first time the award had been made to an institution. Peter Thomas, in charge of Reuters public relations, and Tom Glocer, who not long before had become the Chief Executive of Reuters, were particularly gratified.

I ran into Donald and his wife Claire in the Garrick Club in October 2010. I was amazed to see that Claire was heavily pregnant. She was 47 and he 72. Ben was born four months later. By then Claire was 48 and Donald 73. Not surprisingly the British Press made much of the story.

BREAKING NEWS: HOW THE WHEELS CAME OFF AT REUTERS

In 2003 Brian Mooney and Barry Simpson, former Reuter journalists, published *Breaking News: How the Wheels Came off at Reuters* (London: Capstone, 2003). The blurb said:

> Reuters has suffered a sudden and dramatic reversal of its fortunes. As recently as July 2001 Reuters, Britain's only media and financial information company with a global brand, was riding the crest of a wave following three decades of spectacular and virtually uninterrupted growth. Less than two years later, it was reporting a record loss, with massive staff layoffs and a sharp decline in its share price to the point where it is viewed in the City as a possible takeover target.

The book posed the question: how could Reuters have got it so disastrously wrong? Sir Peter Job, who had succeeded Renfrew as chief executive in 1991 and had retired in 2001, told me: "It's a hatchet job on me. I shall not read it."

The Economist's review was surprising indulgent. It said:

> The frightening thing about the decline of Reuters is that its bosses did not do anything terribly wrong. Certainly they paid insufficient attention to a new company called Bloomberg and they made a few decisions which with hindsight turned out to be wrong, It could have happened to any company, which is what gives an everyman quality to the tale of how Reuters lost £20 billion of market value in a little over three years.

Of my retirement in 1989 the book says: "Few would dispute that he had been one of the most influential figures in Reuters history and a principal architect of its transformation over the previous two decades."

On 7 December 2010 Tom Glocer, who had always been careful never to criticise the previous management, gave a talk to the Reuter Society with the rather surprising title of *Putting the Wheels back on the bus*. Also surprising was that Peter Job attended and took Glocer to dinner afterwards at the Garrick Club.

TALES FROM THE SOUTH PIER

In 2008 John Jessop, a former Reuter journalist who had an impressive career and was the eventual President of Telerate, one of Reuters major competitors, published his memoirs under the title *Tales from the South Pier* (London: Athena Press, 2008). After a number of uncomplimentary remarks about me ("haughty demeanour ... calculated ambiguity"), he concludes the book by nominating an unsung hero of the market-data industry:

> My vote, for what it is worth, goes to one for whom my admiration is substantial. If it falls short of unbounded it is only because I feel obliged to confess, as many others have before me, that I did not personally warm to him. That, I suppose, makes the award all the more genuine. In presenting it, I invoke the words of some anonymous sage at Reuters, whose name I have forgotten. He once said of the nominee: "When the modern history of this company is written, one name above all will be associated with its emergence from the obscurity to which it once seemed

consigned and that is Michael Nelson." I have to agree.

...he invariably picked winners. In doing so he took a series of brave leaps into the unknown. Stockmaster, Videomaster, Monitor and Dealing were all his, and each in its time proved to be a commercial coup, the first three qualifying as triumphs that rescued the company.

BARONESS DE REUTER AND THE BEAULIEU FESTIVAL

By a curious coincidence I met Baroness de Reuter in the South of France. I had become Vice-President of the music festival of Beaulieu-sur-Mer, the village which had been developed in the nineteenth century by James Gordon Bennett, the founder of the Paris *Herald Tribune*. Marguerite de Reuter was the widow of his stepson, Oliver. I suggested to John Fox, the organiser of the festival, that we invite the Baroness, who lived in Monte Carlo. I had first met her at the unveiling of the statue to her husband's grandfather, Paul Julius Reuter, in London in 1976. She was delighted to come to Beaulieu and became a great personality at every festival, always delighted when the mayor drew attention in his speeches to her historical connection with the village. She gave considerable sums of money to the festival. On her first visit we were fortunate that two former Reuter colleagues, Maurice Quaintance and John Ransom, attended and looked after her.

Marguerite – Daisy to her friends – invited Helga and me to lunch at the Hôtel de Paris in Monte Carlo a few months before she died on 14 July 2009 at the age of 96. I represented Reuters at her funeral in Monte Carlo and gave the address. She was buried in Lausanne in Switzerland, where she also lived.

I gave a number of lectures at the Beaulieu Festival, including those on Queen Victoria, the Prince of Wales and Americans on the Riviera. But I found the most interesting the lecture I gave in 2005 on *Russians on the Riviera*, which was politically important, and about which little has been written in English. Here are some extracts:

> The first important Russian to visit the Riviera had helped to murder the Tsar. He was Alexsey Orloff, who, with his brother Grigory, had planned the coup d'état by which Catherine the Great overthrew her husband, the Tsar Peter III, who was later murdered. Grigory was her lover. In 1770 the Russian fleet under the command of Alexsey anchored in the port of Villefranche on the way to fight the Turks, whom

they beat at the battle of Chesme on the Aegean coast of Anatolia. Grigory visited Nice in 1781 with his sick wife. So the Orloffs founded the twin links of the Russians with the Riviera – the navy visiting its ports and its royalty and aristocracy visiting its centres of convalescence.

It was the arrival of the dowager empress Alexandra Feodorovna, widow of Tsar Nicolas I, to spend the winter on the Riviera on 26 October 1856 that marked the beginning of the establishment of the important Russian colony. That she had chosen Nice over such cities as Biarritz, Trouville or Baden-Baden, set the Riviera town apart from its rivals. The Sardinian government attached great importance to the visit (she was also sister of the King of Prussia), gave her a resplendent welcome when she arrived in Villefranche and installed her in the magnificent villa Avigdor on the Promenade des Anglais in Nice. The town of Nice illuminated all the public buildings and asked the hotels and residents to do the same.

King Victor-Emmanuel of Sardinia arrived in Villefranche by ship on 22 January, mounted a horse to enter Nice, rode to the Villa Avigdor and the Empress embraced him.

An event of great significance was the start in mid-March of the construction of a bathing installation for the grand-duchess Helena on the beach of les Baumettes. The grand-duchess, sister-in-law of the Empress, who was staying in the Villa Bremond, was passionate about swimming, so much so that she swam in the nude. The Empress and the grand-duchess were among the first to buy shares in the projected new winter and summer Casino, with its gardens, lecture hall, buffet and sea and spring bathing installations.

We owe the road from Villefranche to Nice to the Empress. A provisional road was constructed for her arrival. On 10 March 1857 she opened the completed road, cutting the tape with a pair of golden scissors. Celebrations included an open-air ball.

The generosity of the Empress to the poor became well-known so she received many petitions, many of which were professionally written: "I am the widow of a retired lieutenant, who served 38 years, have varicose veins in my right leg and eight children." "I have lost all my relatives and have a wound in my right arm which is so dreadful that I have suffered horribly at the Sainte-Croix hospital, which had to amputate." The Empress left Nice on 26 April, having spent no fewer than six months on the Riviera. The grand-duchess Helen stayed on until July, marking her departure with a ball open to the public and attended by several thousands of Nicois, setting the pattern for lavish spectacles for which Russians on the Riviera became famous. She came back to swim the following summer.

But the extravagant visits of Russian royalty to the Riviera were not all what they seemed. They had a political objective. The Treaty of Paris which ended the Crimean war excluded Russia from Europe and neutralised the Black Sea. The Russians needed a base on the Mediterranean to replace Sebastopol. They found it in Villefranche. Soon a Russian naval squadron was anchored in Villefranche harbour and the streets of Nice teemed with Russian sailors. The newspaper Avenir de Nice reported that an English newspaper had written: "One can now understand the residence and the repeated visits of the grand-duchess Helena." "We ... view with great jealousy and dissatisfaction [the appearance of Russia], not as an occasional but as a constant visitor in a Sardinian port," wrote the Leeds Mercury on 21 September 1858. Some English newspapers said the British should boycott Sardinian Nice and stay in French Cannes, but no-one listened. The Sardinian government presented the cession of facilities in the port to the Russians on a lease of 20 years as purely commercial. Lord Palmerston, the British foreign minister, was not convinced. The Odessa Steamship Company, which was to exploit the facilities, according to Palmerston was "a subterfuge employed by the Russian government to evade the Treaty of Paris ... When it wanted to it could transform its vessels into warships."

Villefranche became less important to Russia after 1871 when it denounced the neutralisation of the Black Sea. The Villefranche installations became a Russian study centre for marine life. The centre passed into French government hands in 1934.

MAGDALEN AND REUTERS

On 4 April 2009 Magdalen held its first "Hacks Dinner". Some eighty journalists attended. The largest group consisted of eight current or former Reuter journalists. The dinner was organised by the distinguished war correspondent, Robert Fox, a fellow member of the Garrick.

As I looked down the dining hall I thought how strange it was that two other Magdalen alumni should have worked for Reuters, both in distinctive roles.

James Lees-Milne (Magdalen 1928-31), who became one of the leading English diarists of the twentieth century, lasted six months as the third secretary to Sir Roderick Jones, the Chairman of Reuters. He loathed Jones and thirty-five years later got his revenge with this masterpiece of a description in his autobiographical novel *Another Self*:

He was in stature a little undersized. He was spruce, and dapper, and perky. I would describe his appearance as that of a sparrow were it not for his waist which, instead of being loose, was tight, pinched in by a conspicuous double-breasted waistcoat which he habitually wore like a corset. This constrictive garment gave him the shape of a magnified wasp. His face too resembled that of a wasp under a microscope. It was long and the bulbous nose was proboscis-like. His small eyes darted rapidly in his head in the manner of that insect. They never rested on their victim, yet because of a feverish activity missed nothing. His mouth too was sharp and vespine. His sting was formidable and unlike the bee's could be repeated.

I quote here Lees-Milne's descriptions of his time in Reuters because they are little known in the Company. He recalled that Jones required his desk to be arranged each morning with total exactitude:

> If the softest of the three India rubbers were not found on the left-hand side of the row on the allotted tray and adjacent to the red (not blue) sealing-wax, Sir Roderick's displeasure could be terrible.
>
> When his Rolls Royce drove up each morning to the main entrance of Reuters a bell rang violently in every room and passage of the building to announce the Chairman's arrival. There was a general scurry and flurry of alarm. When it drove off in the evening another bell rang more softly. There was a contrasting sigh of relief and relaxation of tension.

The story I was told about Sir Roderick and his Rolls-Royce when I joined Reuters related to the rubber pads which in those days activated traffic lights. When he left his house in Kensington his butler would telephone the head porter in Reuters to say the great man had left. The porter then dispatched a messenger boy to the traffic lights at the bottom of Carmelite Street and when the Rolls-Royce hove into view the boy would jump up and down on the rubber pad until the lights turned green and Sir Roderick could sail through uninterrupted.

The poor secretary, Lees-Milne, described the effect of Jones on him in a letter to his fiancée: "I groan every morning when the clock strikes 9.45, groan as I enter Reuters, groan as I climb the stairs and carry on groaning until I leave. It is unmitigated hell."

The crisis in Lees-Milne's career in Reuters came one Friday evening:

> Sir Roderick was waiting for the Rolls to take him to Sussex for the weekend. It was incumbent upon me to warn him the moment it arrived. The hall porter rang to tell me the chauffeur was at the door. I forgot to inform Sir Roderick, who was pacing up and down his room, watch in hand. Happening to pass the window he looked out and saw the Rolls and the chauffeur, with rug over one arm, standing patiently beside it. He called me into the room. Angrily he demanded why I had not told him. He had already lost five precious minutes which the Empire could ill spare. Was I deliberately obstructive? Or was I merely a fool? He could not decide which. Neither could I. I only knew what he knew, that it was quite unnecessary for him to be told, because neither the Rolls nor he was ever one split second behind the pre-ordained time.

Sir Roderick worked himself into a towering rage. The slanting sun was pouring into the room. He had his back to it, looking no longer like a magnified wasp but a plethoric turkey cock. Very unprepossessing he was too. But the fine particles of his spit caught in the evening sunlight made a fanlike spray which issued with velocity and subsided on to the pile carpet with the delicacy of the great Apollo Fountain at Versailles. Though the display was in miniature it was no less remarkable than the beautiful prototype of Le Notre's contriving. I was so fascinated by this performance which was being repeated for my benefit with each torrent of invective that I paid no heed to what Sir Roderick was saying, and sat blandly smiling.

A cloud passed over the sun, the Apollo Fountain was switched off, and I heard the turkey cock splutter, 'Well, I can't stop to argue about it any further now, Mr. Milne. We will discuss the matter again on Monday.'

It was thus rudely brought to my intelligence that on Monday I would most probably be given the sack.

Over the weekend Lees-Milne was at a country house-party attended by Stanley Baldwin, the Prime Minister, to whom he unburdened himself about the wicked Sir Roderick and his fear that he was going to be dismissed on the Monday. Baldwin told him to get his resignation in first, but Lees-Milne chickened out and did not resign and Jones did not dismiss him that Monday morning. He eventually fired him on 3 December, although in an uncharacteristically kind interview. He left on Saturday 4 January 1936.

In 1971 Lees-Milne joined the Bath Preservation Trust and was delighted to find that the Chairman was Sir Christopher Chancellor, who had succeeded Jones as head of Reuters, and who disliked him as much as did Lees-Milne.

Lees-Milne died on 28 December 1997 aged 89.

Sir Ian Fraser (Magdalen 1941-42; 1945-46), one of the leading bankers of the second half of the twentieth century, to whom I have earlier referred, worked for Reuters from 1946 to 1956 and was chief correspondent in Bonn. He left to join Warburgs, the merchant bank, became Director-General of the Panel of Take-overs and Mergers and eventually became chairman of Lazards. He was knighted in 1986 (He was a friend of Alfred Geiringer and for a few weeks in 1958 his fiancée, Anne Grant, was my secretary). As I have already noted, he would have made an excellent chief executive of Reuters. Indeed, if he had stayed with Reuters I do not think there is much doubt that he and not Long would have succeeded Cole.

In his autobiography *The High Road to England: An Autobiogrpahy* (Norwich: Michael Russell, 1988) Fraser says that in 1955 Chancellor visited him in Bonn and told him that he was one of three or four candidates for his succession. Soon afterwards Chancellor told him that Cole would succeed him. Fraser says he did not want to build his career on how soon the fat Cole exploded and decided to leave to join Warburgs. Cole told him that if he came back to Reuters he would re-engage him in a significant position, such as his own deputy.

He was probably the first banker to suggest that Reuters should go public and in the late seventies came to present a proposal to Long, Judah and me. The proposal was then before its time, but it was Fraser who prepared the paper dated 19 July 1982 which Alan Hare used to launch the bid for a stock exchange quotation.

Fraser died on 8 May 2003 aged 79.

REUTER TRUST

When Reuters was going public the Reuter Board asked me to bring the principles of the Reuter Trust up to date. I left untouched the provisions that Reuters should not pass into the hands of any one interest, group or faction and that its integrity, independence and freedom from bias should be fully preserved.

The main changes I recommended were:

> 1. Delete the commitment of the owners to "regard their respective holdings of shares in Reuters in the nature of a trust rather than as an investment."
> 2. Change the rather arrogant "to maintain in every event its position as the leading world news agency" to "to maintain its leading position in the international news and information business."

The Trust was greatly strengthened legally as part of the flotation and a Reuters Founders Share Company was established.

However, the Founders Share was attacked by the financial institutions and I spent a great deal of time trying to convince them of its validity. The attacks did not go away and the learned Henry Manisty described to me what happened on the government front:

> The Founders Share became vulnerable every time the protracted agenda over an EU Takeover Directive fired up again. The call for "one share one vote", if carried, could have wiped it out. We pressed the case that the Founders Share should be

viewed as a qualitative rather than economic instrument, designed to protect Reuters core values, but having no economic value of its own. In this way, we sought to distinguish it from the majority of "golden shares" designed to uphold the interests of a particular person, family or other grouping.

When I was working on the revision to the Trust I recalled Rupert Murdoch's comment in a Board meeting that the Trust was not necessary because it was in Reuters commercial interests to be independent. However, many believed he said that because he wished to take over the Company.

The origins of the Reuter Trust lay in the Scott Trust, which was set up in 1936 by John Scott, owner of the *Manchester Guardian* and the *Manchester Evening News,* to prevent future death duties forcing the closure or sale of the newspapers and to protect the liberal editorial line of the *Manchester Guardian* from interference by future proprietors. There was an obligation of similar comprehensiveness to that of the General Confession of the Church of England to run the *Guardian* "on the same lines and in the same spirit as heretofore."

William Haley was Managing Editor of the *Manchester Evening News* and was one of the original Scott Trustees. In 1939 he became a director of the Press Association and of Reuters. In the course of the negotiations in 1941 for the acquisition by the London newspapers, the Newspaper Proprietors Association, to buy from the Press Association half the shares it owned in Reuters, Haley proposed the establishment of a Reuter Trust. One of the purposes was to prevent Reuters being dominated by the London newspapers.

Samuel Storey, Chairman of Reuters, opposed the establishment of the Trust, which he said was no more than a shareholders' agreement which could be undone if the shareholders so decided. Curiously enough it was Storey who, in April 1941, had first floated the idea of a trust, in which such institutions as the Empire Press Union and the BBC could participate. That never happened, although half a century later I proposed that Michael Checkland, the Director-General of the BBC, who had been very helpful to me in achieving Reuters control of Visnews, should become a trustee of Reuters. He did so in 1994.

The staff liked the Trust, which was considered to be a "good thing", and gave the company an aura almost of holiness. In common with my colleagues in management I found it useful when seeking subscription increases from newspapers and broadcasters. We often said we were a "non-profit-making Trust", although cynics in the Company would say that the non-profit was not intentional. It was certainly useful to be able to say that we did not pay a dividend.

David Ure told me that the Trust was valuable in deterring unwelcome predators in the early years of this century when the Company was in financial difficulties.

The 1941 Trust provided that, at the invitation of the Board, the trustees could attend meetings of the Board and confer with the Board and generally be available to act in a consultative capacity with the Board. I am not aware that trustees ever attended a Board meeting.

The Australians and New Zealanders strengthened the role of the trustees when they came into the ownership in 1947. This clause was added to the Trust agreement: "[The duties of the trustees should be] to receive periodical reports from the Board of the activities of Reuters and to make representations (if thought fit) to the Board on matters of general policy and interest affecting Reuters."

I cannot recall any occasion on which the trustees made representations on any issue, other than ownership, or acted in a consultative capacity. This changed as an unintended result of the appointment as chief executive of Reuters of a man who had never been a journalist, in the person of Tom Glocer. On 18 October 2001 Pehr Gyllenhammar came to speak to the Reuter Society. He recounted how Glocer had asked Geert Linnebank, the Editor-in-Chief, to raise with him an issue arising out of 9/11.

The background is explained by the following note in the Daily Briefing, the internal web newsletter, of 19 September 2001 issued by Devin Wenig, President, Investment Banking and Brokerage Services, later to become President of the Markets Division of Thomson Reuters, effectively the old Reuters:

> On Tuesday evening, September 11, as the incredible events of the day slowly began to wind down, I was searching for a way to express all of the feelings of shock, outrage, sadness and concern that so many of us around the world had experienced. I requested of the sign engineers at 3XSQ that they display on the large billboards outside the building an American Flag. This was a simple symbol of corporate solidarity with the U.S. and New York, and in many ways was meant to be a sign that Reuters, as a London headquartered global company, had deep ties with the city and was there to help in any way possible.

Following the display of the flag, we received calls from a number of senior editorial managers requesting that we take the flag down. This was for a number of reasons, including the safety of our journalists overseas and the potential that bias could be implied to our editorial coverage.

After consideration by the management team in the U.S., it was unanimously decided to take the flag down (it was ultimately decided to put up a message in support of the rescue efforts). It was and is clear on reflection that the ideals of independence and objectivity go to the heart of what we are as a company. These pillars cannot be selectively retracted when we feel passion, or when we believe that right and wrong are so plainly clear. In fact, the trust principles are reinforced most powerfully when they are stretched and challenged the furthest. While many of us feel strongly about the events of last week and should not alter those personal feelings in any respect, we should equally defend the position of the Company as a seeker of fact, upon which those personal feelings can be based.

As a New Yorker, and an American, I will wear an American Flag ribbon on my shirt this week, but protect with equal passion the independence, objectivity and critical mission of Reuters.

Pehr Gyllenhammar called a meeting of the trustees, who supported the Editor-in-Chief.

Previous chief executives of Reuters, who were all former journalists, would never have involved the trustees in such a matter.

I commented to Pehr Gyllenhamar after the Reuter Society meeting that the role of the Chairman of Trustees had been importantly enhanced.

The role of the trustees was further enhanced when Reuters came under attack because of its policy of restraint in the use of the word "terrorist". Some Reuter staff were physically attacked in the street by incensed passers-by. Geert Linnebank wrote for me a note about the incidents and the follow-up.

The Reuters Board scheduled a discussion on the subject and on the damage the outcry was wreaking on Reuters business in the US, at a meeting in Paris. At that meeting, the Board chaired by Christopher Hogg regretted the damage to Reuters reputation but was very supportive of Editorial and unambiguous in its attachment to Editorial's independence in matters like this, of Editorial policy, which it confirmed only the Editor-in-Chief was in a position to determine.

Wary of the sustained, often vicious attacks on Reuters in the US but emboldened by the support I received from the Reuters Board, I also presented the issue to the Reuters Trustees at their request at a scheduled Trustees meeting at 85 Fleet Street a few weeks later. At that meeting, Editorial and its policies on the use of the word "terrorist" were given a markedly less supportive reception by several of the Trustees, though in the end the Board of Trustees too concluded that Editorial alone was in a position to set, review or confirm its own policies.

Editorial performance reviews became a regular and core feature of all regular Board of Trustees meetings from that moment on and Pehr Gyllenhammar also instructed his Trustees to schedule regular visits to Editorial offices on their overseas travels, and to produce reports on those visits.

Pehr Gyllenhammar had acquired for the trustees a standing which was unthinkable when I worked for the Company.

Reuters was fortunate that, when Thomson sought to buy Reuters, the Chairman of Trustees was a man of such vision as Pehr Gyllenhammar, who had become Chairman in 1999. He led the trustees to approve the sale. I derived some satisfaction from the fact that I had introduced Gyllenhammar to the Reuter family. Would another man have blocked it by arguing that the sale breached the Trust, which laid down that Reuters should at no time pass into the hands of any one interest group or faction?

The *Financial Times* reported on 2 April 2008 that Gyllenhammar said the trustees had a real issue at first with the notion of handing control to a single interest group. But Thomson agreed to adopt the Reuter Trust principles for the combined Thomson Reuters and volunteered concessions on selling shares that made any unwelcome change of control impossible. That offer was "quite something", said Gyllenhammar. Apart from nomenclature, the Thomson Reuter Trust principles were identical to those I had drafted in 1984.

On 16 May the *Financial Times* quoted Gyllenhammar as saying: "The future of Reuters takes precedence over the principles."

The new agreement between Thomson Reuters and the Founders Share Company had an interesting clause which provided that Thomson Reuters would have:

an office of editor-in-chief of the news services of Thomson Reuters and will provide Thomson Reuters Founders Share Company with the opportunity to consult with its Board of Directors a reasonable period of time prior to appointing an individual to, or removing an individual from, such office.

When I was discussing the Thomson Reuter Trust with Tom Glocer in 2010 he said it was like the Sword of Damocles. It was not important that it should fall, but that it should hang.

Interestingly, the Scott Trust, which had inspired the Reuter Trust, was the salvation of the *Guardian* in the twenty- first century. The newspapers of the Guardian Media Group (GMG), which is owned by the Scott Trust, moved into loss in 2004. The *Manchester Evening News* was sold off and the *Guardian* and the *Observer* were, at least temporarily, saved by the Group's non-newspaper investments.

THE FAMILY

Patrick was born on 20 August 1961, Paul on 27 December 1963 and Shivaun on 30 March 1967.

Paul married Mariana Covarrubias Wonchee in Guadalajara, Mexico, on 27 May 1995. Mariana, who had been born on 17 July 1970, was Mexican. The father of her mother was Chinese. Emilio was born on 4 April 2002, Felix on 19 April 2004 and Alba on 29 June 2009. The children were 3/8ths Mexican, 1/8th Chinese, 1/8th Irish, 1/8th Welsh, 1/8th Dutch and 1/8th Romanian.

Acknowledgements

This book would not have been possible without the help of those listed below:

Adam Black, photographer; Anna Boxer, widow of Marc Boxer; Michael Cooling, Reuter journalist; John Coulter, Lewisham Borough librarian; Ashley Daffin, son of Reuter executive; Robin Darwell-Smith, Magdalen College archivist; Robert Elphick, Reuter journalist; John Entwisle, Reuter archivist; Michael Goldman, consultant; Roger Gough, Reuter executive; Olga Leapman; Henry Manisty, Reuter lawyer; Colin McSeveny, Reuter journalist; Jean-Claude Marchand, Reuter executive; Helga Nelson; Patrick Nelson; Sir David Nicholas, Editor-in-Chief, ITN; Anna Norman, Magdalen College alumni relations officer; Donald Read, Reuter historian; Michael Reupke, Reuter journalist; Patrick Seale, Reuter journalist; Stephen Somerville, Reuter executive; David Ure, Reuter executive; André Villeneuve, Reuter executive.